DATE DUE			

Janáček's Tragic Operas

JANÁČEK'S
TRAGIC OPERAS

MICHAEL EWANS

INDIANA UNIVERSITY PRESS
BLOOMINGTON AND LONDON

Contents

Preface

This book presents essays on six of the nine operas which Janáček completed. I have excluded the early and uncharacteristic works *Šárka* and *The Beginning of a Romance*; and also the satirical *Excursions of Mr. Brouček*, which clearly belong to a different genre from Janáček's other mature music-dramas.

I owe thanks to the staff of the Janáček Archive of the Moravian Museum in Brno, the Opernabteilung of Universal Edition, Vienna, and the British Broadcasting Corporation for making available to me scores and autograph sketches of the six operas studied; the Czech Musical Fund, Prague, for permission to reproduce music examples from *Destiny*; and Universal Edition (Alfred A. Kalmus Ltd.), for permission to reproduce music examples from the other operas. All translations are my own.

The work chiefly reflects my own listening and study; but the ideas which I offer owe something to conversation with many other lovers of Janáček's music. If I cannot acknowledge them all individually, this does not imply any lessening of my gratitude. But particular thanks must go to John Tyrrell, who surveyed the drafts with the eye of an expert Janáček scholar, and has saved me from many errors.

Three final acknowledgements are more personal. This book could not have been begun without the friendship of George Steiner, who first taught me the responsibilities of those who seek to write about great drama; would never have been continued without the encouragement of Donald Mitchell, most patient and enthusiastic of editors; and could never have been completed, but for the profound involvement of my wife Jenifer.

Newcastle, N. S. W.

A Note on the Music Examples

The music examples in this book comprise quotations of melodic fragments, and also representations of continuous passages from the operas. Janáček's instrumentation is so sparing that it has been possible to represent these in short score in such a way that in most cases all elements present in the full score of the quoted extract can be shown. All instruments, including transposing ones, have been written at the pitch at which they actually sound; and some liberties have been taken with the normal grouping of scores by instrumental families, to point up the originality of Janáček's orchestration by arranging on one stave the instruments to which each single element in the musical thought is assigned. Clarity has also been a principal consideration in making these arrangements; and for that reason most of the examples from *Jenůfa* and *Destiny* have been rewritten enharmonically. These are the only two mature operas in which Janáček made extensive use of key signatures; but even in them tonality is so flexible that the corrective accidentals make reading difficult. In all other respects the examples attempt to preserve Janáček's characteristic orthography.

Reference to passages from Janáček's operas is normally made by Act, scene (in Roman numerals), rehearsal figure and bar after that rehearsal figure. But where the context is obvious, only the last two of these numerals are supplied. In *Jenůfa*, *Destiny* and *From the House of the Dead* scene numbers are omitted since the rehearsal figures are numbered continuously throughout each Act.

Introduction

Janáček's tragic operas affect their spectators by a unique blend of emotional and intellectual power. By confronting the causes of tragic action directly, Janáček enables us to see his characters —and through them ourselves, mankind at large in moments of suffering—not merely with compassion but as creatures endowed with nobility.

The action of tragedy is violent. But gratuitous violence evokes neither sympathy nor understanding of the agent. The compelling power of Janáček's theatre is due not merely to the brevity and economy of his dramas, but to the inevitability with which he imbues each major event, from Laca's slashing of Jenůfa's cheek to the closing of the prison doors behind Alexandr Petrovič Gorjančikov.

The medium, and the word tragedy, are Greek. In the classical theatre, as in Shakespeare's, man is no mere puppet of the gods. At the moments of sharpest crystallization—Aeschylus' Orestes with drawn sword before the breast of his mother Clytemnestra, Sophocles' Oedipus on the brink of the unspeakable knowledge of who he is and what he has done—man embraces his fate, choosing freely—by a fierce paradox—to do that which we know he must do. Here there is no melodramatic suspense: at each performance we experience a feeling of release. As the character takes upon himself the responsibility for his action, this moment, deeply expected, is none the less one of shattering surprise for the audience. So too in Janáček; in his first three mature serious operas, the action unfolds to and beyond its climax with the directness of Greek tragedy. And the form remains in the three last stage works, even though it is overlaid there by the patterns of a wider meditation on man and his place in the world.

Classical tragedy carries intense conviction for two reasons: the dramatist's art was close to the centre of ancient Athenian cultural life, and the means available to the playwrights for the description of human experience were rich. Aeschylus and Sophocles could draw not merely on a poetic tradition of complex patterns and a heightened vocabulary deeper in its resonance than that of ordinary speech, but also on a unique expressive device: a hierarchy of gods and lesser powers whose interventions set the human action in a wider context, offering a fierce, direct realization in dramatic terms of the forces which surround us and penetrate our souls, defining the limits of human action.

The re-creation in music-drama of this extreme richness has long been a beckoning possibility. It is given fullest expression by Wagner; in the *Ring*, the poem seeks to refashion ancient legend so that it may furnish the archetypes of experience, while the orchestral music surrounds them; it includes the actors in a cosmos which is at once overwhelming in its emotional impression and also intellectually complex, rich in specific cross-reference.

In his early opera *Šárka*, Janáček attempted a similar synthesis; but success eluded him. His character was fundamentally opposed to that of the German composer, pragmatic and realist where Wagner's was idealistic and meditative. Janáček's mature works do not fail to exploit the vivid orchestral power which Wagner brought to the operatic theatre; but on a far more concentrated canvas. In Janáček, the orchestra's eloquence is limited both by the pace of the dramaturgy and by the abrupt fragmentation of brief, trenchant melodies around the utterances of the characters; the subjective power of Wagner's orchestra is abandoned and replaced by a different balance between words and music. The characters of Janáček's stage stand out as more individual than those of Wagner's late works; his plots are drawn not from myth but from the realities of contemporary life. Intricate, symphonic argument is absent: directness prevails, both on stage and in the pit, even where the libretti proceed far beyond the bounds of everyday experience.

Janáček's work is much closer to the roots of his native culture than Wagner's; the narrative economy and the universal resonance of his operas are both related to their origins. These dramas achieve the inclusive vision characteristic of high tragedy

14

by their nearness to their sources, and the dramatic depth, the avoidance both of eclecticism and of sentimentality, which this made possible. Moravian culture, poised between the deep melancholy of the Eastern Slavs and the cautious optimism of Western Europe, is the source of Janáček's unique synthesis between the ruthless objectivity of the East and the defined, refined strands of Western tradition. He had no predecessors; and his road to the creation of a truly Moravian opera was a long one, the career which led him to write no masterpiece until after his fortieth year one of ceaseless experiment.

Leoš Janáček was born in 1854, tenth child of a village school-teacher and choirmaster. He grew up at the time when nationalism was gaining strength throughout Czechoslovakia, spurred by the increasing weakness of the central government of the Austro-Hungarian empire. Political advance had been crushed in the failure of the attempted revolution of 1848, and the patriotic movement could only express the growing rejection of Germanic influences through cultural means.

Janáček left his native village at the age of eleven, to become a chorister at the school of the Augustinian monastery in Brno; and during his formative years he became increasingly involved in the search for a musical expression of national feeling. As a student he came under the influence of the formidable Father Pavel Křížkovský, choirmaster of the monastery and an ardent patriot who expressed himself through choral composition and the arrangement of folk songs.

Janáček himself began similar work in his own first composi-tions, which date from 1873. But as yet he lacked mature know-ledge of the rural society of his homeland. Two years later he spent his summer holidays for the first time wandering around Moravia: 'fiery coloured costumes, passionate songs ... here was the paradise of my student days. This must have been where the first seeds of *Jenůfa* were sown.'

But *Jenůfa* was not begun for twenty more years. And Janáček should not be thought of as a 'natural composer' who went straight to folk music for his inspiration and sought no other source for his work. During his twenties Janáček's know-ledge of the Western classical repertoire grew extensively, since his work as a choirmaster and music teacher gave him the opportunity to study and conduct major choral and orchestral works ranging from the Mozart *Requiem* and the *Missa Solemnis* to the most recent music of Dvořák. This widening of experience was reflected in his own compositions, which now included small orchestral and chamber works. And in 1879 and 1880 Janáček obtained leave of absence from his job and studied music in the conservatoires at Leipzig and Vienna.

But the atmosphere in each place left him unsatisfied. Siding at this time essentially more with the inclination of his fellow students towards romanticism than with the classicism of his teachers, he yet felt not at one with either. Janáček's 'national fanaticism bordering on insanity' (as his father-in-law put it) grew during these years, and was expressed through journalism as well as in his other activities.

Janáček's contribution during the seventies and eighties to the musical life of Brno was great, and lasting; but the tension during that time is evident in retrospect between his aspirations as a composer and his achievement. The exploration first of pre-classical and then of classical and romantic idioms was bound to lead to artistic breakdown as his sense of the uniqueness of the culture of his native Moravia grew on him in his annual travels; for he was a highly self-critical artist, and it became obvious that none of these idioms could lead to a means of expression for the specific truths which he was beginning to see as within his power. The flamboyant nationalist gestures clearly speak for a consciousness he could not yet express in music. A marital crisis was added. Janáček was forced to artistic silence, writing no music between 1880 and 1884.

He did not find the way out of his impasse till 1888, though in the meantime he had resumed composing, and had written his first opera (*Šárka*, 1887). Based on the Czech version of the Amazon queen legend, it is an odd mixture, symptomatic of the crisis. Wagnerian (via Smetana's use of Czech legend in *Dalibor* and *Libuše*) in the use of heroic myth for subject-matter and the leitmotive technique, its general pattern of sound inclines, disconcertingly, more to Dvořák than to Smetana. And the opera is incongruously brief—its three Acts have a total running time of rather less than an hour. Janáček had a strong affection for *Šárka* in later life; but it is purely a late product of his exploration of Western styles. In fact the last, since in 1888 Janáček set out, in

16

collaboration with the collector František Bartoš, for the Lachian and Vallachian districts of Moravia with the explicit intention of writing down the folk songs which embodied the culture of his native region: words, tunes, orchestration and the manner of dancing each song were notated.

This action was as decisive, and as liberating, for Janáček as an artist as it was a few years later for Bartók and Kodály. Every previous Czech composer of genius, from the Kroměříž school of the Baroque period to Dvořák and Smetana, had found an eclectic method of composition adequate, in creative interplay with the styles and forms of the West; without his long attempts to do the same, and their failure to satisfy him, Janáček would never have realized the full significance for him of the folk songs of his native land, and the possibility of basing a viable dramatic idiom on these sources. Even so his first attempt to do this was a total failure.

But Janáček's opera *The Beginning of a Romance* (1891) must be one of the most fruitful of all artistic failures. In it he attempted to integrate the melodies of folk songs directly into opera—indeed to include many of them, unaltered, in the orchestrations he had devised recently for his *Lachian Dances* and other concert works; and found that the only way to do so—confronted by these vigorous musical episodes to which he simply added vocal lines so that they became arias, duets and larger ensembles—was to abandon continuous opera and alternate formal numbers with recitative.

The plot of *The Beginning of a Romance* is trivial and clichéd, and the music is monotonous. Janáček's lack of enthusiasm during its composition is known, and he disowned it in later life. But it was far more valuable to Janáček's development than his beloved *Šárka*. *Šárka* was inflated, burdened with a ponderous post-Wagnerian style out of all proportion to its length. The new musical manner which Janáček had begun to learn by his collection and study of folk songs could not be absorbed into such a sophisticated Western idiom: a new operatic style had to be developed. *The Beginning of a Romance* showed that folk material could only be incorporated directly into an opera shaped to Western forms by retreating back to the simplest form and setting a banal libretto. This was not obvious in advance; it had to be realized by experiment. Janáček had first to reject the refinements of the West—in actual compositions, and at the price of triviality; only then could he see the way to developing the new kinds of refinement which were possible within a wholly Moravian idiom. The cantata *Amarus* (1897) and *Jenůfa* itself (begun between 1894 and 1896) are the first results.

'I am not concerned so much with their value as collection pieces. They are mainly a means of understanding life . . . they are the unity of song with the hardship of life.' The debt of Janáček's mature operas to folk song is not a mere matter of musical mannerisms and stylistic traits, adding a particular pungency to a sophisticated idiom whose bases are elsewhere. When he wrote (in 1906, and so after *Jenůfa* and *Destiny*) that 'only from living song can "art-music" of a related style develop; I therefore believe that scholarly knowledge of the style of composition of folk song will grow victoriously into art music', Janáček himself had already made exactly this organic development, the entire ethos of his mature operas being based on that of Moravian folk music.

Most Moravian folk songs are also folk dances. Different songs were on occasion given to the same dance, or vice versa, but the dance and the song are performed together, and the dance is a representation, through the stylizations of dance and mime, of the events spoken of in the song. Some enact experiences which are part of all village life—as for example the *Pilky*, connected with the bringing in of winter fuel before the coming of the snow, in which mimed representations of wood-cutting are part of the dance; or the *Dymák* (smoke dance), described thus by Vogel:

> In it a boy kneels on his right knee, puts his left fist on his left knee and with his right fist suggests the blows of a hammer. A girl stands on her toes in front of him and gently rocks from side to side, lifting and lowering her apron to suggest blowing on a fire. To a sudden change of tempo, the boy springs up and they dance a quick polka.

Others are evidently of ritual origins, as the *Královničky* ('Little queens'), danced at the summer solstice, in which two girls, costumed as king and queen and accompanied by a chorus, dance from house to house collecting presents, which symbolize sacrifices to the sun. Others present personal experience in stylized form, as the many nuptial dances, or the 'club dance', in which two waltzing circles, one of boys and one of girls, surround the dancer with the club. When he chooses his girl, all dance a polka, after which the odd boy out must take the club and signal for the waltz to resume. Only one boy is finally left without a partner, and he must pay the musicians.

Such songs are not narrative ballads, sung by a single performer without mime or dance. These performances of song and dance use both media to represent and interpret human experience—daily work mimed in some, ritual or personal situations symbolized by the actions of others—in a way which can only be called dramatic. This impression increases when we look at a folk song which tells a specific story: the text does this as far as possible by the medium of direct speech, placed by the singers in the mouth of the characters. Here Janáček describes one such song, 'The Jealous One', which made a great impact on him, and his feelings when he made his own setting of it for unaccompanied chorus in 1888:

'In a hut, a hiding-place somewhere in a gap in the wild woods on the mountains, lies a young man fatally wounded in the head.

'On one side is a steel sabre, on the other his mistress sits beside him on the clean white bed. In the music of the high mountains the motifs of their icy conversation fall . . .

Will you die,
will you recover,
will you tell me
how long you're going to live?

To the same theme—the poet barely sings his story—the brigand's crafty reply is heard

Give me, my love,
my shining sabre
that I may see
how my cheeks grow pale

'All is silent in the hut—perhaps just a noisy buzzing fly is heard. . . .

19

'Anxiously—for she feels the treachery in her lover's heart
—she gives him the sabre, but quickly jumps aside.

'With her hand on the door, she crouches ready to escape—
but the brigand lies motionless. The jealous man's dying
motif whispers his words

Whoever gave you that advice
loved you truly

'With his last strength, before expiring, he cries out again

I would have cut off your head
so that after my death
no one should have you.

'This work was my introduction to *Jenůfa*! The same place,
the mountains of Slovačko, the same people—and the same
unhappy passion. Three themes which I always heard in their
songs . . .'

The purely technical debts of Janáček's mature style to
Moravian folk music are obvious; but this song clearly influenced
Janáček as much, if not more, by its precise sense of place, its
expression of the fierce, independent character of his people, and
its dramatization of one of the disastrous situations into which
that character led them, as for any musical features. Indeed,
Janáček took this, and several other songs whose subject attracted
him, and provided a new setting, shaping his music and developing it in a style far beyond the capacities of any folk performer.
But he did not attempt to create a drama directly from folk
songs, after his failure in *The Beginning of a Romance*. Early in
the 1890s, while he was editing his folk song collection with
Bartoš, Janáček encountered the play *Její pastorkyňa* ('Her
foster-daughter') by Gabriela Preissová. He realized that this
play embodied the spirit of these songs, on a larger scale; and
began the libretto of the opera based on it, which we know in the
West as *Jenůfa*, in 1894.

Janáček took almost ten years to write the opera—a certain
indication of many changes of direction, since he normally composed his music at enormous speed. And, uniquely, he destroyed
all the sketches; only one page survives. Interruptions for the
composition of the concert overture *Jealousy*, and of *Amarus*, do

not wholly explain the length of time *Jenůfa* took to write. Nor does the fact that Janáček wrote only by night. He had to create a completely new operatic style.

Preissová was not a native Moravian. But her plays show that on arriving in the region she lost no time in understanding the people and adapting her writing to the local dialect. Her 'drama from Moravian village life' has, as Janáček realized, exactly the spirit of such songs as 'The Jealous One': it is in every respect such a song, on a larger scale. The spirited people of Moravian Slovakia, and their passions, are brought to dramatic life just as in the ballad; and the tense, terrible situations of those torn between life and death, presented by the ballad in powerful miniature, are those which recur, treated even more seriously, in every act of the play.

Janáček's music reflects this fact. Just as *Její pastorkyňa* is in spirit a folk song text on a larger scale, so the orchestra with which Janáček surrounds it is a folk song's group of accompanying musicians, expanded, and the opera singers as they act Preissová's story replace the singing, miming participants in the village dance. Janáček's mature music is of course sophisticated far beyond the capacities of any folk musician—if only in the sheer originality of his inventions; but his exultant rhythmic energy and harmonic freedom are exactly theirs, as are many stylistic points. Janáček's is a supple orchestra of stabbing, alien interjections between independent, vivid vocal lines; abrupt, fragmented motifs and their elaborate decorations are the foundation of his style. Similarly, fragments of melody, trills and swirls—admittedly less adventurous in harmony than Janáček's—dominate the improvisations of the fiddlers of the Moravian band. Repetition, pedal, arpeggio and arabesque are the essence of his style as of theirs.

Janáček's orchestration, sparse and consistently insisting on the sharp individuality of the different instruments, is again a faithful expansion of the practice of the folk bands. Janáček realized that direct copying of folk music was inadequate to the setting even of a Moravian play; he therefore devised a re-creation of the spirit of such music in the larger scale of the opera house; a re-creation complete even to the imitation, by the long orchestral commentaries (so difficult to handle in production) which close several Acts in Janáček operas, of the improvised postludes to Moravian folk songs. Western musical techniques are incorporated in an idiom whose bases are fundamentally different. This is true even of the setting given to *Makropulos*, most urban and 'sophisticated' of the texts; and two of the score's finest and strangest inventions make deep, direct ties back to the manner of folk music. In Act 1, one of Marty's interventions elicits an orchestral response consisting of sustained notes for violins and celli, separated by a gap of four octaves with nothing in the centre (53: 7). And in Act 2, the whole intimate first part of the first dialogue between Marty and Prus is founded on elaborate ornamental decorations of the simplest of melodies; by piccolo and solo violin, and in the lower registers by clarinet and solo cello.

Janáček's transformation from folk song to opera is of course one almost beyond recognition; and this is not simply because of the vastly different scale, but also due to the developed, tragic vision which he expressed in his operas.

All Janáček's texts match the manner of the most intense of Moravian songs. Except for *Destiny*—whose words Janáček drafted to his own outline, and which was then put into verse for him—the tragic operas were adapted directly by the composer himself, from a play or novel. And with one exception, they narrate a strong story very much on the analogy of the folk ballad, and against a clearly defined background in the life of the community. The exception is *From the House of the Dead*; and though this lacks any story line whatever, it compensates for this by imposing unity through its powerful evocation of the daily routines of the prison community. Further, this opera is rich in dance forms, and is as a whole an ordered representation of life in a manner finely akin to the combination in folk dance of stylized gesture and pointed, vigorous music.

Janáček's operas have either a bourgeois or a proletarian setting; he abandoned the heroic and mythical world as a serious subject after *Šárka*, referring to it only in the second part (1917) of *The Excursions of Mr. Brouček*, where the poet is made to lament the fact that such themes can, in his time, only be handled ironically. There were strong reasons for Janáček's choice of settings: his origins; his violently egalitarian temperament; the basis of his work in folk song, which as a result of

22

centuries of foreign rule dealt exclusively with the life of the lower classes; and his desire for the operas to reflect contemporary realities. For while he never admitted to the stage works the passionate social protest of many of his shorter concert compositions (indeed, the operas seek universal illumination to such an extent that there is no reference to current events in any of them) there is no doubt that they are addressed to the closest concerns of his audience; they are intended to exclude any element of escapism.

Women and their sufferings occupy the centre of Janáček's stage. Again and again, in every opera from *Jenůfa* to *Makropulos*, a pattern is to be seen in the chosen text: always a young, but mature and loving female is heroine, far more significant than any male character; often she is counterpointed by an almost equally prominent, repressive older woman (Kostelnička, Míla's mother and Kabanicha). And Marty's compelling fascination for Janáček must have lain in the way in which his two archetypes combine in her body, the young Elina imprisoned by the life elixir in the weary, harsh person of Emilia. Often, too, the group is completed by a soubrette, who though less important than the principal male characters is a valuable complement to the introspective, suffering heroine, gay where she is sad and shallow in acceptance of life where she is deep (Karolka, Varvara, Kristina). And in the last opera, which but for an old and raddled prostitute singing twelve bars in the second Act is entirely without female characters, it is the intolerable burden of the absence of women which weighs at almost every moment on the inhabitants of the house of the dead.

That fearful title—borne by an opera in which every one of his lifelong concerns is embodied—evokes the second main subject of Janáček opera. Beside sexual need, man's other inalienable burden is death. In tragedy, violent death. For Janáček, the two themes are bound; the sex that bears children is by that nearer to the realities of life, closer to the renewal in each new generation; and this renewal is the only ultimate consolation in these operas to the living for the reality of death.

Jenůfa and *Destiny* (though contrasted in style, plot and setting) both set out Janáček's three deepest concerns—love, death and renewal—in a clear pattern; in each the love of man for woman, presented in the first Act, leads to a violent death in the

23

second, with the third moving upwards to a closing vision of a better life. Death and renewal are bitterly intertwined in the final scene of *Kát'a Kabanová*, the first of four powerful codas in which Janáček attempts the total challenge of confronting and attaining an external viewpoint on death. And in the last three operas these concerns, only implicit earlier, become overt: the *Vixen* with the original book extensively rearranged by Janáček so that the plot reflects this fundamental pattern through the vixen's life and the renewal after her death by her cubs; *Makropulos*, a play which instantly attracted Janáček, surely because Čapek's much-loved heroine and her fierce quest to recover the elixir by which she can again evade death are a penetrating dramatization of the composer's closest concerns; and *From the House of the Dead*, the opera dominated by the obsessive absence of women and of love, whose whole axis is the tension between the death of the title and the life-asserting motto, 'in every creature there is a spark of God'; and whose close is for one prisoner a return from the house of the dead to freedom: 'new life', as he himself describes it.

Beside this total affinity of concern, the other point which Janáček's chosen texts have in common seems less vital. But it is complementary to his central subject-matter. Each proceeds divisively, evoking a well-defined community as its milieu and isolating the central, suffering protagonist sharply from the remainder of the inhabitants. And in each the modes of conduct of existing society are undermined by the overriding demands of a deeper truth; and this not by a mere gesture of political revolt but by the convincing emergence of truth from and as a result of the action. For heroine or soubrette, the action leads to realization of herself and of her place in the real world. This may be death (as for the heroines of *Kát'a Kabanová* and *Makropulos*); but equally it may, as in *Jenůfa*, be a new, finer life—just as, on a lower tragic level, the forester of the *Vixen* and Petrovič in *From the House of the Dead* attain in the closing scene an enlightenment which gives them the moral strength to lead a better life. Janáček like the Greeks has no inhibition about ending a tragedy in happiness where that is the logical outcome of the events.

The characteristic tension in Janáček's operas, the tension which yields both tragic events and ultimate understanding, is between inner feeling and the impact of pressure from external oppression. It is easy to see why Janáček was drawn to such situations: the conflict in his own youth (finely expressed in the cantata *Amarus*) between the strict régime of the monastery school and the composer's intuitive empathy with the freedom of nature had a profound influence. And they allowed the exploration of reminiscence, guilt, humility and triumph (matters closely bound to the apprehension of inevitability) through which his operas approach understanding of the darkest aspects of their three concerns, love, death and renewal. But to dramatize such a conflict effectively it is necessary to provide both time devoted to the individual whose sufferings they are—and so a close focus on the protagonist—and a clear presentation of the pressures from outside which oppress her. Hence the clearly defined milieu, the cluster of very different characters who surround and oppose Janáček's principals; hence too the lengthy monologues for the central characters, and the preference for texts in which the leading characters go openly to meet their fate, are women and men who act and accept the consequences, not passive in reception of suffering. Through the polarity of suffering individual and oppressive surroundings, the action may lead—when surrounded by music—with inevitability to the emergence of deeper truth.

For such material evidently has universal appeal, obvious gravity and the potential to become high tragedy. Yet none of the texts is in itself tragic. There is the emphatic impression that the characters are people of action, real individuals whose decisions matter: autonomous and so potentially possessing the freedom of will which is one half of the tragic paradox. Yet like all modern prose dramas Janáček's libretti lack the power to convey the compelling inevitability which is the other half. This is not provided by the stark but arresting images which permeate the operas from the relentless mill-wheel of *Jenůfa* Act I to the wounded eagle whose struggles, charged with objective reality, also mirror the hopelessness of the situation of the prisoners in the house of the dead. These have only partial power to bind men, and cannot wholly explain their actions. Nor can the Christian God, who is naturally invoked by many of Janáček's characters but who is not a god of compulsion—indeed not a tragic god, since he is held to give his creation full freedom of will and to dispense mercy when they abuse it. Janáček, marvellously, includes God's mercy in the cosmogony of the operas, comprising it—and Him—in a larger, tragic vision of man.

The texts provide the substantive issues, the aspects of life which Janáček wishes to dramatize; the music surrounds them, illuminating the thoughts of the characters and conveying Janáček's complex vision of the relationships between men and women, the inevitability of action and the place of man in his world.

The opera composer must, ideally, be at once the servant and the master of his text. Janáček solved this paradox, while diminishing in no way the power of the music in illuminating the stage action. He presents operas whose action unfolds directly, with digression, interlude and additional episode of independent value shunned; a musical idiom so rapid that plays are set with the performing time of the opera hardly exceeding that of the original; and a style so concentrated and trenchant that no individual Act is set to continuous music of over forty minutes' duration.

This is achieved by reducing the demands of purely musical logic. The basic logic of all Janáček's theatre work is that of drama, not that of formal musical procedure; indeed his concert works borrow the methods devised in the operas. There is no resemblance to the harnessing of a folk-based idiom to classical and Baroque procedures used in the concert music of Bartók. And the few extended sections for orchestra alone in the operas are similarly programmatic: except in rare instances for specific effect, Janáček avoids all operatic forms, and the large-scale organizing means of abstract music, in order to allow his theatre music to respond as closely as possible to the changing aspects of the text.

Various motifs in the orchestra, sharply marked off from each other by instrumentation, duration, extent of repetition and harmonic character, literally represent and chart for us individual features of the action which Janáček wishes to illuminate. They supply three distinct contributions: first, the wider focus, the deeper elements which surround the action and which at times obtrude on the consciousness of the human participants; second, a precise narration which by dovetailing the repeated orchestral motifs with each other and with an independent vocal line, itself expressing individual character and outwardly-shown mood, reveals the progress of the inner thoughts of the characters and explains the reasons for their words and actions; finally, in the relative nobility and ugliness of line, a clear moral differentiation between the finer and the more vicious thought and word. In this process rhythm and tempo, instrumentation and harmony are inseparable: each of the various orchestral elements is individually conceived on all three levels at once, so as to make its own contribution. Repetition is a central device; each motif remains only so long as the factor which it expresses is influencing the action. The voice part alone, expressing outward character, appears to be a properly distinct element. To imitate orchestral pattern, to initiate a pattern then taken by the orchestra, to pursue a wholly independent path: these alternatives indicate the degree to which a given action is influenced by, initiates (if a motif is first heard in the voice), or is indifferent to inner thought and the influence of others, as registered by the senses. Contrasts within the orchestra indicate conflicts of inner thought. And the whole creates a feeling of inexorable logic in the unfolding of the action.

Elements also occur in the orchestra which draw attention to a larger focus, to frames of reference beyond the characters themselves. And these are the only focuses in which the action—and, in narration of past events, the acts of the people described—are set. To achieve this relentless singleness of aspect—that of illumination—to the text, the libretti shun formal situations, any element of the predetermined or predictable. Similarly, Janáček's avoidance of ensembles is far from arbitrary; such detailed handling of the inner thought of the individual is precluded when a large number of important characters are on stage. Hence his use of confrontations between two characters to crystallize a conflict in the penultimate scene of many acts of the tragic operas, and of monologues to achieve the final release; hence too the fact that the only two large-scale classical ensembles in these operas occur when all the characters on stage share, temporarily, the same simple emotion.

The debate in the orchestra is conducted with sharp moral assessments of the emotions and actions of the characters. Music is a grammar of many ladders, contains many metaphors—stability or instability, expectation and relapse, symmetry, asymmetry, speed, slowness, intensity and relaxation, motion and rest, elevation or depression, simplicity or complexity—the catalogue is endless; and music means nothing, in the abstract. But it is a self-contained system of relationships between such metaphors, all of which it can tie to itself and to the text; and it has effect, emotional and intellectual, on its hearers. Janáček's distinctive genius as a dramatist is that he explores these metaphorical effects as far as possible; he employs sharply conceived blocks of sound, strongly contrasted and essentially independent of each other; by their appearance or disappearance, their clashing and coalescence, their alteration or unchanged recurrence he charts the course of the workings of the minds of his characters; and, by the very fact that all these blocks are placed in collage in the one, whole medium of the orchestra and on the single ladder of the tones, he sets every action in relation to every other action. By adding intrusive comment, external points of reference on the same axis, the means are complete; Janáček's operatic style, surrounding his actors with the rich, unified world of this orchestra which binds together that which is within them and that which is outside, has the potential to be the medium of tragedy. It supplies at once the hierarchy which orders the action on an objective framework of description and the essential moral axis, the sharp ordering of actions and characters as noble or ignoble, which makes sense of our experiences.

And it has that potential to an unprecedented extent. There are few operatic vocabularies which abandon the claims of music's own logic so extensively, in order to gain a flexibility which can use every aspect of music to convey understanding of the unfolding action. Janáček's only danger is that, as his idiom grew more violent in expression, and more thorough in its orchestral reflection of dramatic logic, musical relationships within each work might become so tenuous that all overall consistency would be lost and the intended unifying medium become a mere collection of unrelated fragments. The unfolding collage—and it was just this, as the building up of much of the music through successive sketches can be seen to have been conducted, literally, as a montage—might collapse, the ever-flowing succession of new material yielding a whole less meaningful than the sum of its parts.

The danger is avoided—by two means, one almost beyond

analysis but the other soon revealed. Each of the operas inhabits, in an indefinable but quite definite way, its own sound-world, closely related to the subject and setting. While none of them could ever have been written by any other composer, the differences are striking: *Kát'a Kabanová* and *From the House of the Dead* somehow characteristically Russian, the *Vixen* warm and luxuriant where *Makropulos* is astringent and acid. More definably, as Janáček's idiom grows more sparse and fragmented, a subtle binding is introduced: the late operas all possess a motto-group, a significant pattern of notes by whose transformations meaning is charted, and round which the disparate materials, grouped, gain order. So as diversity grows greater, an ever more subtle unity is imposed; and—wrongly but quite understandably —critics have gone so far as to speak of monothematicism in *Makropulos* and *From the House of the Dead*, confronted as they are with the endless, ingenious and disguised recurrences of a single pattern. These configurations do not limit, but offer both a basic framework and a vast, ordered resonance. It is wrong, in general, to speak of leitmotives, attached to or describing a particular person or thing; the Wagnerian cross-reference is against the essential ethos of Janáček's music, in which all is direct, the phrase makes its desired impact without any conscious effort by the hearer to recall its appearance and remember its previous associations. Recall is loose and rare; in Janáček's music the new is the constant expectation, of no less significance than that which, on occasion, is related to previous material.

The potential, then, for tragedy. But the actual attainment? Autonomous characters in naked confrontation with the inevitable?

'The art', Janáček once declared, 'of dramatic writing is to compose a melodic curve which will, as if by magic, reveal immediately a human being in one definite phase of his existence.' Janáček sustains this emphasis on character not in isolation but in action in a situation, through rigorously controlling the material admitted to the final draft of the opera so that nothing superfluous to this aim is heard. He never meditates at large on the implications of his action, but always maintains this stance of objective, uncondemnatory yet committed and involved, carefully paced narration of what the characters are thinking and feeling. The composer neither caresses, indulgently, the souls of his characters nor assaults rhetorically the sensibilities of his audience, but stands midway between classical impersonality and romantic involvement with his subjects. It is as if Janáček were totally conscious that the orchestra is his intermediary between stage and audience, that it *accompanies* the action, not merely trivially but in the deepest sense.

And it is through the (as Janáček implies) almost magical manner in which his music supplies insight that the characters in his operas have autonomy and independence despite the force of the pressures depicted by the orchestra. From almost every aspect this art exhibits or mirrors the tragic tension between freedom and relentless control. Janáček sought to realize character by capturing it in action at particular points—Jenůfa's reflections after Jano has left in Act I come to mind, Kát'a's monologues, or the interventions and reminiscences of Marty as Kolenatý tries to describe the Gregor lawsuit to her in *Makropulos* Act I; the music goes to extreme limits in expression of what the character feels in 'a definite phase' of existence—while the composer rigorously denies both libretti and music diversions to illustrate character or theme in general, at the expense of the action. Again, his vocal lines are free to the point of violence in the intervallic tension permitted to express emotion, but are never allowed decoration for the sake of purely musical pleasure, oversetting the orchestral primacy. And this 'power in restraint' is complemented by that of the fragmented technique whereby vocal lines of this directed energy are enveloped by an orchestra which is highly powerful in assertion, yet which never swamps the vocal line and almost never supports it, but leaves it independent. Both elements have unassailed strength.

But Janáček does not perpetrate a naïve division, assigning the communication of free will to the voice and inevitability to the orchestra. The orchestra, representing the pressures on the characters, in the very same notes also charts the workings of their minds as they react to them. The vocal line presents the narrow, irreducible 'I': the orchestra depicts the pressures on that self both of internal thought by the individual and of outside agents, other people and physical forces. And because of its double function, at once, if desired, 'within' and 'outside' the individual, the orchestra can reflect the tragic paradox, both supporting the freedom and nobility implied by the vocal assertiveness of the characters and at the same time charting the forces which compel them mercilessly.

At each point of crisis, sentimentality is absent; Janáček's music seizes on the single, central thread, extracts the words concerning this from the book, and constructs a unified argument of words and music which concentrates solely on what is happening at the immediate moment.

Every one of Janáček's libretti gave him the chance to portray heroes and heroines fully aware of their predicaments, choosing not blindly but in as much knowledge as a human being can have of the inevitable consequences of their decision. When approaching the composition of his last opera, Janáček explained the attraction of Dostoevsky's criminal prisoners for him in simple words which would stand for any one of his leading characters: 'these splendid people—suddenly something comes over them, and they have to suffer'. Such is—and has always been—the unique manner of tragedy: the blend, on equal terms, of savagery and tenderness—the extreme polarities of the human spirit—in the evolution of situation and action to, and sometimes beyond, a disaster which, though superficially unexpected, is none the less deeply expected by the audience.

Text and music, then, are inextricably combined in communicating the inevitability of action. This enables the music—always powerful and intrusive—to carry the main burden of establishing a wider setting. Localizing, specific reference is at times needed, and the clattering mill-wheel of *Jenůfa* Act I, the storms, river voices, wood-nymphs or wounded eagle which assume meaning in the later libretti have undiluted force, set as they are on a musical axis together with the people to whose lives they have relevance; and they are at once qualified and elevated by the music. These elements are 'symbolic' enough to make loose talk of Janáček as a realist or naturalist absurd; but the word should not be used without qualification. Symbolism is bypassed, such objects having at once the larger resonance of the symbol and a full significance for what they are in themselves. We should speak rather of real phenomena which, congruent with the experience of the characters, yield wider overtones. In this there is a directness and economy, at once naïve and profound, which makes it possible to speak of Janáček as in a true sense a realist,

31

a dramatist who seeks immediate, unflinching confrontation with life.

And the absence of a systematic mythology or religious ethic from the operas is transcended by the role of the music. For the setting of events in the single focus of the music, and its achievement in linking the human world, bounded by the narrow confines of the self, to the areas beyond us which the Greeks described as divine, goes beyond the musical explication of obvious, substantive elements. Linguistic subtleties in the libretti, dangerously inadequate in themselves, are complemented by, and find a home in, music of this degree of response. This is the final reason why Janáček's operas could exist as tragedy at a time when no audience could be depended on to hold a single religious framework: Janáček's pantheism plays a crucial role in enabling him to achieve tragic stature. To be tied to a framework of belief would have been a constriction in an age where no one religion was any longer universal over the area for which symphonic music has meaning. Janáček's vision—and his published aphorisms make plain that he saw God in everything that lives and breathes—possessed a deep sense of the wonder of nature which is perfectly mirrored by the direct style of his music, natural in its unpredictability. And from the embracing powers of the music spring the sources of strength and vitality; Janáček can encompass and include the varied religious beliefs expressed by the characters in the stories he sets, believing in—and asking his audiences to believe in—at once all of them and none of them. All gods are included in a pantheon in which everything that lives has in it something of the divine, the marvellous. Again very Greek; Janáček's 'jiskra boží' in the motto of *From the House of the Dead* is, without qualification, *to theion*—the spark of God. The music enfolds the characters of the stage, and together they offer—without any tension—a whole which has meaning to any who can feel with European music.

Viewed and heard from the West, Janáček appears to be in simultaneous advance and retreat: Wagnerian passion, intensity and lyric power without the hypnotic effect, Italian objectivity but the *verismo* constantly marred by overt stylization, 'modern' harmony—especially in the late operas—alongside the retention, as a possible element of musical vocabulary, of the richest touches of romantic harmony, and much else. But every opera is homo-

32

geneous. We must adjust our perspective. We have to do with works which are neither advance nor retreat, and are not to be measured on the scales of any evolution. Janáček's operas have specific dramatic aims, those of tragedy; in realizing them he proceeded, musically, in directions of his own which explored the implications of a number of contemporary and classical views of the possible roles of music; and he grounded them, uniquely, in the narrative technique of Moravian folk song.

Janáček's position was such that this particular achievement was possible for him at a time when it was almost impossible elsewhere. Subscribing to naturalism sufficiently to avoid the attractions—and the dangers—of allegory, he was yet incomparably beyond the sphere of *verismo*. Janáček's sheer thoroughness and richness of detailed musical insight enabled him to go further, to introduce and integrate into his dramaturgy textual 'symbols' of larger implication and to handle convention with a freedom which is at moments astonishing. The higher seriousness combines with the truth to popular experience, which remains (there is no aloofness of art) in works which, for this reason, are at times as witty as they are profound. And this fusion is paralleled by the total fusion of drama and music. The tragic forces, within and around human beings, whose compulsion defines the limits of conduct, are embodied in forms and patterns of action; and in Janáček these forms have been combined so that they mix inextricably, in a manner totally different from that of any of his contemporaries.

Jenůfa

The mountains of eastern Moravia are moderate in height; though the upper regions are rugged, the valleys have none of the enclosed, confined feeling of the Alps. Only the remoteness of the upper villages, the endless conifers of the descent to the lower regions, oppress.

And—at the end of the nineteenth century—the strict religious morality subscribed to by the inhabitants. Act I of Preissová's play is set in the yard of a village's water-mill, source of wealth and therefore of social status to the feckless young hedonist, Števa Buryja, who has inherited its ownership. Števa has seduced Jenůfa, who works at the mill; and the stage seems set for a confrontation between him and Jenůfa's foster-mother, a formidable lady known throughout play and opera not by her name but by her title—Kostelnička, sextoness, and high in the hierarchy of the village's respect. Preissová makes the miller speak eloquently, early in the Act, of Kostelnička's own maltreatment, as a young woman, at the hands of her husband, Števa's uncle; and some interpreters have gone so far as to see the play in terms of class: Števa's seduction of Jenůfa has been read as a political critique, of the bourgeois 'gentleman's morality' of those who rely on their inherited wealth to abuse those who must work to live.

The indications on which this interpretation was built are minimal. The authoress 'wrote what she saw and felt' and considered politics to be outside the sphere of drama. The opera goes even further. Not only does it ignore the story's potential as a vehicle for analysis of class conflict, it avoids the dramatic possibilities of the struggle between religion and amorality.

There are no references to Kostelnička's past life, and a lengthy

34

scene between her and the mayor's wife, early in Act 1, is eliminated. There the play established her proud devotion to Jenůfa —but also her piety, strictness and severity. In the opera, however, after passing almost unnoticed across the stage, she does not appear again until her later, dramatic intervention in the action. And there the issues are very different.

Janáček removes Kostelnička from the centre for the first half of Act 1, asks us to take her moral strength, her role as guardian of the village's strict morality, for granted. And so the focus of the story shifts to the young woman who by this becomes its heroine. The Western title is—for the opera—appropriate: *Jenůfa*. And with this change the fourth principal, Laca, comes into his own—Števa's half-brother, jealous of him, as the opera opens, both for his inheritance and for his girl—observing the events penetratingly, but from behind the veil of ignorance of Jenůfa's pregnancy.

The shift in emphasis is intellectually neat. Both play and opera end with Jenůfa and Laca transcending the morality of the village as they achieve one after the other a depth of maturity in which unforgettable personal injury can, if the reasons which compelled the agent are fully and lovingly understood, be forgiven. The opera takes place in a closed community. These two people are alone in escaping the grip of its values; and they do so only after their characters have developed in the course of ardous suffering. It is therefore appropriate that the action should invite —and sustain—attention to them, from its outset; and a flaw in Preissová's original that she does not achieve this single-mindedly.

But there is far more to Janáček's adaptation than this. When the opera is complete, all characters have been shown to have received their deserts, on the most profound level; and all have progressed, morally, as far as they are capable. In the development of those who go furthest, each successive stage of growth is shown by the music to be the necessary result of the impact of their experiences. This is the opera's constant theme, aimed at by the composer from the opening; Janáček's music therefore focuses such a depth of insight on the situation of Jenůfa and Laca in the first Act that it reshapes the direction of the whole work. And in consequence, what was sentimental in the first Act of the play becomes deeply pathetic, and what was dramatically striking becomes tragic.

35

As the curtain rises, Jenůfa stands alone, apart from others, shading her eyes against the setting sun and looking into the distance, waiting. Today Števa is before the recruiting board. If he is not drafted, she trusts she will persuade him to marry her. If he is taken, her condition will soon be evident to all; and the village's judgement on the unmarried mother is pitiless, the solutions of our larger, secular societies beyond reach; the disgrace will drive Jenůfa to suicide.

So stated, the predicament is moving—but not tragic. Even the confrontation between Jenůfa and the village, foreshadowed here but ultimately evaded, would produce no inner tension, no paradigm of a tragic act, chosen yet inevitable. Janáček supplies another framework, larger than that of village morality, for Jenůfa's predicament; and as a result the opera's opening scene becomes universal in import, transcends the local limitations of the play.

Early in the Act Jenůfa, complimented by her Grandmother for her *rozum*—a complex word embracing both intellectual understanding and common-sense practicality—replies, with a sigh:

Alas, dear Grandmother, that good sense of mine
long since flowed away somewhere in the millstream!

Janáček fashions this moment, orchestrally, into one of the most intense penetrations of a character's mood in Act I. And with reason. For the opera seizes from the outset on this image of the millstream, and uses it to make tragic sense of Jenůfa's predicament. Orchestrally, the Act is dominated—from the very first bar, and at every lull in the action—by the emergence of a relentless, quiet C flat hammering from a xylophone concealed onstage, as if in the mill buildings. As if it were the mill-wheel; so that in the opera, all that happens in Act I is measured against the implacable flow of the mountain stream, the inevitable passing of time and the rhythm of work of the mill. Against this background the focus is different. Jenůfa's pregnancy appears not as transgression (as she herself sees it now) but as the natural consequence of the desire of an adolescent girl: her shame and anxiety in Act I become, in hindsight (to which Janáček will soon assist us), merely guilt, imposed as one of the village's strongest fetters; the force which will sweep it away becomes a torrent of

36

love and violence, through which she will mature immeasurably.

Act I lacks any other structural device; no other music but the insistent xylophone recurs so pointedly from scene to scene. So the implacable flow of nature is the only focus in which the music sets the action. Nature includes human nature: in the moment of self-realization cited above, the text explicitly links Jenůfa's 'lapse' to the natural flow. But beside this certainty—and that of the growing life in her womb—the heroine is as the opera opens ignorant of other, equally natural developing events: that Števa has had no lasting love for her; and that Laca loves her nearly to desperation. Jenůfa's hope of having retained Števa's love is unmasked as a fragile, self-protecting delusion; at the same time as this is revealed, so too is the increase of Laca's love and jealousy.

Janáček sees these as the two guiding threads of Act I: for he devotes the central energies of his music to portraying the developing contrast between the two characters, Jenůfa ever more self-protecting and vulnerable, Laca more and more aggressive as the Act proceeds. Števa's return, and its disastrous consequence in Kostelnička's intervention, seem almost parenthetical, an abrupt intrusion of the outside world into an Act which is essentially a sequence of clashes, progressively more violent, between two people: Jenůfa, with the Grandmother as her confidante, and Laca with the old miller as his.

The Act, then, is fundamentally a matter of three musics: that of Jenůfa and her slowly eroded illusions; that of Laca in his mounting aggressiveness; and the xylophone which measures both against the relentless unfolding of time—and so enables Janáček to show all this in later Acts as part of the inexorable progress of their growth to adulthood.

As the opera begins all is adolescent impatience, expectation, apprehension; and the events before Števa's arrival unfold with a concision and clarity which are hard to parallel even today from tragic opera. The opening pace is rather that traditionally associated with *buffa*, but even there few major operas other than *Le nozze di Figaro* spring to mind in comparison. In a brief prelude which leads directly into the action, Janáček expounds the musical essentials for understanding the first Act: the xylophone flow, with an anxious, semitonally circling theme implying the anxiety which it generates; an agitated central section whose opening figuration is soon to be taken for his own by Laca in his

37

first monologue; and an autumnal close whose rapturous cello descents, heard now only as rural tone-painting, soon become associated with Jenůfa's illusions. Expectation is matched by fulfilment—but an illusory fulfilment, as this autumnal calm is too easily attained. And so it is natural that the xylophone re-appears beneath these figurations as the curtain rises.

The pace is now of the essence: musically, each guarded, vulnerable moment in which Jenůfa seeks to withdraw herself is a rallentando, set like an island in surroundings of agitation and commotion. The accompaniment to her opening prayer is tense and sinister: it conveys as Jenůfa's both the semitonal circling and the agitated spiccati of the prelude; and so adds resonance to her predicament, showing it as a logical growth from the meaning of the xylophone of the opening.

With Laca's intervention the action proper begins; but Jenůfa decides to ignore his taunt, and turns away to apologize to her Grandmother for not working:

I shall make up for all of it.
I just remembered about my rosemary,
that it's fading;
I went to water it in the stream.
And if it should wither
look, Grandmother, they say
that all the luck in the world would go!

Janáček responds to the adolescent superstition of the text, clothing all this in precious textures, repetitive and fragile; the music becomes languid and even the vigorous movement with which Jenůfa turns away from Laca at the start is seen, musically, as introversion, a movement into a cocoon of self-indulgent despair.

Janáček now contrives a full revelation of Jenůfa's underlying emotions, both to show that her plight is to develop into something worthy of serious attention, and to foreshadow and explain in retrospect the depth of character to which she grows in the remainder of the opera. And the text provides a fine opportunity. A young shepherd-boy, Jano, enters. Jenůfa has taught him to read, and he begs for another exercise, recalling to Jenůfa a lost world of childhood rewards and punishments; his enthusiasm rushes the musical action on, catching even Jenůfa up in his ecstatic orchestral figuration. She gently puts him off; Jano returns, exultant, to his work. But the orchestra is ominous, unexpectedly sinister under the Grandmother's comment:

How much you enjoy it!
And you taught Barena to read too!
You've a man's sense, like your foster-mother:
you should have been a teacher.

And the action is suspended for Jenůfa's reply (Example 1).

The orchestral response is profound and complex, uniting many threads of the opera's action. The high tremolo of the violins looks back, to the anxieties of the opening prayer; the bass clarinet forward, to the young mother with child of the crucial moment in Act 2 where she cries out in her sleep. As the text makes the tie which explains in retrospect the dominance of the xylophone, the clarinet imitates, and takes from the vocal line's insecurity, the sliding descents from the end of the prelude; the imitation unmasks them as insecure, the tranquillity attained there—and again in the incident with the rosemary plant —as illusory. The orchestral response is therefore explosive, the abyss of possible tragedy before Jenůfa fully revealed as fragments of themes from the rosemary scene and from her prayer swell in agitated transformation. Calm is only gradually, tentatively restored.

Laca's position is the reverse of Jenůfa's. If she is subconsciously trying to retard the action, he is advancing it beyond the pace it would otherwise have. But his desires distort his character as much as hers, and the outcome is no more what he has desired than she.

Again, as with Jenůfa, the revelation of this potentially tragic position is careful and gradual. The two essentials are laid down at once: fiercely aggressive, outward-facing music of barely controlled violence erupts at Laca's first intervention in the action, a monologue ostensibly directed at the Grandmother but evidently racked with something more. It is not his Grandmother whose fondling of Števa's hair, 'golden like the sun', has caused Laca this eloquent pain.

Against the violence, the tenderness and depth. The miller will soon tell us that the aggression is not the whole man, rather an uncharacteristic mischievous manner assumed in Jenůfa's pre-

Ex. 1 (1.20:1)

sence; and it is vital to the plot that we realize this as early as possible. Preissová is therefore not slow to hint at this: the first encounter of Laca and Jenůfa ends with a rueful acknowledgement from the heroine that behind his sarcasm is the insight of his 'penetrating eyes'; but Janáček is impatient, and moves even faster. The slow middle section of Laca's opening monologue, where he recalls his emotional deprivation and misery, evokes a richness of feeling—simple, rapturous, obsessive figurations high in the register of the celli. This is a vital pointer to the development of the action, counterbalances immediately the danger of thinking of Laca purely as a man of natural aggression.

Laca, like Jenůfa, is supposed to be working. He is engaged in lopping a branch into a whipstick—a singularly frustrating activity when, as in this case, the knife is blunt. Preissová offers a parallel: as Jenůfa's work is shirked, while she delays in the illusory world of the fading rosemary plant, so Laca's becomes more and more frustrating, mirroring the increasing frustration of his love for her. But Laca's work is more closely involved in the action. The Act is framed round his three contacts with the heroine, each more tense than the one before, and in each of which she rebuffs him with increasing vehemence: the first, in which he touches her with words alone, and Jenůfa temporarily tames him; the second, in which he touches her with the whipstick, childishly tweaking her headscarf; the third at the end—and menacingly increased in power by the long delay—when he abandons his work and transfers his knife from the frustrating stick to the face of the intolerably frustrating girl.

Janáček is alert to the symmetry between the first two encounters. Just as he has used the aftermath of the first for the revelation of Jenůfa's character, retarding the action in accordance with her inclinations until the return of reality in the passage printed as Example 1, so too the aftermath of the second is used to reveal Laca's. Laca plays with Jenůfa's headscarf to Example 2,

Ex. 2a (1.22:1)

Ex. 2b (1.23:1)

Ex. 2c (1. 24:8)

a motif of classic Janáček versatility which only gradually takes
on its full meaning as the scene unfolds. First appearing (2a)
with the miller's entrance, it might there seem only to characterize him. But in retrospect it is entirely the music of Laca's
frustration, even there—for the miller asks 'What are you doing,
young man?', and the motif rises to explosive violence in explanation of Laca's reply. Then a high version (2b) accompanies the
exchange between Jenůfa and Laca as he tweaks her scarf—
undermining the impression that the episode is merely playful.
After Jenůfa leaves, the miller praises Jenůfa's attractiveness—
and the theme here (2c) is a 'meno mosso' transformation of the
same figure. The connotations are then in no doubt: this is music
of the power Jenůfa has over Laca; and by now the cumulative
effect on him is that Laca is forced into revealing his love.

The revelation is simply contrived: Janáček just makes Laca
repeat, to a different, deeply emotional vocal line, the last clause
of his sarcastic retort to the miller 'Me! You can just see for
yourself, how much I love her.'—And the music, by transforming
2b into 2c, has already made us see the scarf incident in a deeper
light; the playfulness is suppressed, violent passion. The rallentando is therefore momentary: now that the energies driving
Laca are fully established, this same music rushes on, propelled
by his obsessive vigour and explaining his open declaration:

> But, miller, he hasn't got her yet, he hasn't got her yet. If
> he has been taken today at the recruiting station, there will
> be no wedding. There will be no wedding.
> MILLER: He's not drafted!

Janáček's *coup de théâtre* (contrived by a massive cut in the
play) completes a pattern. Laca has overreached himself, and his

defeat at this moment is as crushing as Jenůfa's apparent triumph. The opera's exposition is over.

The ironies here are complex. Števa's evasion of the draft is predictable: luck goes along with his wealth to flout justice. But (for reasons not yet evident) it will not bring the outcome which Jenůfa hopes and Laca fears. As the drama breaks out of the tissue of hopes and fears surrounding the question whether Števa has been drafted, Janáček crystallizes the situation in a short, harsh and agitated ensemble for his vocal quartet, almost grotesque in the violent way in which it binds together Jenůfa's desperate joy with Laca's outrage and barely concealed fury. Kostelnička prefigures her role in the next scene: her brief entry breaks the circling chain of emotions which the news evokes, and the suddenness with which the musical fabric collapses as, passing rapidly across the stage, she simply asks with total disbelief 'Števa not drafted?', shows how fragile and temporary those emotions are. Laca, in an expressive stage direction, 'takes off his hat and returns to work', Kostelnička goes into the mill-house. The orchestra, after a brief eruption as Jenůfa begs to be allowed to remain and not to have to follow Kostelnička, falls silent.

These facts alone would secure for the next episode a feeling of digression: Jenůfa and Laca retire to the sidelines; the old miller and Grandmother, the only other characters we yet know well, are silent. But there is more. Števa, returning festive from success with the drafting board, is accompanied by a band of musicians, and a male-voice chorus of recruits. When the main orchestra resumes, it is to support, maintain and finally adopt a melody which has been dictated by Števa and his group; accepted also by the female mill-workers who come out to meet them as they return—so creating the opera's first scene with full chorus. A totally new mood invades the stage and the pit, imposed from outside. The mood is strikingly, unmistakably characterized. For the first time in *Jenůfa* the music presents a sustained consistency of key (A flat minor), an even rhythmic drive, and a steady growth of consistent orchestral textures. The recruits' folk song gradually becomes audible as they approach; and its text gives precision to this total contrast from the world of Jenůfa and Laca; an uncomplicated, irresponsibly optimistic outlook on the future:

43

All who want to marry
are afraid of war,
and I'm not marrying—
I'm not afraid of war.

Števa—who proposes to avoid both alternatives—joins none the less in the song, adding with particular enthusiasm to the refrain 'and that's the end of love!'; he enters drunk, with flowers given by other girls in his hat, and to this reckless text. He has reverted to or—on a harsher but more justifiable reading of the play— never left the irresponsibility of adolescence.

The point is not lost on Jenůfa. She realizes that she must halt the momentum of these massed, dancing young people; and does so, with three gigantic calls on his name. And in the moment of calm so imposed she has her last moment of peace in Act 1. She summons all the energies of her introverted, self-cherished love to her appeal 'My darling, Števa, Števuška'; for so the music tells us, as the darkest orchestral instruments meditate on Example 1a. And then the pain—tellingly illuminated in the music—sweeps her over the brink into the unforgivable re-proach: 'O Števa you're drunk again!'

With this the love of Števa for Jenůfa is dead, and he insults her mercilessly. Her later attempts—in the closing scenes of the Act—to pretend otherwise are heard, musically, as totally futile and become, in the last scene with Laca, simply dangerous.

But Jenůfa has no time to appreciate the tragic loss of this moment, her first words in the opera with Števa. In her defeat he and his music resume control. After flaunting his wealth and his other women before her, Števa with adolescent superficiality and drunken fickleness decides to heal the breach. He commissions 'Jenůfa's favourite song' from the musicians, and persuades her to dance with him to it.

It is a measure of her desperation that he succeeds. But Janáček does not illustrate her motivation in the orchestra. The song-text, openly symbolic, tells us plainly enough what Jenůfa is doing— comforting a fallen idol. And so Janáček concentrates on the action: the orchestra goes wild, conveying the hubris as a drunken 'hero' and a pregnant heroine attempt a fearsomely difficult brigands' dance.

Kostelnička intervenes, and tremolo violas on C flat recall the musical world of Jenůfa's anxieties from the start of the opera. But it is fatal to understanding here to follow the first impression which this gesture gives, that of a return to reality after Števa's gay diversions. Kostelnička is no more in responsible control of events than Števa. Indeed, her music rapidly shows that she is hardly in control of herself as she hands down her rebuke to Jenůfa and forbids the marriage unless Števa can stay sober for a year.

Janáček's dramatic position here is tenuous, and only the richness of musical reference saves him. Despite his drastic cuts, Kostelnička's rebuke must have behind it not only her own severity but also the full force of the village's morality, and establish her as its (admittedly harsh) guardian. But the opera, equally, cannot confront us unprepared at the opening of Act 2 with Kostelnička's obsessive, 'moral' hatred of Jenůfa's child, her brooding on Jenůfa's sin. Janáček therefore exploits the orchestra's ambiguous position when more than one character is on stage: read outwardly, the music here illuminates the impact on Jenůfa of the disastrous prohibition, as a public event of such severity that she dare not disobey; read inwardly, there is barely controlled strain to be heard in Kostelnička's mind as the patterns by which she gropes towards a verdict repeatedly explode in a flurry of woodwind. With this preparation, the apocalyptic orchestral gestures when Kostelnička calls down divine sanction —'God will surely strike you, if you disobey me'—yield the necessary irony: both the almost physical impact of the new, unlooked for defeat on Jenůfa, and the nail which Kostelnička, in ignorance of Jenůfa's pregnancy, is driving into the coffin of her own vision of the order of the world.

In this way the opera successfully avoids having to be specific on a matter in which the play has much to say—why Kostelnička is so severe. And by cutting all reference to Kostelnička's past experiences, Janáček avoids having to express in Act 1 a clear attitude to the village's strict morality. Judgement is clouded in Act 2 by the fact that there its only representative is Kostelnička, whose sensibilities are of course warped. By Act 3, the 'stone her' ensemble presents the village at its most unpleasantly severe. A fierce contrast is thus attained: for by then Jenůfa has developed to a position where she is able to transcend the village's code.

That transcendence will be achieved by understanding, born

from a vision of the future. Lack of such vision is what Kostelnička and Števa share, a self-confident willingness to act irrevocably, regardless of possible future consequences. And this
fact—their relative superficiality now, in comparison with Jenůfa
and Laca, on whom our attention has been fixed—explains how
they come and go with little explanation and can still plausibly
wreak disastrous effect on the main action. Kostelnička, her
intervention accomplished to her satisfaction, leaves; Števa leans
drunk and silent against a pillar; the musicians are chased off;
and the quartet ensemble regroups, to close off the Act's grand
opera episode as they began it.

But again the crystallization is premature. It is made in a
medium uncharacteristic of Janáček's mature work; a fully
worked out vocal quartet with chorus, treating one musical
theme and one text—'every couple must overcome their sufferings'—in a traditional manner which (as Janáček acknowledged
later in life, somewhat apologetically) indulges the purely musical
argument of the ensemble at the expense of dramatic timing.
This fact alone indicates that the quartet can in no sense be a final
summary; it is too alien to the overall idiom of *Jenůfa* to be
authoritative. And Janáček redeems his dramatic 'lapse' by
fashioning out of the simple text and placidly flowing melody a
miniature drama in which Jenůfa, coaxed by her emotions into
joining the ensemble and forcing the melody to a height at which
it can express her anguish, is joined there by Laca; but ignores
the congruence of his emotion with hers, and leads the other
characters to acceptance and musical resolution. As an immediate response to what has just happened, the quartet is perhaps
adequate; but not in relation to all that has taken place in *Jenůfa*
Act 1. As the mill-workers leave, and the sentimental ensemble
ends, reality returns. Disclosed under the last embers of the
theme as it plays itself out is the inexorable xylophone, now long
unheard, on its customary C flat.

Logically, perhaps, we are now only one scene from the end:
Jenůfa and Laca in their final confrontation. Instead Preissová
offers first a scene in which Jenůfa begs Števa to marry her, and
he, maudlin drunk, promises with hollow rhetoric not to desert
her, 'if only for your apple-blossom cheeks'. All that seems to be
gained is an added motivation: Laca overhears the end of this
scene as he returns, and it therefore implants in him the idea of

slashing Jenůfa's cheek to make her unattractive to Števa. Jenůfa's reproaches are predictable; Števa's responses unpleasant. Why does Janáček retain this scene?

The xylophone's recall to reality is a recall to the issues of the opera before Števa's arrival—issues exacerbated, of course, by his drunken dance and Kostelnička's intervention. One of the effects of recent events has been to shock Jenůfa out of the languid torpor in which she has shielded herself from Števa's true character. Her intervention in the quartet—whose text is not a banality to her—is the first sign of this development; and the total desperation to which she is now reduced is finely illustrated by Janáček, who makes her repeat herself again and again, in florid and futile coloratura against musically irrelevant pedal points.

And this total desperation is necessary, if the inevitability of Laca's act in the final scene is to be established. Preissová's first Act is not in itself high tragedy; Laca's closing action remains merely plausible—if only too much so. Janáček's final scene achieves tragic inevitability, chiefly because it rests on the gradual development of *both* principals over the whole Act, to a point at which, hardly in control of their actions, they provoke each other beyond endurance. Laca's feverish agitation is, of course, the main component of the disaster; but—as will be seen —only slightly less important is Jenůfa's complete despair. That is why this scene with Števa is necessary: reduced to abject grovelling, suicide threats—and even finally to impotent physical assault against a man she now knows to be ridiculous and feeble (and whose promises she rightly discounts)—but who yet is her only hope—Jenůfa is in a state to make the one mistake that will provoke Laca. And she does. In the last scene, with the hopeless aggressiveness of the really weak, she flaunts her love of Števa before Laca to a lilting, defiant dance rhythm. The effect of this lie—that Števa is a better man than Laca—is terrible. As the embers of the dance theme burn themselves out in the orchestra, a low B is revealed. Laca simply, ironically repeats her boast: 'you can take pride?'—and from then on is driven into himself, is meditating within himself rather than talking to her.

For this reason the last scene is, truly, Laca's; and the culmination of threads gathered early in the Act and held since his scene with the miller. Against his interests and against his deepest

47

wishes Laca, tormented beyond endurance by Števa's praise of her 'apple-blossom cheeks', slashes Jenůfa's face with his knife and destroys their beauty.

Janáček explains, with devastating clarity. Števa, as he leaves, praises her beauty to a loud, rhetorically simplified, repetitive and brassy version of Example 2, showing, of course, that Jenůfa's appeal to him is the same as that which had provoked Laca, but in the eyes of this lesser man generating the oratorical, hubristic pride of one who thinks he can control a woman's beauty, and own it. He is soon enough deflated; the by now frankly menacing xylophone C flat returns after these flatulent textures as he goes, and now for the first time is joined by other instruments: violas attack the same rhythm and pitch, as Laca comes forward to confront Jenůfa, showing that the human action has finally attained the pitch of the inexorable flow of time and the mill-wheel. But the penetrating tie of total illumination has been made a few moments earlier, as Števa for the first time promised to stand by her 'if only for your apple-blossom cheeks'. Janáček accompanies this with the ecstatic high cello slides first heard at the end of the prelude, and totally tied by their use in the rosemary episode to her adolescent, near-virginal beauty. After this, Laca's slashing of those cheeks takes on precise meaning: he strips from Jenůfa, already too mature in mind for Števa, Števa's chosen token of the physical beauty for which he values her. Pure jealous violence? But subconsciously, Laca is taking the first step to making Jenůfa worthy of his deeper, inner love.

In the final scene, Janáček illustrates this complex psychological point powerfully. The moments before the deed are anguished beyond description; but Laca's power is such that he can deflect the xylophone, for the first time, from its customary B or C flat: thrust down a semitone, it creates the most intense of several tritone clashes with which Janáček illuminates the anguish of the moment, the deeper man's crisis as he meditates on the superficiality of the shallower. And the tritone is the characteristic interval of Act 2. With this irrevocable violence, the action is lifted on to a higher plane of seriousness. A point which is frighteningly illustrated as Laca cuts Jenůfa's face. Janáček blasts with four brutal horns through the delicate textures of Act 1, shattering the autumnal lightness which is the dominant mood of the Act and prefiguring the astonishing, permanent increase in the opera's intensity from the beginning of Act 2.

His action shatters every care of Jenůfa's, every hope of Laca's own—and forces both of them, in temporary disgrace, to retire from the closed nineteenth-century community from which they are eventually to escape; retirement in which they both mature. So this furious hurling of the opera's idiom from ambiguous, often triadic eloquence to the ferocious clarity, fluidity and tension of the harmony of the two subsequent Acts establishes a deep congruence with the stage drama. But Janáček has a final task: to set Laca's act in perspective. In tragic perspective, for the question is: accidental or deliberate? Preissová's text carries, split between the spectator Barena and the miller's closing comments, the paradox that is at the heart of tragedy, that it is both; inevitable, and willed—but an undesired accident and so freely chosen. And Janáček's music arranges the closing moments so as to order and give authority to this suggestion. Barena's theory that Laca hurt Jenůfa by accident—a desperate attempt to keep what has happened within the bounds of the community's experience—is backed by Laca's repentance, which is presented simultaneously, and sincerely reiterated; but the orchestral image, rushing downward scales for strings, shows the ebb of such energies in the chaos and panic after the deed. A constantly shifting pedal, together with an upward turn in the rushing strings, soon chronicles Laca's gradually increasing nausea; and the backward-looking images are dissolved in the forward-looking realism of the ending. The tension breaks, and Laca takes to his heels as a flash of brass violently breaks the textures. Looking back, Laca's is a young man's act of folly, easily repented; looking forward, it is naked, adult violence for which deep forgiveness is needed. The second view is given, in the miller's mouth, the separated chords of a curtain line, not because it contradicts Barena, but because it looks forward, to the second Act and beyond. 'Don't run, Laca! You did it to her on purpose! On purpose!'

Laca has already run. In the immediate aftermath, he cannot face the consequences of his action.

With Act 2 we are plunged into a different world. Winter in place of autumn; an indoor setting; and a drama of fierce intensity, leading to hideous crime. It is played by the four principal characters alone, with the village only an unseen presence separated from Kostelnička's home by the snow. Jenůfa now bears the visible scar of Laca's knife-slash, and has confessed her pregnancy. Kostelnička, unable to bear the disgrace, has concealed her, pretending to the village that she is away from home; the lie is the first sign of the strain imposed on Kostelnička by the tension between her severe moral standards and her foster-daughter's 'sin'. Of the two women one is unable to leave the house, the other has little reason to do so. We have left the world of men, reckless, ever-active, their actions to be moralized on by old women, suffered by the young; the course of the drama has been taken beyond their control, become locked into a world dominated by women, stiffling and enclosed, heavy with the responsibilities of children and of marriage. The two women stand firmly; the men who visit the cottage do so hesitantly, anxious—in different ways—about the burdens and obligations which may be imposed on them there. Janáček gathers all these aspects of the changed situation into one arresting gesture, plunging us with the ominous opening bar into such a world and maintaining throughout the Act a sustained level of intensity almost without parallel in modern music-drama.

Janáček, unlike his male characters, enters the world of *Jenůfa* Act 2 without hesitation; for him as for Ibsen, the enclosed, domestic room is among the truest stamping-grounds, in the modern world, of high tragedy. With the men diminished in role by the setting, Kostelnička comes into her own, and now achieves dramatic importance equal to that of the heroine. Her murder of Jenůfa's baby, studied with penetrating insight, is the chief tragic act in *Jenůfa*; and by its position, central in the running time of this Act and of the opera, this becomes the pivot on which the action turns and round which the central meaning of Janáček's opera is displayed.

For with Jenůfa and Kostelnička as balanced central characters, Act 2 is able to dramatize at full strength the moral issues latent in their roles in Act 1. As Kostelnička loses real moral stature through the course of this Act, Jenůfa is shown gaining it. Strain distorts Kostelnička's morality into an insane parody of itself, while Jenůfa grows in her sufferings. The turning-point is Kostelnička's departure from the house; after she has degenerated into blasphemy and murder a monologue for Jenůfa follows immediately. It provides a counterbalance and contrast, since in it she begins to throw off the shackles of dependence on her foster-mother and grow towards self-awareness and moral self-sufficiency. At the time when this has been achieved, in the closing scene of the Act, Kostelnička's guilt causes her total breakdown.

Musically, this subject-matter is foreshadowed immediately, and the contrast between the two women is laid before the audience in the first scene. The prelude offers two violently contrasted themes:

Ex. 3a (2.0:3)

Ex. 3b (2.1:1)

and their associations are rapidly made clear after the curtain rises: 3a persists under Kostelnička's questioning ('Why are you always going to by the window to pray, like a lost soul?') and Jenůfa's reply, but is dissolved in a reprise of 3b as Kostelnička confesses her inner restlessness. The contrast is patent: the clarinets, circling placidly in thirds, indicate a person who, if restless, is in inner calm, accepts her mental turmoil and has no will to be anything but what she is now. This is shown by the way in which the melody is repeated, with each reprise running smoothly into the start of the next. 3b, in contrast, is explosive, an irreversible movement: it positively invites development into a new, animated, explanatory phrase. This is exactly what it receives: Kostelnička launches into an extended monologue, venting her shame, fear and anxiety during Jenůfa's pregnancy and childbirth, and her anger at Števa's having ignored the whole affair. Preissová gives the opportunity for a total contrast between

51

the two women: as Kostelnička concludes this outburst, Jenůfa starts from her chair towards the bedroom, fearful that the baby Števuška has woken from sleep. But he hasn't, he is sleeping: 'he is so lovely and quiet; in his eight days in this world, he has never once cried.'

Kostelnička's monologue was set to agitated transformations (4a, b, c) of a single, angular, strained motive, her vocal line little more than declamation; tonality was grossly unstable throughout. The text's insight is expressed directly; difficult though it may be to realize, both women are talking about the same subject— Jenůfa's baby. To the mother he is a person, while to Kostelnička, obsessed with her vision of the moral disgrace of Jenůfa's sin and Števa's desertion, it is a thing. Persons are less easy to hate. Janáček backs this vision powerfully; the contrast is acute as Jenůfa and her baby become the focus of orchestral attention: under descending violin tremolos an unutterably beautiful melody, 'dolce con espressione', unfolds itself serenely in B flat major on violas and clarinets. But the music is not merely a matter of static tableaux. Kostelnička continues to mutter protests against Jenůfa's love for the child, but her motive is reduced by the force of that love to tame querulousness (4d); and when Jenůfa returns it is transformed into a version as beautiful as her own theme (4e): and it is this which persists.

Ex. 4 (2.5 to 2.9)

A further, violent outburst is similarly tamed—this time by an accelerated, swirling viola version of 3a. A dynamic situation, then, in which Jenůfa's moral worth tames Kostelnička's distorted vision of the events. Jenůfa has the power to do this simply because of the natural force of her motherhood, of the harmony of mother and baby; the lyric expansiveness lavished both on this episode and on the orchestral 'good-night' music which surrounds Jenůfa as she goes to bed at the end of the scene are vital to understanding of the Act. Janáček is beginning to set up a true counterweight to Kostelnička's perverted religious 'goodness', in the inner goodness which Jenůfa has acquired through mother-hood, the unity with nature which motherhood confers. The use of harmony in this music, the contrast between tonal consistency in the orchestra's complex hymn to Jenůfa's beauty and the 'unnatural' dissonance of Kostelnička's shame imposed by human moral criteria, is at the essence of the opera's meaning.

But Jenůfa's goodness is acquired too late, and in too passive a form, to prevent the tragic events of this Act. Jenůfa is tired, weak; tends in this scene not to contradict her foster-mother but only to dissent tacitly. Further, Kostelnička has prepared her a sleeping-draught, which she takes as she goes; the stage is Kostelnička's, from now until the moment of disaster.

Preissová provides a series of monologues, framing and punctuating Kostelnička's two confrontations—with Števa, and with Laca; Janáček fashions these, with fine response to situation, into a precise study of a gradual loss of moral control, graded in intensity from the fury of this first scene to the blasphemous hysteria and insane visions of the last monologue. And so explains, profoundly, the murder of the child. The most drastic means are not shirked: Janáček is, uncharacteristically, willing to risk drowning the voice in *tutti* sound at the climaxes; and predominant throughout Kostelnička's music here is the interval of the tritone, its disruption of tonal sense in the musical argument closely parallel to the breakdown of Kostelnička from the authoritative calm of her first words in the Act to the broken, isolated woman who murders the child.

Janáček's study begins the moment Jenůfa has left the stage; the first monologue characterizes Kostelnička's hatred for Števa and his child, musically, with a startlingly new vehemence: this is not a cold, rational hatred, but a surging, almost physical nausea. And the libretto presents a drama of ironies and of rapid reversals: Janáček is given the opportunity to illustrate not only the intensity of the hatred but also the reason for it. 'I've got no choice but to give Jenůfa to Števa, into misery—and also humble myself before him.' The pathos with which Janáček sets the first part of this protects the audience from a vital mistake; the first cause of Kostelnička's torments in this act is not her own pride, but her love for Jenůfa. The reminder is necessary; the cause is shortly to be buried under the effects, and will not be regained until the vast, understanding forgiveness of Jenůfa herself in Act 3 recovers it.

With Števa, Kostelnička follows her own prescription. But her mask of placid persuasion is in danger of slipping from the out-set: the vocal lines are excessively tense, out of proportion to the text. And the open appeal to which his cowardice provokes her is desperate; the accompaniment is a sustained tritone tremolo; and that, combined with the bare continuity of the melody in the upper strings, is firm indication of her pain. The appeal is too emotional; it is inevitable that Števa should reject it.

This scene is a study in overreaction; for Števa too is carried away beyond his intentions. Here he has been freed from his stereotype role in Act 1. The weakness and the willingness to evade any responsibility remain; but the wholly hostile view is now eroded: Janáček wants us to understand and sympathize even with his weakest protagonist. Under Kostelnička's re-proaches, Števa expresses regret about the child; and the tritone falls of the orchestra acknowledge that the pressure on him was a real one. And when he confesses his helplessness, a horn chorus expresses sympathy. There is sympathy, too, in the way in which his outburst is generated from a stab of mental pain, caused by Kostelnička's mention of the child. But he is carried away; his responsibilities have become too much for him; his fear of both women leads him into furious denunciation first of Jenůfa and then of Kostelnička, and the orchestra's reckless gathering of momentum shows how he loses control. So too Kostelnička, who in reply, provoked beyond endurance, is prompted to 'a horrible outburst'. Agony leads, for her as for Števa (but no longer for Jenůfa), to disastrous action. Števa makes his escape.

Kostelnička is stilled by Jenůfa's cry in her sleep, which raises her for a moment to Jenůfa's moral level as she attunes herself to the deep peace of the sleeping young mother. But she broods on her situation. Alternately repressed and stimulated by events, it is natural that Kostelnička's next outburst, when Jenůfa settles again, leads in the text to a vision of the child dead—and, musically, to an orchestral outburst which, correspondingly, is unprecedented in its violence. But now the pattern of ever-increasing tension is altered. Janáček brings out the irony in-herent in Laca's arrival, apparently as Kostelnička's saviour but in fact to drive her over the brink; the action is seen as slowly running down towards the disaster. We hear Kostelnička, exhausted, assent to the gentle flow of the reassuring conversation; she has always favoured Laca: his loyalty matches her desire to save Jenůfa. And the final, fatal error is one she could never have predicted. Trapped by the fact that he comes as if the answer to her prayers, caught up in the flow of the music to whose accompaniment he declares his undying love for Jenůfa and so willing herself to agree with him, she misses—fatally—the underlying rhetoric (all too audible to us) which lies behind and joins together his assertions; and when his love is put to the test, and he is told that the Jenůfa whom he idealizes has borne a child of Števa's, he falters. Kostelnička, desperate, feels she has no choice but to utter an irrevocable lie.

Janáček marks the moment with turbulent chaos in the orchestra; for a moral universe is as shattered by this act as by the slashing of Jenůfa's cheek in Act I. But this time the act is not self-contained: the consequences of the lie are not within itself; they are worked out in subsequent, immediate action. Janáček takes advantage of the fact that after Kostelnička has hurried Laca out there is a further monologue before the central act: he slows the pace of the action to a halt, and uses Kostelnička's final monologue to review and gather in one all the sufferings of the first half of the Act.

The monologue which leads to the murder of Jenůfa's baby is of classic simplicity. With the grave calm of a tragedian in complete control of his powers, Janáček makes no attempt to remind us of the respectable, authoritative Kostelnička of the opening. Instead he gives us an old, crushed Slav woman, stripped of every feature of personality, utterly alone in a vast emptiness. Out of the cruel separations of the silence appear three groups of notes for tremolo strings; circling, recurrent traps of thought which slowly connect, begin to overcome the mental paralysis caused by the knowledge that Laca will soon return. As Kostelnička's thoughts link up, agony and reminiscence begin to lead her towards action. For each group but the third closes in an impasse; but with the third 'in that way I would redeem her life', love for Jenůfa breeds the idea of destroying the child.

Never referred to, of course, in those terms. Preissová is as acute as Janáček: Kostelnička passes to the thought in oblique allusions, and from those to euphemism and blasphemy: 'I will carry the child to God.' Janáček hears the descent to this blasphemy as crucial; he breaks the chain of reasoned musical argument with a powerful intervention of the horns just before this line of text, and sets it and the rest of the scene as a crescendo of madness. The blasphemy is the measure of Kostelnička's moral descent; it is as deeply shocking as it is deeply appropriate that the final collapse of the village's spiritual guardian should be expressed in the language of the God whose values she had fought to uphold.

By position the strategic centre of the opera, this moment is also its nadir: the point in the plot at which all the worst consequences of the opening situation have taken place, and from which the overall movement is upwards, to resolution. But it is a long upward movement. The last scene has seen a crescendo to the horrific triumph of evil, and the positive elements, as the second half of the opera begins, are of the most tenuous: represented, in fact, by one disgraced, disfigured and at this moment drugged and physically weak girl. For this reason Janáček offers a total contrast: from Kostelnička's dissonant tutti to a single solo violin.

Still, the immediate gains are rapid: though the action is, at this moment, at its most hostile to her—Kostelnička is murdering her child—Jenůfa has already been established in this Act as measured, calm and noble, by her music in the first scene. So it is not implausible that now, after the opening, helpless dependence, Jenůfa rapidly begins to take stock of the situation for herself. The rises and falls of the violin melody chronicle her mind's surges of thought and its relapses into drugged obedience; and almost immediately we are confronted with the beginnings of extroversion and independence.

The means to this are characteristic of the composer and central to the understanding of this work. Jenůfa's independence and clear-headedness come at the moment when the violin sustains its top notes and decorates them—a moment which is attained as Jenůfa opens the shutters and contemplates the night, with moon and a canopy of stars shining for the poor. Looking out into the night, harmonizing herself with nature, Jenůfa for the first time in the opera considers the predicament of someone other than herself.

The gain is consolidated. Janáček interprets Preissová's play as offering him a pattern the reverse of Kostelnička's in the first part of the Act: each successive shock inflicted on Jenůfa leads, not to greater agitation, but to deeper calm. Already there has been one such moment, as Jenůfa absorbed the fact that her foster-mother is not there; and now a feverish search for her baby, whose climax is a desperate vision of Števuška's danger, is succeeded by a greater peace: Jenůfa's Ave Maria is set to slow, undulating arpeggios, musical images of massive calm and stability which powerfully influenced Alban Berg, so vividly are they echoed in the opening bars of his violin concerto as the expressive portrait of the purity of his 'angel', Manon Gropius. And which convey in *Jenůfa* not only peace of mind, equilibrium and the ability to face the human suffering to which the prayer's text makes reference, but also—as three octaves are spanned in the rise and fall of the melody—the new expansiveness of Jenůfa's sensibilities. Her prayer, its heartfelt depth a shattering surprise, is yet natural after the scene at the window, and it sets up both an immediate, firm counterbalance to Kostelnička's blasphemy and an image of inner strength in Jenůfa which is essential to make credible her response when Kostelnička returns.

Again, a blow which should shatter her. And the impact is heightened by a ferocious irony: just before Kostelnička tells her her child is dead, Jenůfa creates for herself a joyful image of Števa, accepting his child, bringing it back and staying, won over by its lovable nature. This is the last self-created illusion in the opera; from now on, the movement is to the full revelation of truth. The impact of the particular truth revealed now is of such force that Jenůfa regresses, briefly, to dependence, her head buried in her foster-mother's lap. But again the restored calm is correspondingly greater in proportion to the degree of impact; the section which is often called Jenůfa's 'lament' is in fact a refusal to lament; a total, at first faltering, absorption of the fact of her child's death; its depth of response again totally 'unexpected', but yet a logical advance from the acceptance of universal suffering seen in the prayer scene. In Janáček's wandering thirds for woodwind can be heard both a tender questioning and a true acceptance. And Kostelnička's attempts to make Jenůfa grateful for her freedom are stilled.

In the last scene of the Act, Laca returns, pledges himself to Jenůfa, and is accepted; Kostelnička blesses the newly engaged couple. Preissová is well aware that even in the compressed time scale of this fast-moving Act, the scene is near to psychological implausibility: a considerable amount of dramatic time is needed on Jenůfa's first meeting with Laca since he wounded her, to establish the depth of his love for her, and for Jenůfa (whose integrity is absolute) to accept it for a fact, to abandon the hopes and affections which for an Act and three-quarters have been centred on Števa, and accept Laca despite the fact that she does not love him. Preissová's text therefore enlarges on these matters. Janáček, however, rightly senses that the Act must be concluded within a very few minutes to retain a proper dramatic balance; he therefore cuts heavily, including all of Laca's affirmations of the depth and constancy of his love. The libretto's final scene looks totally implausible on paper; but Janáček solves both the problems musically. Laca's new sincerity and depth are simply taken for granted in this scene as it stands—but this does not matter in the opera, since Janáček more than makes up for this by the power of his setting of Laca's declarations in the scene between Jenůfa and Laca alone early in Act 3. And this leaves the orchestra here free to concentrate on the other problem, Jenůfa's rapid change of heart. Insoluble and unsolved in the play, it has already been partly transcended in the opera. Jenůfa's music in Act 2 has already taken her character to a depth far beyond that of Števa and his world; her references to him can therefore be set lightly, almost parenthetically. Combined with careful pacing and the utmost psychological subtlety, this enables Janáček to transform her response to Laca here from the implausible to the inevitable.

Laca's first appeal is set to music of almost reverent devotion; but the music sees her initial response to him as paralysed by shame, her attempts to talk to him as distant, embarrassed. But the music flowers; the sheer goodness of heart embodied in Jenůfa's attempts to thank him leads in the orchestra, in her mind, to an explanation:

I used to think very differently about life
but now perhaps it is as if I stood at the end of it.

Janáček sets this as a deep contemplation of herself and her predicament, showing a Jenůfa of far greater depth of insight than ever before; over a bitonal pedal and dragging ostinato, the whole-tone scale from C rises and falls in what appears to amount to a clear, considered rejection of Laca by a woman who sees herself as trapped by dishonour. But the dolcissimo flute doubling of the last line indicates that this is not all that is in Jenůfa at this moment; and in rebuking Kostelnička for her optimism, she is obliged to apologize to Laca. Now, moved by his renewed appeal, she turns from implying she is an unsuitable bride to asking whether Laca really wants her as she is. After the deep introversion of the whole-tone passage, the music flowers out in solo violin, belying the import of these words. Jenůfa is desirable: and in the very act of asking him whether he wants her she has moved from tacit rejection to presupposing that she might accept. And so she is committed.

The Act closes ferociously, Kostelnička reduced to breakdown. Nature rebels as a pointer to the action of the next Act: the outburst is provoked by the outrageous arrogance of Kostelnička's 'I've done right, considering everything'; a true marriage cannot be based on an undiscovered murder, and Kostelnička disintegrates from blessing their engagement to hideous curses against Števa and against herself. The music reuses the crucial horn phrase in which her sanity was destroyed in the monologue leading to the murder; and so makes clear that she is undermined by the weight of her guilt. She is reduced to an hysteria in which the storm, blowing open the window, is for her the hand of Death.

Janáček is able to gather into this moment the whole burden of the Act: Jenůfa, going to close the window, exclaims, 'Ha, what a wind and frost!', and the vocal line gives us the alert, innocent young woman, at one with nature, whom we saw in her own scene at the window. It is the measure of the outrage, the unnatural distorted world of this moment, that this cry is brutally drowned in the *fff* crescendo of Kostelnička's orchestra; for her moral reading of the storm is correct, prefigures the role of nature in the discovery of her crime in Act 3. Kostelnička's terror is backed by the excruciating, protracted agony of the curtain music: the sheer terror generated by this Act cannot be cut off, the pent-up horror must be released in the music. This Janáček does, and so forces us to witness a closing tableau of utter contrast between the two women. A contrast which carries over to inform the meaning of the final Act.

In theory, the third Act is weak. Kostelnička's crime is discovered, she confesses, and is forgiven. Laca and Jenůfa begin a new life for themselves, on a deeper plane. Hardly enough material for a full Act; nor is there the linear intensity of the argument of Act 2. Add to this the traditional (though surely false) feeling that a tragedy must have an unhappy *ending*, and it is easy to feel that with *Jenůfa* Act 3 the level of achievement has fallen.

The impression might be compounded: for much of the early part of the Act Janáček is content to follow rather than to lead; the contributions of the music in the previous Acts establish most of what Preissová now writes as the natural consequences of what we have seen, and there is little in the first half of this Act which demands exceptional illumination from Janáček in order to make the resolution credible on the level of high tragedy. But Preissová's wedding preparations are not carelessly written: they put quietly before us a number of points which are necessary, if the attitudes of all the characters when Kostelnička's crime is discovered are to be understood. And her decision to set the discovery of the dead baby on the wedding day of Jenůfa and Laca enables Janáček, in the discovery scene, to offer a pattern of outrage leading to revelation which, merely ironic in the original, becomes in the opera a classic sequence of tragic appropriateness. By the end the achievement is clear: we are offered a closing Act of immense grandeur, less dark but no less profound than that which precedes. And the relative lightness of the opening adds to this impact.

In the play, the turning-point of the action, the moment at which the inexorable path towards the emergence of full truth begins, is the entry of the shepherd-boy Jano with the news of discovery. In the opera the mark is a little earlier: Janáček welds this news firmly back on to the scene before, the blessing of the young couple by their elder relatives; and this is itself linked back to the song sung by a group of girls from the mill. In effect it is their excited incursion which, musically, begins the chain of events leading to Kostelnička's confession—a close sequence of contrasts designed by the composer. If, then, we are dividing the Act into events and preliminaries, the preliminaries occupy only the first five scenes of the libretto. On inspection there are only three scenes of importance before the mill-girls arrive: the opening scene; that between Jenůfa and Laca alone; and that between the two couples, Jenůfa and Laca and Karolka and Števa. Each has something to contribute.

The opening takes us back into the community, restores, with its character parts—the mayor and his wife, the shepherdess—a sense that the tragic action is not being worked out in a moral vacuum; and the three parts, sharply and humorously depicted by Janáček, do much to make the village and its people a reality to us. This is important, since the place of the villagers in the denouement is token: morally inadequate to the shock of Kostelnička's guilt, let alone to the acts of transcending forgiveness which follow her confession, their role at the end is the silence of the uncomprehending spectator. But there is no point in showing the reduction to silence of a cipher; the scene shows us, with understanding and sympathy, the kind of people who cannot rise in and to the events of *Jenůfa*.

The contrasts are already large. Janáček also takes advantage of the scene to consolidate the picture of the two women offered by the closing tableau of Act 2: Jenůfa yet more calm and strong, and now with the new note of a true, well-founded optimism in her voice; Kostelnička distraught, dependent on Jenůfa (her music here recalls that of Jenůfa's mental paralysis towards the end of Act 2), craving almost overtly some form of release. Her role in dispute with the mayor's wife over Jenůfa's preferred, simple wedding dress is set as a deliberate, self-imposed animation, and the sense of release is overt when Jenůfa and Laca are left alone, and the drama's music reverts to its customary seriousness.

For here there is much to communicate. Laca's love must be fully established on the deep level at which the resolution of the opera will be conducted; Preissová adds to the character the new element, that of remorse and forgiveness, which when reciprocated by Jenůfa will conclude the work; Janáček responds to the deep sincerity of both partners with a music of piercing tenderness. Their vocal lines are interwoven with a continuous cello melody of the utmost beauty, which hints at a deep affinity between them and so points forward to the transformation in the finale of Jenůfa's pity for Laca into love. Laca too has developed: the sincerity of his affirmations is in no doubt, as the exultant E major descents of the brass culminate not in a rhetorical climax but in a precise diminuendo to the almost sanctified chords of Laca's new understanding and forgiveness of Števa.

To drive home the point, establish the depth of Jenůfa and Laca, Preissová has Števa and his new fiancée, Karolka, join them. Janáček takes the opportunity to fix precisely the moral character of his protagonists, sweeping aside the music of deep love and setting Karolka's greetings in such a way as to bring out mercilessly her shallowness and vain self-satisfaction. Teased by her, Števa declares that if she deserted him he would have to kill himself; Janáček hears the hollow rhetoric in this, and after so setting it responds with a tender orchestral melody to Jenůfa's comment, 'There, Števa, she is that true love of yours.' Jenůfa is not being naïve. On the contrary, suffering has given her the moral perspective to be entirely accurate: in Janáček's Karolka, Števa has a bride on exactly his level. The village's judgement—and Karolka's own—when the truth becomes known is harsher.

The four young people stand, as a tableau now precisely etched by the music. Events surround them. First, the hubbub as the guests return from their inspection of the trousseau; then, still more commotion, as Barena and her girls from the mill interrupt, chattering excitedly. Calm is only restored when they begin to sing their song for Jenůfa. It is the last calm which any member of the village is able to impose on the protagonists—but it is deep. It moves Jenůfa profoundly—unsurprising, since the text treats the eternal conflict of mother and daughter, the liberation from parental dominance which marriage confers; more finely, the influence of the melody infects the whole room, since—elevated from the lascivious to the sublime by the raising of pitch and the gradual taking by the violins of their mutes—the mood changes seamlessly as Janáček transforms the melody of this song into the accompaniment for the blessing of the couple.

This transition is powerful, for Janáček emphasizes by these means the total unity of the village's activities: the wedding is an age-old ritual, embracing both the permanent joy of the contest between a mother's authority and a daughter's desire for independence, and the sublimity of Christian blessing. The blessing is administered by the senior relatives present; first by the Grandmother. But as Kostelnička moves forward in her turn, to perform the ceremony 'just like a priest', the clinching outrage of this threat—that the potentially deep marriage of Jenůfa and

Laca should be blessed by the murderess of Jenůfa's child and founded on a lie—is prevented. A noise outside frightens Kostelnička, and she retreats from the kneeling couple. The orchestra has already told us why: disrupting the integrated textures of the music for the Grandmother's blessing, the descending brass figure of Kostelnička's visions of persecution in Act 2 steals in. What was foreshadowed there now becomes real.

A massive 'ensemble' grows from this destruction of the village tableau, a concerted gathering of forces of a kind only repeated once elsewhere in Janáček—also for a scene of confession—*Kát'a Kabanová* 3.i. The technique (in profound contrast to that of the Act 1 quartet) is quite unclassical: the scene achieves a level of intensity which is wholly novel, integrating into its textures utterances of greater and greater hysteria. The crescendo is seen as a sequence of separate, cumulatively more intense episodes, small tableaux each of which is marked off by being accompanied with a different ostinato figure. And the final climax is generated simply by adding extra forces and a second equally trenchant motif on top of the crescendo of the last and most aggressive of the ostinati. The power of the whole lies in the precise dramatic appropriateness of each transition to a further level of intensity, the dreadful plausibility with which the whole village passes from ignorant apprehension to misinformed mass hysteria, and the crisis is reached in which Kostelnička must confess to save Jenůfa's life. Karolka's bathetic line, 'Števa, it's awful . . . . the wedding is spoiled . . . . if I were the bride, I would cry' is followed, with dreadful poetic appropriateness, by the shriek with which the real bride, Jenůfa, responds as she recognizes her child—and so wrenches the sequence into its next, tenser stage, a battle between Jenůfa and Laca, who tries to calm her; and Jenůfa, fighting herself free in a reckless, Oedipal quest for truth regardless of the consequences, precipitates in the orchestra the insistent return of the descending notes of Kostelnička's vision of persecution at the climax of Act 2:

Ex. 5 (3. 46:2)

These in turn thrust the action into its final phase, as what was seen there becomes reality: as Jenůfa's reckless concern drives her on to identify the child conclusively, the orchestra shows how her energy goes out of her control, and is transferred to the crowd; they begin to gather and draw the obvious conclusion; she has borne an illegitimate child, and murdered it to escape disgrace. Example 5 returns over the final ostinato, and the attack which is so clearly what the phrase conveys is joined:

Stone her!

As the musical expression of Kostelnička's torment recurs, so too Preissová's constant image of oppression in Act 2 becomes real; only Laca's strength of character stands between Jenůfa and summary injustice.

But the fearful tension created, as Laca stems the crowd and the massive movement of the ostinati is halted, is pressure not merely on Jenůfa but also, unknown to them, on Kostelnička— a fact reinforced by these references to the second Act. Her confession and humble self-justification bring release of all the accumulated, falsely directed pride which led to the murder; and to mark this moment Janáček permits himself, almost uniquely in *Jenůfa*, the classical release of a cadence from dominant to tonic. And with this the opera moves into its final phase.

Here a pattern is imposed. First Jenůfa, then, inspired by her, Kostelnička and Laca, find strength to forgive the wrongs they have done to each other and so rise, morally, to a position far above that of the village's conventional morality. They do not find that strength—as is so often, and so wrongly, said—in suffering or remorse: there is nothing in *Jenůfa* of the redemptive Wagnerian *durch leiden lernen*. It is through depth of understanding of the reasons why others did them wrong, a depth given by harmony with nature, that Jenůfa finds the strength to forgive and Laca to love; and it is in acknowledging that natural strength in her foster-daughter that Kostelnička finds strength to suffer the penalties of law.

Such understanding is not to be attained at once. For Jenůfa to forgive Kostelnička's crime instantly would be the action either of a thoroughly superficial person or of an implausible saint. Instead, the harmonics of horror which overlay Kostelnička's narration of her crime, explaining the moral paralysis of all

64

present, erupt into a furious gesture of revulsion in Jenůfa. This breaks the spell, assures us that Jenůfa (like Laca, who is to follow the same pattern when he asks the forgiving Jenůfa if she is out of her senses) is human; and Janáček takes advantage of the ensuing turbulence, the fact that the major characters have withdrawn from orchestral attention into silence, to group to-gether and dispose of those who will not be able to rise to the truth which will evolve from Jenůfa's necessary silence now: Karolka, timorous, near-fainting, her only instinct to reject Števa and return to dependence on her mother; Števa, his fate pronounced by the shepherdess: 'no girl will ever take him . . . not even if there were an honest gipsy!'

Those who know Janáček's later, tragic exploration of the theme in his song-cycle 'Diary of One who Disappeared' will know the depths of disgrace involved, for a village boy, in taking a gipsy to wife; Števa, condemned now below even that, falls far lower than the Karolka to whom, in Jenůfa's earlier, generous judgement, he was more suited.

Only three voices are heard in the rest: the villagers are silent, uncomprehending spectators of that which is played out between Jenůfa and Kostelnička; and then they are absent from the opera's final ecstasy—for it takes Jenůfa and Laca for ever out of their world.

To the music of Example 6 Jenůfa approaches Kostelnička, and bids her rise from her knees. The harmonics of the horror of the deed, assimilated by Jenůfa after her moment of revulsion, are now heard transmuted into a lapidary triad; and from its depths the strength to forgive rises in the woodwind figure. Just as Aeschy-lus' avenging furies become of themselves the Eumenides, the *kindly ones*, at the close of the Oresteian trilogy, so here the horror itself, when assimilated with full knowledge of the truth, becomes the source of a forgiveness which is as deeply expected as it is shattering in its surprise and degree of understanding:

My foster-mother—now I understand it—she does not de-serve your curses. Don't condemn her! Give her time to repent! Even on her the Saviour will turn his face!

The setting is majestic, Jenůfa's authority and calm understand-ing as overwhelming as her logic is inexorable: Janáček therefore modulates from the sharpness of Kostelnička's outcry to the

c

Ex. 6 (3.55:1)

naked simplicity of the resolution. Jenůfa's total autonomy and control of her world are reflected by the movement of the music, in the span of this penultimate scene, over the sharp keys from E to the blinding C major tutti of the close.

But there is an apparent digression before that end is reached; and in it we proceed to the centre of the opera's meaning. Overwhelmed, Kostelnička begs only for forgiveness:

If only you will forgive me—
now I see, that I loved myself more than you.
Now you cannot call 'Mother dear, ah mother dear!'
You could not inherit my character or my blood
and now I turn to you for strength. . . .
I want to suffer, suffer!
Even on me the Saviour will turn his face.

Here we reach the paradox which is at the heart of the opera. Jenůfa, who has sinned against the roots of the village's morality and is morally worthless by its standards, can alone provide Kostelnička with the strength to accept what the law must inflict on her and gain moral redemption. A paradox of wide implication; for Kostelnička's authority is that of the village's structure of inherited moral strength; and in its breakdown the relationship between the women becomes crucial. Jenůfa is not Kostelnička's true daughter, has not inherited her strength; was as the opera began her weak, errant and dependent foster-child. But she has within her a new, different strength which has no outside source; as this is now realized by Kostelnička, her literal insistence, that Jenůfa can no longer speak of her as of a real mother, becomes utterly right. Janáček illuminates: as Kostelnička begins the fourth line of the plea, the orchestra is progressively more animated by the rising scales of Jenůfa's Example 6, until the 'digression' culminates in its logical conclusion, the authoritative, ecstatic return in C major of the music which conveys the scene's warmth and the total gift of the younger woman's strength to the elder.

Jenůfa and Laca are left alone, and Janáček's setting encounters its last and greatest challenge: to recoup the action and cap the shattering climax of the penultimate scene with a greater still. This is accomplished with almost unbelievable delicacy and authority. Janáček sees Jenůfa here as he saw her at the end of Act 2, her outer determination to discourage Laca undermined by her honesty, forcing her to acknowledge that theirs is a deep harmony which must lead to union. The melody to which she attempts to persuade him to leave her is fragile and delicate: gaping hiatuses between its every return show her exhaustion, the difficulty with which she finds the words to argue against her own deepest inclinations; and in the very act of saying good-bye

67

she reveals her forgiveness for what he has done to her. But just as she can bear all suffering, so now can he. When two people understand each other so deeply, love is born, and it is inevitable that Laca should accompany Jenůfa from the village as she, in the final line of the opera, acknowledges for the first time that she loves him. 'Love led me to you—that great love, with which God is content!' The closing gesture coalesces the cleansing of all the wrongs that have been done, the maturity of Jenůfa's love and the recognition of Laca's into a vast image of love; and Janáček, who has done so much in this last Act to make real for us the nature of 'that great love', portrays the harmony of Jenůfa and Laca as they attain it in music of unutterable grandeur. We are given assurance of their subsequent happiness, not as a cliché but as a certainty for the couple, whatever their physical circumstances.

We are offered in *Jenůfa* the most intense and concentrated of Janáček's operas; a music whose grip on the audience is relentless, with little wit but the savagely ironic, and whose few moments of light relief do nothing to dim the high seriousness of the whole. The colourful milieu of the first and third Acts, perfectly and truthfully evoked, is set in deliberate opposition to the depths explored by the music; it should not be allowed to disguise the truth. *Jenůfa* is the narrowest in concern of Janáček's tragedies, more single-minded even than *Kát'a Kabanová*. But with narrowness may come depth; and in the distance travelled from first curtain to last, the span of the development of the action and the characters, *Jenůfa* is rivalled among Janáček's later creations only by *Makropulos*. This opera presents a profound, precise study of how people are led to do tragic acts against their will, in a world where real moral strength is seen as being acquired by some people in their sufferings: to confront truth is to suffer but, for those who are capable, to understand that pain is to grow. The process is precisely observed, rooted in reality, far from metaphysics; and Janáček's understanding extends equally to the more shallow characters; even Števa is portrayed with compassion.

In this opera only three people rise: Jenůfa and Laca to a mature, adult understanding of themselves and others, and Kostelnička to a true humility in which she can welcome into herself the outside world's verdict on her crime. Externally learnt, human standards are useless: the triumph of the close spreads outwards from a young woman who has gained her strength from her harmony (half accepted, half imposed) with nature. *Jenůfa* might—if the libretto alone is read—offer us a strange, implausible and unpleasant meaning: that human beings can attain maturity only through such sufferings as Jenůfa's. But this is to disregard the music: when the work is seen as a whole, strength is shown to be given not by the sufferings themselves but by the depth of response and of understanding to which they give rise. The wonder of *Jenůfa* is the promise that if sufficiently sensitive and understanding of others, we may by our own experiences attain, as Jenůfa and Laca, a moral maturity which is sufficient in itself, and which does not need—indeed rejects and goes in love beyond—the standards of any given community. A promise of marvellous hope, to Janáček's spectators as they go out into the night: for are we not all, in some or every aspect of our lives, moral children, Števas or Karolkas, dependent for morality on others, lacking to a greater or a lesser extent the inner strength to respond nobly to disaster?

Destiny

Jenůfa was well received in Brno, but repeatedly refused a production in Prague. And Janáček chose a very different setting for his second tragic opera. The new work was set in middle-class society; its plot was suggested to Janáček by some actual events, and he created his own libretto. He outlined the dialogue, and it was made into 'Pushkinesque verse' at his request by a young schoolteacher, Fedora Bartošová.

The text is rich, almost excessive in its wealth of imagery; the plot less coherent or cogent than that of *Jenůfa*. Critics and directors have by and large seen little to admire in *Destiny* except the quality of some of the orchestral inventions; and the only two productions to have been staged (both thirty years after Janáček's death) presented the action of the first two Acts as a flashback, splitting the hero's narration from Act 3 into two parts to make from it the prelude and epilogue to a two-Act opera.

And so they destroyed, irrevocably, the essential development of Janáček's theme. This is a music-drama as closely knit as his other tragic dramas; and like them it unfolds its theme gradually as the opera progresses. The subject-matter is intimate, personal but strong and significant; the theme is reminiscence, and the artist's attempts to recapture completely his most intense past experiences of love.

This theme grows gradually from the start to the complete dominance which it attains in the later pages of the score. We are denied the beginning of the love of Živný and Míla, offered instead for the first of Janáček's three 'romantic pictures' the return of Živný to the spa at which they first met. Živný seeks, for the purposes of the bitter, vindictive opera which he is creating on the theme of his first love, which he sees as a betrayal, to capture that episode by returning to the place at which Míla abandoned him. Not only does she come there, but they are obliged to meet, and it is made clear in the development of the action that their affinity is in fact so deep that they must reunite and marry.

The reason for their parting was not betrayal but the opposition of Míla's mother: implacable and permanent, this opposition is treated as a datum from before the action begins; and so, like the prior events assumed in *Jenůfa* and *Makropulos*, brings the action at its opening nearer to crisis. Inextricably mixed with the inevitability of their love is the inevitability of its destruction, and this surfaces to colour the end of Act 1: in Janáček's vision their love is destined both to be fulfilled in marriage, and to be destroyed. Janáček portrays as the means to destruction not something grand, romantic or heroic but the domestic, banal and in its final moments grotesque hatred of Míla's mother (who, because slightly distanced, is seen as an agent of an impersonal fate) for the composer. Unnatural, unrealistic and, in relation to *Jenůfa*, a clear departure towards the world of *grand guignol*, the passions of this woman (she has no name but 'Miss Míla's mother', although Míla herself is given a maiden name, Valková) are the catalyst of the opera. At the end of Act 1 she is seen to be maddened by the reunion of Živný and Míla; in Act 2 she is completely insane, and her tirade against Živný is concluded by an incident as grotesque as, in Janáček's setting, it is inevitable: hurling herself from a balcony to her death, she takes her daughter with her.

Míla's death—itself brought on, like every major action in the opera, by anguished recollection—is an inevitable stage in the development of the opera's main theme: Živný's work has developed new tendrils, thrown out a new vision not of bitterness but of tender re-creation of the reality of their love, one which will do justice both to their division and to the fullness of their reunion. But there is a psychological block. Živný finds himself unable to complete his work: Míla's death now savagely opens the possibilities of completion, as it thrusts Živný bereft into the mania of desire for immolation by storm.

In Act 3, conservatoire students play over Živný's score, which is to be given its première that evening—unfinished, and ending

71

with a dramatization by Živný of the death-wishes that closed Janáček's Act 2. Tension is increased by the approach of a storm, and the entry of Živný. If the creation of his own opera could not, even after Míla's death, lead him to full re-creation of the reality of their past, the story of it which the students win from him brings the vision of her before him in such intensity that he suffers collapse. Yet the denouement is sternly objective in its denial of our perverse expectations: that past which we have never seen, though we have participated in the gradual deepening of its recovery, is refused us; the ending of Živný's opera—both the closing pages which would enable the whole affair to be comprehended and the totality of recall—still elude him, as they always must: 'that is in the hands of God and remains there'. Destiny has led through the atrocious loss of Míla to hopes of recall of the love of Živný and Míla; but even the most total recall possible must inevitably be cheated, and Janáček—who has already shown comprehension of a living being as fraught with difficulties—will not let us see Živný's vision of the dead Míla, powerful though it is, as in any way more satisfying. Živný lives on, with nothing but these useless memories to sustain him.

Luhačovice is a spa about a hundred kilometres east of Brno, which Janáček used to visit; the idea for this opera was generated in his mind by a true story which was told to him there, and it is the scene of Act I in all but name. It stands at the upper narrowing point of a wide valley, shrouded by conifer forests which extend into the distance over the rolling hills which surround it. Contrasts of sun and shade are, on any fine day in summer or autumn, intense. This fact, often mentioned by Janáček in his feuilletons and correspondence, is the focal, generating point for both text and music: as the curtain rises the spa is enveloped by the heat of the sun, which when it attains full strength in the second part of the Act will be seen to promote and further both love and lust. In preparation for this, it is seen at the opening as the source of health and spiritual renewal for all the people who have gathered there. Renewal will be a key image of the text, preparing for a violent contrast to the memories and passions which haunt Míla; and there is music to match the association of this text image with the stage picture of the sun streaming through the trees in the first bars of the prelude; there the sun's delicate, sharp A major tracery is the overlay from which, after only a very few bars, springs the robust, vulgar waltz to which the spa visitors promenade when the curtain rises. The entry of this waltz yields a simple juxtaposition which establishes the idea of renewal, in contrast to which the burden of reminiscence on the principals will be defined.

Ex. 7 (1.0:9)

Already it is possible to see that a structural technique similar to that of *Jenůfa* Act 1 is involved. Janáček introduces immediately a strong association between a physical phenomenon and a musical motif, both of which are to underlie the emotions of the characters; and so foreshadows a development analogous to that made by the use of the recurring xylophone in *Jenůfa* Act 1: in both cases an autumn day passes from the heat in which passions are generated to a disastrous conclusion in the dusk. And the difference from the *Jenůfa* technique is less striking than the similarity, and can be explained from the different dramatic situation. Janáček's xylophone remained the same, reappeared always—until wrenched out of true by the traumatic pressure of events just before Laca's slashing of Jenůfa's cheek—on its obsessive C flat. That was because its function was to remind the audience of the increasing pressure of implacable forces, unchanging elements from the past, whose effect the characters sought to ignore. In this opera there is no tension of that kind: the whole focus is on the inevitability of each step of *changing* feelings and relationships, which become heated and intimate towards the mid-point of the Act; and the physical image which Janáček seizes on, and elevates to prime importance by chronicling it with the orchestra, is an evolving one too. The sun's inexorable progress to the most intense heat and beyond it into the

73

dusk is therefore paralleled by the evolution of the melodies associated with it. Janáček begins with this almost incoherent tracery, and declares the full form of the melody only as the sun reaches its most penetrating elevation.

The promenaders are, visually, colourful and varied, and their concerns as they take the air and the sun are trivial or effete; but their joyful waltz is entered into sincerely, and there is no attempt to distance the audience from them; Janáček extends his understanding to every character even of this diversely peopled opera. Nor are they introduced just for contrast with Živný and Míla: they are entrusted with the introduction of the second main idea of the Act and of the opera. At the climax of each of the two choruses hailing the sun some students and schoolgirls stand on a bridge and call across the valley for an echo—which is returned at pitch, after a moment's delay, by an offstage chorus. Echoes are the second dominant image of the text: Živný has returned to the spa 'for the echo of the voice, which resounds through the commonplace gloom of my life'; and the love of Živný and Míla, as well as his artistic work, are seen throughout the opera as a quest for the echo of response in others. Here, the fact that the uncharacteristic device of ensemble is used gives fair warning, in Janáček, that the chorus is over-confident, that the effect is to be irony: the echo's regular return, half a bar later, of their hymn mirrors the reciprocal response of joy which they are confident the sun will bring to every one of them; but a gift of roses from an admirer brings to the most elegant and beautiful of them all, as she enters, an echo in response which is the reverse of joyful:

Living memories supply for me their furnace.
Bitter memories!

—and when Míla turns to promenade with the others the music belies her socially correct surface calm; ominous semitonal movements threatened since she entered explode into a fortissimo eruption of the waltz melody, reinforced fiercely—and with a lack of restraint in the percussion which is rare in Janáček—by the use of a tam-tam.

The technique is superficially like that at 'Alas, dear Grandmother, that good sense of mine . . .', early in *Jenůfa*. But the means are different, the tension being released purely orchestrally, with uncharacteristic vehemence, and with a general pause at its close. And this is because a stage gesture *cannot* express her passion. The character's silence, the indicative power of the orchestra alone, are required by the opera's setting; the use of its own waltz as the climax of the heroine's reminiscence is designed to show that the fashionable milieu is not just a milieu, alien to the protagonists, but a re-creation of the past in which she met Živný at the same spa, and so contains all her memories. And the explosion supplies a new level of feeling: we are to be alive to the tension between social convention and inner passion—which is why the score calls the *prima donna* 'Miss Míla' throughout. Where Jenůfa could speak directly of her feelings, even if she did not speak the whole truth, Míla must remain silent or speak—as she does a few moments later, when Živný appears in congruence with her recollection—obliquely and poetically, in lines which are characteristic of the pointed, allusive manner of the text:

> The wind makes scattered leaves circle, and who
> knows where they land?

This is the nearest the issues come to surfacing verbally in public: passion cannot be expressed vocally in this Act. But Janáček welcomes this, for his whole theme is now the issuing of reminiscence in action, which is a constant preoccupation of his; and the setting of the first Act therefore calls for three distinct, contrasted dramatic modes: that where Živný and Míla are alone, with a music of piercing intensity; that where society is proceeding with its normal life, with a music of a more relaxed and lighter kind; and the places where the two principals are, uncomfortably, involved with society. Interruption of the lovers by others is one effective dramatic possibility exploited by Janáček; another, more subtle, is a multi-layered unity such as is attained at the close of the Act, in which the similarities and contrasts of situation, impressed simultaneously on the audience, add up to a total theatrical communication of great power.

I do not propose to discuss in detail the rest of the early encounters between Živný or Míla and their acquaintances. Something must however be said about the scenes later in the Act where the stage is left to spa society, since these have been much criticized. After Živný and Míla have met, and Živný has claimed—and been conceded—his right to Míla, all has been said that can be said: Živný and Míla must rediscover each

75

other. Janáček wants their relationship far advanced, their practical rediscovery of loving enhanced before he may put in their mouths the two great monologues which occupy much of the close of the Act, and lead us to the realization that their marriage is both inevitable and doomed; he therefore makes them leave, to do so out of our sight. Love-making can neither be spoken nor staged. To fill the dramatic time until they can credibly return, till the sun reaches the full heat where the utmost intensity can be unleashed, he must call on his spa people; and the scenes in which he does so have been seen as among the weakest in any Janáček opera.

Yet not all absurd, nor irrelevant. Janáček's operas are inclusive, illuminatory: they seek to encompass the life which is their theme—to embrace it, as the composer used to put the point. He does not offer in a serious opera six consecutive scenes occupied by people whose concerns are light-hearted for no dramatic reason; nor would it, as much writing on this opera has tended to assume, be a blunder in itself to place frivolous, shallow people on the stage. We must try to see why they are there.

The position of these episodes in the course of the Act shows their main dramatic purpose at once. These characters dominate the stage between the passionate declaration by Živný of the inevitability of reunion with Míla and the two great monologues in which they—and we—reach full understanding of the depth, and the doomed nature, of their love. Janáček is clearly therefore pursuing further his strategy of illuminating Živný and Míla by contrast; developing by itself, to let us see it, the alternative focus of the society which is the setting for his hero and heroine. The precise nature of the opposite pole from Živný and Míla is only gradually revealed, and reaches its full extent only in the complex last pages of the Act; but the process is begun here.

After the schoolmistress, Miss Stuhlá (her name means 'prim'), has come and gone, mocked by the students on the forecourt, in her slow but successful attempt to muster her colleagues for a rehearsal, the music takes on a strange luxuriance, midway between the original sun tracery and its full flowering—more than just to mark the tipsy entry of Dr. Suda and the painter Lhotský (old friends of Živný); schoolgirls and students gather round them in the heat, and the making of a 'banner' from an umbrella draped in ribbons of the Czech national colours binds the proposed outing—which is unchaperoned—in a meretricious unity, while the 'la la la' of the schoolgirls improvising as they make the banner is set disturbingly—at once with charm and with a complete absence of innocence. As students, girls and one or two others gather round the doctor and his musicians for the outing, the precise nature of the luxuriance is revealed: lascivious flirtation is the mood foreshadowed.

More is to follow, in the next scene: this injects the beginnings of the unpleasantness which Janáček will develop to the full in the leaders of the outing when they return. Miss Stuhlá and her fellow teachers are heard through an open window rehearsing an atrociously banal ballad; Suda, egged on by the students, parodies them and is joined in deliberate attempts to provoke the schoolmistresses by the rest of his party.

It is at this moment that Míla's mother makes her first solo appearance, almost as unremarked as Kostelnička's in *Jenůfa* Act I. She is searching for her daughter, and is brushed off by Lhotský: there are more important matters for him than her real emotional need:

LHOTSKÝ: Miss Míla? (shrugs shoulders half-heartedly, turns round) Waiter, menu! Menu!

—which all happens in collage with Stuhlá's replies to the abuse.

Refusing to develop this new theme of the unpleasantness of the spa people any further, or to do more with the mother than just inject her into the situation (his only concern here is exposition), Janáček sweeps the outing party to their exit by showing the connection between the gentle lasciviousness which he has introduced and the dominant element of the milieu: the sun, which in the first scene caused renewal of spirit, is here presented in a new aspect, shown as the cause of their sensuality (musically, this is shown by the adoption for the close of Example 8 of the twist which ended the girls' 'la la la'); and with this move on to what will be a main plane of the Act, it gains—in its first form— the figure which will dominate the score, as Suda—having vanquished the forces of sobriety—proceeds to sing 'a little song to the sun'. He is joined by the students in the refrains, applauded by the girls, as everyone leaves for the outing (Example 8):

Ex. 8 (1.29:5)

You golden sun of ours
though you have only one little eye
yet you see enough!

You golden sun of ours
though you don't have a heart like us
you too have pleasure enough!

You golden sun of ours
move only a little further
until we call 'enough'!

Need I point out that it is the last verse, begging extra time for their pleasure, which is emblematic? For the tune goes into harmonics: we are at the heat of the day: 'The sunshine floods the spa; in the shade of the colonnade guests recline here and there.' It only needs the stylistic contrast inherent in the reintroduction now of Živný and Míla to move from this to the closest concerns of the Act, from lust to love.

The opposite pole from Živný and Míla is, then, not just petite bourgeoisie, outward-facing while the central couple are absorbed in themselves, but, more precisely, light-heartedness, lasciviousness; an affair is lascivious precisely when it is not taken seriously, when the participants feel no necessary bond between themselves. Janáček spends so much time on the society in which they move in order to set Živný and Mila in this focus; for the fact that there are compelling bonds between *them* is the feature which distinguishes them from their surroundings, and the most intense musical energies of the score are devoted to exploring the nature of those bonds. For the destiny of the opera's title is shown, in the first Act, in the inevitability of their reunion. This is fully established only in the great dialogue after their return to the stage; but the musical unfolding of the concept of destiny dominating this opera begins earlier and, as is customary in Janáček, takes place gradually. We must retrace our steps, to the first meeting of Živný and Míla in the opera's action.

Míla's recovery, just after her first entrance, from the over-whelming access of reminiscence which floods her when Lhotský presents a bouquet is short-lived: an ironic horn call greets the appearance, in congruence with her reminiscence, of Živný in the distance, and Suda and Konečny, who are both of Míla's party but are old acquaintances of Živný's, describe him to her. Míla, disturbed by seeing him, and seeking to avoid a meeting, can—in the social conditions which Janáček has already established—do only one thing: she begs her companions that they should all walk on further. Various stage directions follow in the libretto:

Míla and the others walk in such a way that they are bound to meet Živný. Živný, alone, goes far from Míla, Konečny and the other onlookers; his appearance is revealing, and in fact again conceals emotion. He sees Míla with the society people accompanying her and recognizes Konečny.

Restrained step of Živný and Míla. Her gaze has a strange splendour, questioning—entirely fixed, calmly, on Živný. Konečny's expression discloses the question 'why are you here?' Živný brings his steps to a standstill, feels that he cannot avoid them, greets them.

The conception, of course, is Romantic; but the treatment is only superficially so. As we would expect after the first climax of the opera, this sequence, in which the characters are silent, is treated by supplying an expansive orchestral interlude to depict its various stages (Example 9).

The music is richly and specifically suggestive. The ostinato (a) communicates by its repetition the inexorable round of the pro-menaders; (b), which is crucial in the remainder of the opera (it communicates throughout the rising of a reminiscence in the character whose emotions are being illuminated), grows from this and shows by its way of leading into the emotionally intense (c) how Živný and Míla are gradually being forced against their will, by the emotions summoned up in each by the reminiscences of re-encounter, to a point where both inevitably slow their pace;

79

Ex. 9 (1.14:1)

and finally, after the successive returns of this melody, each time animated by the ostinato, have led through a climax of full intensity to calm acceptance, they are succeeded by rising tremolos of apprehension on the notes of (c). These precede, throughout the score, attempts to understand the feelings stirred up by reminiscence. And, after the two have been left alone, Živný's measured, calm explanation of his return, 'I come for the echo of the voice, that resounds through the commonplace gloom of my life . . .' is introduced by a recall of this music. The way in which Janáček wishes us to see the action is now clear; the facet of destiny which has made it inevitable that they should meet again is the power, once it has been aroused, of recollection.

But these early moves, intimating the ideas which Janáček wishes to express in the opera, create expectations which must be fulfilled later, if he is to succeed in the Act's aim of making the reunion of Živný and Míla appear inevitable. Can he establish credibly the well-worn idea of the compelling power of love when reawakened by the presence of the loved one? Failure would make the promenade music seem portentous and overloaded; success will yield a convincing transition to the deeper problems dramatized in Act 2.

Janáček tackles this problem head-on, writing as centre-point and climax of the Act, two extended, complementary monologues of recollection for the protagonists. Two bars of transition after the departure of the excursionists are enough to launch a great scene enclosed emblematically by the motif of the sun. This reaches 'white scorching heat' in the stage direction at the mid-point of the scene—between the monologues—where Míla's text is 'I want the scorching heat, would that the sun might burn away my grief', which is the clearest allusion after the opening chorus to the sun's role as a movement parallel to the emotional realities of the Act:

Ex. 10 (1.34:1)

The full extension over its widest range of intervals, the symmetrical balance—with an interval of a perfect fifth to the apex —which the motif now attains, and its appearance at the beginning of each of the monologues, indicate that now the sun is to be seen, at its full, as renewing love. Both characters prove the depth of their love by the expression of sentiments overpoweringly urged on them by the force of their reminiscence, and this issues at the end of the scene in a declaration of reunion which is then to be seen as inevitable.

This stage of the drama is successfully accomplished: Janáček's art develops in this scene a new dimension of intimacy, presaged in *Jenůfa* only by the brief scene between Laca and Jenůfa alone in Act 3. Consider the text first. Živný is a composer, his 'artistic temperament'—or hypersensitivity—has already been hinted at, and will steadily be brought out yet further over the course of the two subsequent Acts; this is seized upon, his monologue used as the vehicle for an intimate description of the experience of lovers, dominated by the metaphor of harmony.

It is not merely an appropriate metaphor for a composer to use. The movement in Živný's monologue is of course from the first moments of love, with their dissatisfactions, to the delight of union; but it is characteristic of Janáček's consistent orientation towards the feminine that the fullest realization of this idea should be not in his part of the scene but in Míla's reply, as she

81

tells of her dreamlike recollection of their happiness in Prague: there the languid motion of the music will show what harmony is, and through it the meaning of ecstasy.

Živný's monologue comes first, and like much of the second Act addresses itself directly to the tragic force of the opera's theme of recollected love; its compelling power is established in music of relentless modernity of insight. The scene evokes the first music of full intensity to occur in this Act; and Janáček's generosity of invention is reckless. The result is that the complex point is carried effortlessly: each has established that they understood, both when separated from the other and when recollecting their past experience together, the meaning of ecstasy; therefore, that when together they had been in love. This, deeply proved, makes their illegitimate child seem, at the end of the scene, to be utterly right as the bond between them; and the contrast with social convention which this implies yields a smooth transition to Janáček's coda, where the energies set up by confronting Živný and Míla, in their present position, with society are engaged.

For here the moral axis, paramount in this Act as in every work of Janáček, is presented complete. After the dialogue, the opera's exposition is completed, and Janáček can argue a conclusion with great strength in the four closing scenes, simply by bringing all his characters on to the stage: the Act ends with contrasting focus upon contrasting focus, qualification upon qualification. Dusk falls, blaring horns announce the return of the excursion, and under a circling violin tracery which dissolves the stability of the monologues all the terms of deep love on which Živný and Míla have reunited are corrupted: a rendezvous is arranged with a young widow; Konečny reads to a female companion verses from an inflated love poem—parodying Živný's artistic aspirations and his language; and two young men comment sarcastically on the liaison of Živný and Míla. Lechery and cynicism are thus established as the values in which the returning excursionists are united, for the orchestra slides at this point into its closing movement (Example 11).

As the day drew on, the sun tracery of Example 7 crystallized into two related melodies—the perfect, symmetrical Example 10 and Example 8, morally diminished by the tone and semitone fall at the end of each phrase, and by the demisemiquaver twist

Ex. 11 (1. 46:21)

that replaces this on the third phrase of each verse. Now the theme is the sun theme, split into its most basic components— the almost toneless children's trumpet outlining the rhythm, the harp's shapeless arpeggios incorporating the harmony. This precisely communicates the barrenness of their merry-making— and the flute melody is corrupt: it is a diminution of Example 8, complete with the twist used to reanimate its *perpetuum mobile* at the end of each four-bar phrase. Only when Míla is drawn into the conversation are the styles homogenized by the theme's re-currence in the pure Example 10 form. The reason is that the gossip about her which she hears over Example 11 drives Míla to beg Živný to take her away. But it is only now, after he has begged her to ignore the opinions of others, that a full declaration of their love comes, supported by the transport of Example 10 into the highest harmonics (recall of the most radiant heat)— because now we can see their love in full perspective, defined by contrast to the affairs and liaisons of the others. So deep is the definition that this direct method shows precisely how Živný and Míla are different from the spa people, and what they have in common with them.

But the harmonics are as much those of tragedy as of triumph; for equally, with full acknowledgement comes the first full ex-pression of Míla's fear that her mother will not endure 'the light of my purification'. This metaphor, tying music and text, points up acutely the distance between Míla's vision of their love and *any* description society could muster for an illegitimate liaison; and it comes at this point precisely *because* in the full form it has

83

reached in this scene it is plain to Živný and Míla by how much their love flouts social convention. So the slide now, as the last of the excursionists return, is even more acute than its predecessor: a rising figure of four or five notes, first evolved as the excursionists began to gossip about Míla, crushes the sun melody, and a ferocious climax marks her refusal to join the party as Suda shepherds them into the hotel; the sun, the theme that is leaving (and the light of pure love which is now overshadowed), is crushed by the new chords which will underlie the tenuous, slow oboe line tracing the mother's anxious wanderings—for Míla's premonition is fulfilled immediately: as Míla and Živný leave together, the mother wanders on.

Yet, as the mother is in acute contrast to anyone else on stage (her presence is now ignored by the excursionists, except that someone tells her Míla has eloped with Živný), so Janáček provides a focus yet further in the opposite direction to end the Act in its most extreme contrast: brutal, brilliant, and bearing directly on the theme of the Act. The sun has set; the promenade's electric lights go out; and a student is heard in the distance pleading with a young girl to kiss him, to stay. Bells underline their dialogue, playing gently to illustrate love apparently at its most innocent, its most pure. This moment fades as the girl appears to reject him—but both disappear together into the dusk, and now the helpless five-note rise of apprehension appears in the violas. The effect of the new moment—the light innocence, yet that of full sexuality—on the mother's sensibilities is total: the sequence of chords ends, assisted by the flood to her mind of the first half of Example 10, in a sustained, harsh A major; then, with a sudden decisive rise in pitch and flattening of key to D flat major, she goes insane. The music has told us that it is love at full flower, as in the sun, that has sent her mad; Janáček points the degree of her aberration (confirmed in Act 2) by showing us that to her a natural phenomenon is deeply abhorrent.

My Míla with Živný? With Živný?
No no—with utter misery!

Act 2 takes place in one of Janáček's most characteristic modes: the enclosed domestic scene (Živný's study), the cast temporarily reduced to the principals, away from the glare of public opinion, and the action about to be irrevocably advanced in the intensity of such an atmosphere. As in *Jenůfa*, the increased tautness of the libretto under such conditions, and the fact that the audience has by now had a chance to understand the basic concerns of the opera, enable him to proceed without the use of any one strong idea binding the physical and the musical action, such as the group of evolving motifs associated with the sun in the first Act: the music, while occasionally allusive, is a continuous stream of new, locally illuminating inventions.

The manner is familiar, but the devices are very much those of this particular opera, designed to trace its own individual patterns of action. The emphasis now begins to move more and more in the direction of the power of reminiscence as written—that is, of Živný's opera, whose score he is looking over, and pages of which actually precipitate the climax of the Act; the idea that the marriage is doomed because socially ostracized fades, its work having been done with the onset of insanity in Míla's mother.

The prelude virtually foreshadows such a change of focus, with its dialogue between the stable, self-enclosing loops of the violent rising figure first heard at the end of Act 1, and a new, introspective slow theme for oboes:

Ex. 12 (2.0:1, 2.0:5)

And the opening of the Act is given over to an extended monologue for Živný, his wife looking on and his six-year-old child Doubek playing in a corner. Homogeneity of style and a post-Romantic melancholy are prominent here; for the actual problems of life and of youth have been left behind with Act 1, while there remain the artistic problems of rendering Živný's insight into them—the mental problems which are created after Act 1 and its events have been assimilated. 12b, developed rhapsodically, is the main idea of these pages, in which Janáček's music explores one of the moods in which he is at his finest, that of exquisite tenderness, edged and bittersweet.

85

But it does not dominate the score. Živný's legacy from the past consists of two kinds of music: the happy, optimistic pages composed after the reunion, and the bitter, agonized score of reproach composed after Míla first left him. In allusions to the newer score, 12b predominates; but the qualification, the stabbing fall of the horns as he turns to the older, bitter pages is indicative:

Ex. 13 (2.5:5)

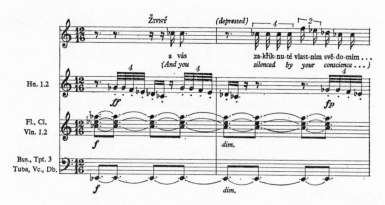

Shortened to six notes—and inverted to convey the inward-facing depression of the memory of these pages—Example 12 is here crucially tied to the painful consequences of their inexorable union; and the dialogue between these two wholly opposed kinds of thematic material—between the bitter force of inevitability and the rhapsodic, musing wandering of pleasant memory—established here, returns to clinch the coda of the Act.

But the past cannot be viewed wholly as artistic material: it has legacies in the real world as well. Janáček's device for conveying this is the crux of the opera. Živný is made to recall, improvising at the piano and so in song form, Míla's reply at the time to his premonitions of their parting:

... an echoing forest are our souls, in pain
my soul called yours to it in echo,
and mine was veiled in anxiety until
yours called, so that I'd come back again,
so that I'd come back again!

86

Míla reacts to the close of this recall 'with an expression of un-controllable unease', which leads for the last line of text with irresistible harmonic impetus to a climax at the extreme of both grandeur and ferocity (Example 14).

As the violins enter, the recall leads *both* to Živný's triumphant hailing (*Fatum* set to a perfect fifth descent) of the inevitability of their marriage *and* to the ironic exclamation, a minor second below, with which the mother, offstage, greets this before proceeding, under the sustained high harmonic of lunacy, to a parody of the entire song. (Janáček's original proposal for conveying the double vision was even more extreme than her sudden, unprepared entry here: the mother was to sing the entire song a minor second below *at the same time* as Živný—an effect which, as John Tyrrell has said, would make the parallel minor ninths in *Wozzeck* sound tame in comparison.) And catastrophe occurs at the end of the Act when this sequence to the two utterances of *Fatum* is repeated for the third time.

The whole special vision of this opera, the naked opposition of the poetic or Romantic interpretation of life and the insane, ironic rebuttal, is seen at its most direct here, and vitally so, since this passage establishes the mood which must be adopted by an audience if it is to understand how Janáček sets the movement to Míla's death. But one more element is introduced into the picture. After the mother has returned to silence, Živný in a further monologue of vivid, stabbing motifs and surrounding emptiness describes the growth of his furious, slanderous artistic response to Míla's apparent desertion of him—developing hints in Act 1 into a picture of the inadequacy of both to destiny; this mounts to the most intense climax of the Act, as Živný sets upon his old manuscript and tries to destroy it; and an utter contrast is then provided by the re-entry of Doubek, asking his mother, 'Do you know what love is?' This becomes a major theme of the rest of the opera—*do* Živný and Míla really know what love is? *Can* they know?

The handling of Doubek here, with variants of 12b in the first violins and oboe to impart a caressing gentleness to the texture, reminds one at once of Jenůfa's Števuška in the first scene of *Jenůfa* Act 2. But the technique is different. Števuška was introduced in order to polarize the emotion of two adults, and the contrast between the utter naturalness and beauty of the mother

Ex. 14 (2.13:17)

and child, conveyed by Janáček's setting of Jenůfa in the scene, and the violence of Kostelnička's emotions, vexed by the thought of its illegitimacy, was employed to emphasize the aberration of Kostelnička's position, while the scene as a whole advanced her hatred of Števa himself as the father responsible for the child's existence. In the libretto, Janáček's position here is strongly reminiscent of the *Jenůfa* scene as I have described it—except that it is Míla's own sense of guilt that is racked by the innocence of the child.

DOUBEK: Do you know what love is?
MÍLA: My child, I know, oh I know!
DOUBEK: You don't, you don't.
Jean and Nanny love each other!
Jean and Nanny!
MÍLA: But really? Jean and Nanny?
—Yet my offence is real, already you
are not silent about it.

Jean and Nanny are the family's servants, and they overhear the last part of this sequence, 'peeping, frightened, in from the door'. Míla takes the boy's playful denial as showing that he has already learnt to think of love as something which no one who deserts the beloved—as she feels she has—can truly understand. But the music is strongly at odds with this text. The intensity of the passions recalled in the preceding scenes between Živný and Míla has done nothing more thoroughly than proving the intensity and depth of the love of Živný and Míla; and the persistence, under Doubek's questioning, of the 12b group reminds us that he is the child of that love, while the elegiac calm with which these motifs play—they are the slowest elements in Janáček's collage at this point—backs Míla's assertions with the fullest authority of the past, especially since her vocal line is integrated with these groups.

But the child's question does not simply re-establish the genuineness of Míla's feelings, in contrast to the accusations that she is impervious to love which Živný has just described, and repented. There is no counter-element in the music: Míla's last line is set without orchestra, and the only other theme in the collage is a nervous four-note descent to express the shyness of the servants as they overhear. The emotions Doubek awakens are

89

unreal; the text may at the close recall Kostelnička, but here there is no real opposition in Míla or anyone else onstage to the feeling that her love is innocent and good: the scene cries out for a contradictory force. The result is that the mother's abrupt entry for the final scenes is, after this enigmatic close to the vignette, deeply expected.

Janáček here attempts something so extraordinary that no critic has argued that he is anything but simply mistaken, far beyond the limits of what is dramatically viable. Tragedies rely on the welding of elements into a coherent, inevitable chain; rely, that is, on the tragedian's having, and communicating to his audience, a profound understanding of his characters. But the insane person is, almost by definition, someone whose actions are so irresponsible that they cannot be understood. How can Janáček successfully make sense of a madwoman's actions?

The entire axis of this Act is contained in the sequence which I have printed as Example 14. There we saw that the destiny which runs through this opera is consistently seen, with an originality which stretches our mental response to the limit, both straight and ironically; that Míla's early love-letter, claiming an inevitable bond bringing her and Živný together, is set straight, and in such a manner as to show the nature of the bond—and hailed by Živný as the manifestation of fate; and also set ironically, for the mother, after she has ridiculed Živný's claim. This double focus, at the heart of the opera's vision of conduct, is established for this act by that crucial sequence—so the audience should be prepared to see it in the closing scenes as well. If so, they will be able to understand Janáček's music.

There are only two elements: Example 10 and Example 14. The mother enters declaring, 'I'm not really crazy', accompanied solely by Example 10, played at at least twice its original, natural tempo and thus merely grotesque. What she says is true; and the effect of this accompaniment is to remind us why. She is certainly unbalanced; but what unbalanced her—and is now running through her mind—is irrational obsession with the union of Živný and Míla in the heat of the spa, the events dramatized at the end of Act 1. What this music tells us is that she comes onstage obsessed; and once we know this we can see the onward movement of her mind as inevitable just as much as any sequence in the mind of a sane person.

What actually comes next is an ironic reprise of Example 14, its chord-sequence, so precisely fateful in character, stretched to accommodate the final parody of Míla's letter—for so much of the force of this scene derives from the compelling power of hearing the chords leading up to the word fate for the *third* time, with all the associations of finality which that number has; and also accusations against Živný of having seduced Míla. The third appearance of the sequence is fearfully qualified, Example 10 being dovetailed in fortissimo in the trumpets to the four bars of the 'fate' cry to convey the glory of their love.

Grand gesture *and* irony—the double vision is intolerable, and Janáček sees the need for a strategic calm before the final climax. The mother rejects the claims of fate—for her whole role is that of both an example and a parody of the idea of the opera, that recollection issues in action. She is convinced that Živný married Míla for her money, and as she retreats towards the door with the threat that he will get none of it the *pp* calm is gently invaded by endlessly falling, reiterated figurations for the strings and mysteriously irrelevant chords for the woodwind—illuminating the mother's wary retreat but also implying the element of irrationality which is the other component of Janáček's picture. This is followed by the sudden breaking of the texture, 'con moto' passagework as the mother, struggling with Míla on the balcony, drags her to her death.

The death of the heroine is, then, seen both as absurd—a grotesque, unpredictable outrage—and tragic: an inevitable act. No critic has appreciated that Janáček was seeking such a double perception, despite the fact that considered as an attempt at either one of these modes on its own the scene falls down completely. Yet it is obvious that the double focus is maintained. Given the mother's obsession, her actions throughout the section are illuminated with the same thoroughness that Janáček gives to the conduct of sane people. Yet she is not sane. But, as she says herself, she is not 'completely crazy'. Her actions, then, though they include things no sane person would do, have a strange logic to them—indeed, it is often said that the mad are more logical than the sane. This is all the authority Janáček needs to show credibly as inevitable the sequence of events just described; and the music sees them *both* as the inevitable consequence of the union, via the mother's obsession, *and* as an irrationality, a grotesque absurdity which has no justice to it. No catalyst other than a half-crazed person could plausibly contrive this focus; but equally, no other focus could yield the perspective necessary for the third Act, where Živný's attempts to write an autobiographical opera in which this event is seen purely as tragedy are first qualified ironically and then shown to be ultimately impossible.

Yet such a vision must predominate now, in counterbalance. How else can the death of his wife be seen by Živný, at the moment after it has taken place? So 12a emerges in the aftermath of the disaster to convey its remorselessness; 12b, in the highest strings over rippling arpeggios, comprises Míla's elegy; and a steady motion edges the music towards its maestoso conclusion —gathering and frustrated. 'It is lightning, with pure brightness' sings Živný of the catastrophe—and we realize, against the music's inexorable logic at this point, that lightning is arbitrary; the opposition of text and music brings out yet again the double focus. Now Živný calls down upon himself the thunder which must follow it—begs, that is, if we remove the metaphor, for the inevitable sequel to follow. That sequel is already foreshadowed: the removal of the substantial Míla opens the way paradoxically for the attempt to recover her memory even more totally; and Živný's heroic defiance, expressed in the vocal line here, is generated from the double nature of the event he has witnessed: who would struggle against fate? But who would not defy a fate which operates with such absurdity?

The difficulties of third Acts are notorious, and even *Jenůfa* provides an illustration of the problem. Many otherwise successful stage works are fatally weakened by the fact that even the right ending seems, obstinately, to be tame in comparison with what precedes: spontaneous and natural growth from the previous events seems not to be enough. In music-drama, the additional medium makes it possible to supply another level of control, to counterbalance the almost imperceptible loss of force which afflicts even the finest plots at this stage by increasing the level of musical tension gradually in the finale. Janáček always took extreme care in the strategic planning of his operas, and in particular in the grading of the musical response so that each Act concludes more tensely than its predecessor; but the third Act of

Destiny assaults its hearers with a uniquely terse abruptness, assuming from the outset a vigour and animation only rarely foreshadowed in the previous pages of the opera.

The paradox of human existence which Janáček illuminates by this means has not received the understanding it deserves. The prelude in which this vigour first manifests itself is the introduction to a passage of Živný's opera, from which we hear two extracts performed (in concert form) by students of a conservatoire. In the first Act of Janáček's opera this score was merely alluded to, a subject of half-informed conversation by Živný's acquaintances and given only the most cursory references by its composer himself. In Act 2, it is physically present as a score, though nothing is played from it; here we hear part of it for the first time. So the score of Živný's opera gradually comes further within the apprehension of Janáček's spectators as *Destiny* progresses. But while Živný's subject, of course, is the first love of Živný for Míla, and the tragic consequences of that liaison, Janáček's own subject, which is rather different, has also been evolving: Janáček's opera studies three different, successive stages of Živný's attempt to recapture his love for Míla. But the paradox should now be obvious. The movement of the work is steadily towards increased knowledge by us of Živný's attempts, and towards greater or, at any rate, more extensive success in those attempts. But at the same time Živný's actual contact with the events which he is trying to recapture becomes more and more remote, and the death of Míla (now, in Act 3, between ten and a dozen years in the past) has removed the last tangible link —the loved one and her own memories. It is thus far from surprising that Živný's attempts should have reached a blockage— precisely at her death, as we soon find out—since the passage which the students are playing over, the conclusion of Živný's opera, is a dramatization of those emotions of *his* hero which correspond to Živný's own desire for apocalypse at the end of Janáček's Act 2.

The complexity of this plot is only apparent—and much more so on the printed page than in performance. This is because it rapidly emerges in the course of Act 3 that Lensky (Živný's hero) is Živný himself, and while Živný is not Janáček himself (the composer who wronged Míla's real-life prototype, Kamila Urválková, by writing an opera exposing his affair with her was

93

called Čelanský, and Janáček was only involved in the events as a sympathetic hearer of her account), Janáček treats him as if he were, assimilating him by extension of the way in which all songs sung in Janáček operas, even when an original tune existed to the words, receive new settings. There is no distinction between 'Živný's music' and Janáček's own style, and an effect of surprise is achieved when what might be taken at first for a vigorous opening chorus composed by Janáček *in propria persona* turns out to represent a rehearsal of another man's music. The difference between Janáček and Živný lies elsewhere—in the text. Even the strongest critics of Janáček's collaboration with Bartošová will concede that they do not permit their own characters to use imagery as preposterously banal as that of the cockerel flying home to under the eaves, the wind ruffling his tail as a storm gathers—which 'Živný's librettist' uses as simile for man's powerlessness before the hand of destiny. The wild, macabre satire of the dance set for organ and strings, with which the students relieve their feelings after breaking off their read-through of Živný's opera, seems a natural response. Once again, the ironic view of Živný's aspirations is prominent.

Yet the balance remains delicate. Not all of the text imagery of the Živný 'extract' is extravagant Romantic rubbish—Janáček will transfer to Živný's own mouth the picture of the aged, shattered linden which follows the passage about the cockerel, and imply that the composer drew it as an image for his opera from personal experience; the text for Živný's tenor solo, defiantly imploring destruction by lightning, is distinctly more expressive than that for Živný himself doing the same at the end of Janáček's Act 2; and this fine balance is completed when we look at Janáček's score by his provision for 'Živný's opera' of unequivocally serious music, with writing for male chorus of a quality not to be equalled again in the tragic operas before *From the House of the Dead*. What exactly is going on?

The device of the playover by the students enables Janáček to achieve an overlap with the end of his own Act 2, omitting the ten years which intervene: Živný's invocation after Míla's death for the lightning and thunder to overwhelm him is heard again here, in his own artistic version of it—and is fulfilled, for today there is a storm gathering; and it will, later in the Act, overwhelm

Živný himself, at the moment of the highest intensity of his recall of past experience.

This dramatic scheme, which would be naïve if it were to be presented straight—neither tragic nor modern, but a weak melodrama—becomes very different in the context of *Destiny*'s first and second Acts. The action is worked out in Act 3 as a development of the double perspective introduced in Act 1 and at the heart of Act 2; and a gradual development takes place within the Act itself. Consider the stage action first. After the ironic dance, already mentioned, with which the students respond to the conclusion of their run-through of Živný's opera and to the approach of a storm, this ironic attitude to Živný's work continues, first in the affected, over-elaborate chorus in which they declare that 'we will all be coming' to the première that evening, then in the way that, as their fellow-student Verva (who has private information) tells them a little about the background to Živný's opera, the chorus to begin with listen attentively (over hushed orchestral tremolos, to establish their mood, in the lowest strings), but the sopranos soon become impatient, wanting to get rapidly to the bottom of the business by going to ask Živný himself to explain: 'let's leave their mysteries'.

However, the half-distanced, half-fascinated involvement expressed here is the beginning of the destruction of the ironic approach; Verva now plays them a passage from Živný's opera. This turns out to be identical with Janáček's Doubek scene in Act 2, with an overlay of string octaves held to convey the mystery of recall; and the reaction is much warmer; the men are totally involved, taking up the refrain 'D'you know what love is?' with full strength on Janáček's original, powerful melody, while the girls, their reaction remaining distinct as before, comment on Živný's dramatic idea 'that is clever, Jean and Nanny'. The young women are none the less shown to be moved by the scene as much as the men. Their comment is dovetailed into the same four-note fall which in the orchestral music of the original scene conveyed the hesitating, wondering reaction of the two servants themselves; and the same emotion is shown by this to be present in the girls now. So after this heightening of the response of all the students, the stages from their bafflement at Živný's appearance, through involvement in his narration to the end, the

95

blatant terror of people totally and directly disturbed by events, are totally convincing.

The pupils are of course a surrogate audience: their moods are to guide our moods, their view of the action to reflect ours. It follows from their closing mood that the opera's final perspective on its action is tragic. And this is the inevitable outcome; the music makes plain as the Act unfolds that Živný's loss is real, and no other response would then be appropriate or adequate. The dramatic strategy which Janáček has adopted has also got a momentum of its own: given such a platform as Živný's appearance before an inquisitive stage audience provides, Janáček is virtually bound to launch one of the great, impassioned—and therefore serious—monologues which occur near or at the end of each of the tragic operas, from Kostelnička's confession to Šiškov's story. (This explains the otherwise curious under-use of Doubek, whose introduction in this Act as one of the students creates expectations which are unfulfilled.) But the effect is to complicate the meaning of this Act, to make what Janáček seeks to say intricate and difficult. Živný leads the students, at first baffled and ironic about his opera's portentous claims to trace the workings of destiny, through a journey of insight; seriousness comes only with deep understanding, and, apparently paradoxically, understanding comes only with idealized reminiscence. The significant word here is idealized: Janáček seems to be saying that such is the intensity of feeling in recollection that even the banal, the trivial and the bizarre there become serious events.

To see how this is done, and understand how the evolution to this point of view is made into a convincing, inevitable sequence, we must confront the music directly at some crucial points. Janáček begins by exploiting the dramatic convention by which Živný's style (and indeed, later, part of Živný's opera) are assumed to be identical with Janáček's own; and he can use this convention to secure two main points on behalf of his own opera, while ostensibly only relaying a portion of Živný's. The opening, as I have mentioned, is extremely tense, rich and strange; and the working out of the four-note violin figure of Živný's storm to accompany the text, 'It is not safe to challenge the agent of God', followed by the use of Janáček's own rising trills of apprehension on the Example 9c notes of inevitable involvement before the words (of the aged linden tree shattered by the storm) 'its seasons have rotted it', establishes the tie between the onset of the storm and the working of destiny, long before Janáček can either make this point seriously for himself or reveal its nature—the crucial revelation which is congruent with the illumination of the lightning-flash. Establishes it so well, in fact, that Janáček can go further and foreshadow the end in 'Živný's tenor solo' while ostensibly only dramatizing on Živný's behalf the events after Míla's death. A solo violin—which will reappear at the denouement of Janáček's own opera—provides the link between memory and revelation. Beginning only with a slowed-down version of the storm figuration, it leads inexorably into demands for lightning to come, picturing the hero's move from remembrance to desire with precise conviction (Example 15). The animating element is the extension of the violin solo's pattern to four quavers, in the third bar, introducing the high G flat which calls for a lower level, a filling-in of the texture; and the lower voices precipitate simultaneously the rushing arpeggios of desire and the parallel fifths of the storm in the horns, echoed by the violas as the voice enters.

Živný's experience in this Act will be an act of recall: to bring the opera's balance down in favour of seeing this seriously, Janáček contrives to suggest the immensity of the emptiness which such an act must traverse, using a device almost without parallel in his music before *Makropulos*—wildly figured violins alone and high above the stave—as Verva reports that Živný delivered the score to the theatre without a last Act. This device will be used again in developed form when Živný enters, together with the moving theme 'Do you know what love is?' from the scene the pupils have just played over, here given on violas and cor anglais. There the motif seems almost to sum up in a nutshell the essence of his experience—and of his quest: his knowledge of loss, so much greater than any the students can have—but also his continuing search. It is characteristic of Živný that the orchestral phrase which announces his entry is associated vocally with a *question*—prefiguring the inconclusiveness in which the opera ends.

Živný's statement about the ending of his opera, 'It is in the hands of God and must remain with him', reported by Verva, provides the next stage to understanding (and these words, in Živný's mouth, also provide the affirmation which closes

D

Ex. 15 (3.7:13)

Janáček's opera). The theme is designed to be inconclusive—and so reduces the students and the orchestra to virtual silence. Then spacious string octaves with leisurely descending bassoons convey the depths of mystery and of the past which begin to open before the stage audience. When Verva begins to talk about Živný's opera, he has a captive audience. But it is of course the recall implicit in playing over the Doubek scene as Janáček set it which clinches the movement to seriousness. We have seen enacted what we now hear; the action recalled by this section of 'Živný's score' is totally recalled; we *know* this, for we saw it enacted with this music to illuminate its nuances.

After Živný's entry, the main burden shifts, as these last moves have predicted, to making the students—ever the mirror for our involvement—begin to understand seriously Živný's position. Since the advancing of the stage action now is so bound up with recall, the musical device of recalling music from previous Acts makes the crucial tie—for it is so rare in Janáček that such material sounds out clearly in his operas, in which the normal expectation is to hear completely new material at each point. As Živný narrates 'Lensky's' new faith in life after falling in love, it is natural that a horn call should bring back for the last time the cadences of Doubek's childhood question; and the end of the same section establishes a far more important pattern: violin figurations derived from Example 9b, but with no closing fall—already associated in 'Živný's opera' with the passing of time in the quest—are associated in this narration with the rising of inspiration from the points at which love's penetration of the soul ends. First, inevitable patterns are apprehended by the stage audience; then, the theme is the tracing of such patterns by the artist. The link is crucial to making credible Živný's later collapse under the agony of narrating what is, after all, experience of his own which he has already to some measure assimilated by writing his opera; and it gives the students now their first serious understanding of him ('Do you understand? He is telling us his own grief'). It is this new association of the rising pattern which lets it explain later—in the form, familiar from the previous Acts, of rising tremolos for unaccompanied violas—Živný's having turned in rage on Míla in the abusive pages written in his first turmoil, after her apparent desertion of him.

'How can I forget you? A last sob, a last groan. Snatches of melodies, snatches from lips grown pale.' This is how Živný finishes his narrative of his love for Míla up to the time of her death. The violence of the imagery (and the stage direction, 'convulsive spasm of grief') demands a corresponding violence of musical response; and receives it, so shifting the opera on to a final plane of intensity which it does not now desert. *How* is the significant word of the present text: the inevitability of the meeting of Živný and Míla, and of its consequences, is now taken as established; and so the focus in these last pages will demonstrate the inevitability of his search in the emptiness after her death, and of the recall we are about to witness—so leading inexorably into the denouement. This is done with compulsive power. Much is conveyed simply by the force of animating the orchestra with the convulsive ostinato which gives birth after two bars of ostinato alone to the great maestoso whose opening is printed as Example 16: 'He crept out to seek the music (of God), that it might drown his whole soul/and there, where aged lindens trembled in terror/he went to find God.'

Ex. 16 (3.31:2)

The music prefigured in octave violins, echoed with limpid clarity by the trumpet, is of course finely related to Example 10 (it is a sorry testament to the commentators that both are solemnly labelled 'fate motif' in more than one study of the piece). It is related because both motifs figure the impact of a celestial light on a sensitive, responsive human being in whom there are emotions which can be congruent with it: in Act 1 the sun, and here the lightning. The intensity of the light, the inspired equilibrium of the spirit when it is illumined by it, are the matter of the phrase, as can be heard in its calm but inexorable rise and fall. And it forges the link which completes the chain: Živný's visions, welded in his brain by lightning, are shown by the music to be of the same stuff as the ardour of his love for Míla when she was alive; lightning, seen clearly only in twilight and dark, is the more intense vision—and also the more tragic—after the clarity of day, the happiness of life with Míla, is past; the vision to follow this will be one of Míla, in all intensity, and with the same binding power on Živný that their meetings in her lifetime possessed.

So it is: a fearful combination of textural imagery—twilight scatterings of silver as the background, Míla's white angelic face complete with its golden locks (night against day, past against present), Živný's defiance, 'in ecstatic madness' of the storm which has made all the students cower by the organ at the back —with a fierce array of motifs of reminiscence in the orchestra leads to an overwhelming climax: lightning strikes, the lights fail and Živný falls stunned before the combination of total recall and present congruence with nature. After which there are only four elements in the score: the scurrying viola and later violin figures, narrow-intervalled, which chronicle the tense emotion of the onlookers; a complete recall of Example 15, introduced by an extension of the violin solo, now elevated to the sublime as Janáček's own illumination of Živný's total recall of Míla in tears; a recall of the questioning theme to which Verva had suggested to the students that 'this is music, perhaps, from the last act', and Živný overhearing reiterates his conviction, now as certain knowledge, 'that is still in the hands of God and will remain there!'; and the fierce close that follows, in which the rhythm of the brass is generated from that of the setting of the last words, reinforcing 'and will remain there', and the declension into terror of the students is represented by the repeated four-note cadence of Živný's intonations. The ending is entirely repressive, as the violins' identical repetition in each bar of the four-note figure shows: it holds back the 'and will remain there' theme from full resolution, reinforcing the text with its graphic, direct musical image of the failure of the recall to develop. Živný has reached the limits of recall in a moment of ecstasy as nature is congruent with his expectations; but destiny leads no further, life offers no grand secrets even in such a moment, even to a composer.

It is extremely difficult—even after this extensive discussion—to make a final assessment of such an unusual work. But the attempt can be made. *Destiny* remains unpublished and its score is not widely known; but its constructional technique is that of the mature music-dramas—unlike Janáček's other two unpublished operas, the early and uncharacteristic *Šárka* and *Beginning of a Romance*. This technique creates an unparalleled fusion of music and drama, and can therefore only fully be judged by combined criteria, those of music-drama; and so judged, *Destiny* offers moments which are finer than anything in *Jenůfa*, and dramatic sequences whose theatrical power Janáček was rarely to equal before *Makropulos*.

As to the poetic diction of the text, *Destiny* inhabits to a considerable extent the perilous, visionary climate of some Czech poetry of the time—entered elsewhere on a large scale by Janáček only in the cantatas *Amarus* and *Eternal Gospel*. But, except in the closing pages of the work, the characters who speak in the high style are viewed, partially, with irony precisely because of the elevated attitude they adopt; and in those last pages, when we must sympathize closely with Živný or miss the point, banality and profundity must stand or fall together—for both are inextricably mingled with the music.

Janáček did not wish the allusiveness, the looseness and the inconclusiveness of *Destiny* on himself for no good reason: the work confronts problems which *Jenůfa*, with its direct plot of evident, immediate seriousness wholly avoids. The emerging theme is the power of recollection, a highly abstract theme, and it must be crystallized—in the figure of an artist; the artist is, understandably, placed in his creator's own profession; self-indulgence and narcissism are the first dangers, though Janáček avoids both. The delicacy and intangibility of the theme mean that direct serious impact of the kind made by Kostelnička's murder of Jenůfa's baby is virtually impossible. As too is continuous advancement of the plot. So the work, like all Janáček's subsequent operas, attempts a mixture of styles, in which side episodes not apparently involving the main characters or the main theme are designed to contribute as much to the illumination of the subject-matter as anything else—though more obliquely.

Destiny, then, is a serious opera on the intertwined themes of a love bound to attain fulfilment but equally bound, by its opposition to social norms, to disaster, and of the paradoxical way in which reminiscence, consciously pursued, both hinders and helps action and eventually, when free of any contemporary living reality to bind it, gains power out of all proportion to the events remembered. The presumption of such a pursuit is recognized, and the artist concerned, and the intense love affair between him and Mílá, are consistently viewed with ironic qualification supplied by the words and actions of other characters. More deeply —and this is the crux of the opera—the same focus extends to the destiny which gives the work its title. Claims to trace the workings of destiny in the events are made, mocked by people or events—and yet substantiated in the action. No crucial event in the work before the catastrophe of the last five minutes—which is itself inconclusive and baffling—is dramatized without text, music or both qualifying it so as to produce this double focus: life is seen as serious, as involving catastrophes caused by inevitable patterns of events and which elicit deserved emotion; but all claims to trace the patterns are qualified by the tragic fact that such claims—or the catastrophes themselves—are simultaneously seen in ironic focus, as trivial, bizarre or both.

To create a work of such malignant double focus, to set it in the stamping-ground of bourgeois melodrama and to endow it with a hero drawn from a province of extravagant Romanticism may seem—it is a matter of taste—a shocking aim for the creator of *Jenůfa* to have embarked on almost immediately after the completion of that opera. Yet there is no doubt that he did so; little doubt that he succeeded. *Destiny* has as much to offer as any other opera of Janáček; and the vision of the inevitable which pervades it is decisively modern in comparison even with *Jenůfa*. No other composer of the period could have come anywhere near Janáček's degree of success, and the few inelegancies of working out are owing to factors beyond his control: I have in mind that some of the opera's points could, perhaps, be carried with total effectiveness only in a non-naturalistic stage convention not available to a composer in the first decade of our century —in particular the almost surreal, at all events grotesque and difficult role of the mother, so hard for audiences to accept with the right blend of seriousness and alienation.

The claim might perhaps be made that Janáček overstretched himself, departing from the mode of *Jenůfa* in too many ways at once, with *Destiny*'s inconclusive ending, its expressionist elements, the construction of a libretto from Janáček's own prose outline, the absence of folk elements and the new musical style— for here the nineteenth-century harmonic opulence of some passages of *Jenůfa* never occurs; the lucid, lyric beauty of the score is that of an accumulation of motif in his later manner, and the characteristic predominance of sixths and fourths begins here too. It could then be held that Janáček achieved the aims of *Destiny* only in the later operas, which blend the uncompromising directness of *Jenůfa* with the grotesque elements introduced first, and so disturbingly, here. But if the opera *is* for these reasons to be seen as a failure (this is not my view), it is a failure on the grandest scale, in an act of complex, rich and stimulating vision.

Kát'a Kabanová

Kát'a Kabanová alone, among Janáček's tragic operas, begins slowly, serenely. But the measured, elegant argument of the opening destroys itself: the melody breaks down within a page into explosive violence. And the turbulence persists to the end of the prelude: it is relieved only by a few moments of fragile peace, shortly before the violent, unsatisfying close. All this takes less than five minutes; and in those minutes the whole emotional course of the opera itself has been prefigured, from Kát'a's initial, self-imposed calm through a gradual breakdown into the naked unrest of the confession scene, and beyond, through the brief peace of her final moments to a brutal death. The concision speaks for an authority new in the composer's work, leads us to expect an opera of clarity, of precision and of integrated, complete achievement. That is what we receive: *Kát'a Kabanová* is Janáček's most direct tragedy, unfolding its story with classic economy. The line leads directly from the potentially disastrous opening situation to the savage, negative conclusion.

Janáček had taken no tragic opera beyond preliminary sketches since completing *Destiny* in 1906. The outbreak of war in 1914 had forced the abandonment of a projected production, and in the meantime he had been struggling for years to complete the first section of what was to become a satirical opera in two parts, *The Excursions of Mr. Brouček*. But the eventual Prague success of *Jenůfa* stimulated Janáček to full self-confidence and new inspiration: he first completed the *Excursions* (writing the second part in eight months; the first had taken eight years) and then began to search for a new tragic libretto. Alexander Ostrovsky's *The Storm* was suggested by a theatrical friend; and it appealed powerfully to the composer. The opera's simplicity is that of a work of consolidation: here Janáček reassembled at full strength the tragic powers which he had first found in *Jenůfa*, and welded them to the acute vein of satire which he had developed in the intervening years. After this successful work he was able to advance; and the last three operas have other virtues: they are wider in focus, and different in their dramatic aims from *Kát'a Kabanová* and its predecessors. *Kát'a Kabanová* is the last of Janáček's works to be obviously and directly high tragedy.

Its simplicity has not prevented fantastic misunderstanding. Commentary after commentary has seen the heroine as a pure soul, who does what she believes to be right and is hounded to death by a malevolent or indifferent community. This interpretation of the opera will not stand.

Ostrovsky's play, a classic of the Russian stage, does offer a tension between the individual, Kát'a, and her surroundings. The setting is Kalinov, a small town on the Volga in the 1860s. It is ruled despotically by a backward, self-appointed 'aristocracy' of rich merchants. Everyone else is forced into hypocrisy and self-repression by dependence on them. The sufferings and eventual suicide of Kát'a are used as a vehicle for a powerful critique of the merchants and those who submit to them: Ostrovsky exhibits the town's *mores* in an extensive series of monologues and vignette scenes given to a varied cast of characters; and he uses the young woman's pain chiefly for the contrast it makes, the reminder that there are other, more idealistic worlds than that of the society against whose injustice he was protesting.

It has often been observed that Janáček's adaptation of his libretto reverses this relationship: it is designed to focus chiefly upon Kát'a, and diminishes the role of the town to that of a distorting mirror for her predicament. But there is more. Reducing the play from the sprawling Russian five-Act form to his customary three, Janáček cut the text extensively. The cuts remove motivations superfluous in view of the insight Janáček's music supplies; but they are also consistently designed to remove the more obtrusive, specific period details; and with them goes the whole thread of social commentary. Janáček was not interested in criticizing the society of Russia sixty years before he wrote. So the extensive dialogue of the servants Glaša and Fekluša, and the scenes for the half-crazed old lady with two valets all disappear;

Kuligin, a wise old man who is the chief vehicle for Ostrovsky's choric comment on the action, is reduced to a cipher; and the opera's stage directions do not even insist on a vital social detail—that Boris alone wears Western dress, pointing up his position as an outsider in the provincial society. Minor characters, and even some major ones, are weakened and simplified: Kudrjáš, though taking over many of Kuligin's lines, becomes little more than a young intellectual rebel, Dikoj is softened, is less than wholly an unpleasant and self-pitying bully. The effect is to blur Ostrovsky's rich outline of the town's society as a whole, and to sharpen the extent to which the tragedy is an interaction between three pairs of people: the merchants, Kabanicha and Dikoj; the superficial couple, Varvara and Kudrjáš; and the more profound couple, Káťa and Boris.

Janáček cuts, adapts, compresses characters into one with great boldness; and in the final result Káťa's development through the action to the point at which she takes her life stands out as the main thread of his swift, almost breathless libretto. Even her lover, who defies the community no less than she, hardly intrudes upon this focus: if Káťa is the Jenůfa of this tragedy, Boris is no Laca. Indeed, Janáček takes the extreme risk of making the hero conventional at best and at some moments self-dramatizing and self-deluding: Boris is only just strong enough to be credible, and vigorous characterization by the interpreter is necessary. As Janáček's heroines become more powerful in the later operas, his tenors become less significant: Boris is only a step away from the ranting, inadequate Gregor of *Makropulos*. The opera thus comes near to being a tragedy of unworthiness, Káťa giving her love to a man who does not deserve it. But not completely: Káťa alone, and the outrage of her death, are central; and to this Boris's character is irrelevant, beyond the fact that he loves her.

The primary focus is the tragic tension which causes Káťa's death. And this tension has frequently been misinterpreted. It is not a tension between her values and those of the community. Káťa's predicament is not that she does what she believes to be right, and suffers for it; it is that she believes deeply that adultery is wrong, and when she is driven by love for Boris into committing it she is shamed by the consciousness of what she has done, the destruction of her values, into taking her own life. The community, in Janáček's adaptation, is reduced to a crowd of

107

compliant loafers, a grotesque irrelevance. And Janáček's sharp characterization of the other two pairs of principal characters places Kát'a's inner spiritual conflict in a precise, relevant context. For the two merchants—ludicrous characters, finely realized in Janáček's music with the satirical devices which he had developed in *Destiny* and the *Excursions*—claim (hypocritically) to uphold precisely the same morality as that for which Kát'a dies, and attempt to impose it on the community. This fact yields ironies throughout the opera: explains Kát'a's meekness in the face of Kabanicha in the early scenes (what can you say, when you agree with the sentiments of a hypocrite on whom you are totally dependent?); and leads to the overwhelming irony of the closing scene, where the fate to which her own true conscience and morality lead Kát'a can be acclaimed as justice by the hypocritical Kabanicha for exactly the same reason—that the heroine has paid the penalty of adultery. Hence, in large measure, the grimness of the conclusion: Kabanicha's self-satisfaction is outrageous, but grows so organically from the moral bases of the heroine and of the opera that there is no suggestion of any prospect of retribution on her and her kind.

In various ways, everyone but Kát'a has come to terms with the rule of the merchants, accepting their petty autocracy in return for material security. Even Boris, who in the first scene reveals real agony in his need for spiritual independence before his youth is past, meekly accepts his uncle's demands right to the end, where he is exiled to Siberia. Many suppress their misery in the traditional Russian fashion—with drink; so most prominently Kát'a's husband, Tichon. An alternative way of life is offered by the amoral, hedonist young lovers, Varvara and Váňa Kudrjáš. Living like Boris and Kát'a to the extent that they follow love where it leads them, they yet follow the safer paths of the false, hypocritical morality; for like the merchants they believe in doing what you want—as long as you are not caught doing it. In this way they stake out a middle-ground and strike a balance with the other two pairs which yields, even in the libretto alone, a highly effective dramatization of the moral issues; better laid out even than the libretto of *Jenůfa*.

And the music supports this spiritual ecology, eloquently and simply. Matching and responding to the prominence of its delicate, spiritually beautiful heroine, Janáček's orchestra is dominated, during Kát'a's music, by the softest, most caressing tones of strings and woodwind—which makes this the most sensuous and eloquent of the tragic operas. The same instruments are also employed—with considerably less grace—in the illustration of Kabanicha's taunts; and this precisely supports the text's vision of her morality as a perversion of Kát'a's. And—again appropriately—the music of the third pair, Varvara and Váňa, is marked off, sharply distinct; only in the double love scene of 2.ii, where the four young people are more united by their shared emotions, do Varvara's four chords for flutes and celesta become integrated into the musical argument. And the amoral couple are further isolated, by the fact that they alone make extensive use of folk-like songs, and that their vocal lines, even when not consisting of actual quoted songs, are lighter and gayer than those of the other characters.

But if the music of the groups of characters is clearly differentiated, this pressure towards incoherence is equally sharply counterbalanced: the work is bound together, thematically, with an intensity not paralleled in any other opera of Janáček's. One motif dominates the score, in two contrasted versions, first stated in the prelude (Example 17a, b):

Ex. 17a (1.i.0:5)

17b's associations become clear in the last scene of Act 1: the bells evoke the troika which is to take Tichon to Kazan—and with him the last outside restraint on Kát'a's passion. 17a, which recurs at almost every major crisis in the action, has naturally—in view of this fact and of its gloomy character—attracted the label 'fate theme'.

The label is depressingly crude. Janáček's examination of the inevitability of action is always subtle and penetrating: no one theme can speak 'fate', rattling its sabre to remind us of the presence of destiny. We should be alive to the uniqueness of the

Ex. 17b (I.i.3:1)

device; for though *Kát'a Kabanová*, like all the late operas, practises ingenious transformations of theme into theme, it is alone in being dominated by a motif so strident, distinctive and unvaried as this. Here for the only time in Janáček the score's emphasis is as much on a repeated motif as on the expectation of something new; the spectator is made even on first hearing to note and assimilate the points at which this phrase occurs. For this reason I believe that Daniel Muller was near the truth: for him this theme evoked the spirit of old Russia, the binding force of the iron circles of tradition (a feature largely withdrawn from the libretto by Janáček's cuts). This pattern and its constant recurrence convey the atmosphere of a closed society; though virtually impossible, the ideal of escape is constantly before the minds of the subject characters. In this work, social convention binds and constricts the spirit even more than in *Jenůfa* and *Destiny*. And the effect, as the opera proceeds and the motif becomes more trenchant at each appearance, is to remind us of the limits of action: the drama's delicate triangle of morality, false morality and amorality is conducted within unalterable, close bounds— from which, for the heroine, there is no escape but death. And in the musical balance between the variety of the individuals and the monotony of the theme which conveys their repression lies, I would suggest, the profound, surprising beauty of the suffering expressed in this opera; a work which plumbs the depths of human misery in a manner equalled only, perhaps, by *From the House of the Dead* and Alban Berg's *Wozzeck*.

Ostrovsky's play is called *The Storm* after its climactic scene: prompted by the sight of frescoes of the fire of Gehenna, and sharing the belief of the other Orthodox characters that 'storms are a punishment for us, that we may feel the power of God', Kát'a is prompted by a particularly violent thunderstorm—and the accusing, sinister appearance of a half-crazed old lady accompanied by two valets—to confess her adultery. Janáček largely strips the play of its theology, removing the old lady and reducing the debate between the rationalist Kuligin and the Orthodox characters to a few short exchanges between Dikoj and Kudrjáš. But the storm remains, as does the skeleton of the debate; Dikoj sings the line just quoted, contemptuously ridiculing Kudrjáš's plea for the installation of lightning conductors and his scientific belief that storms are 'just electricity'. And the fact that it remains is fascinating—for Janáček does not need metaphysics to explain Kát'a's actions, when his powerful music illuminates her declension into the desire to confess, and indeed every step in her psychological progression in the opera. Further, Janáček himself was pronounced, indeed fanatical in his rejection of conventional religion. The storm should not be read as symbolic: it is a real storm which in Janáček's adaptation infects everyone, at the end of the storm scene, with a mass hysteria initiated by Kát'a: they all rush, scattering, into the storm.

And there is no doubt which side Janáček supports in the dispute between Kudrjáš and Dikoj. Atheist and rationalist though he was, Janáček accompanies Dikoj's claim with the sonorous orchestral music of the actual storm (Example 23), which proceeds inexorably to affect Kát'a and cause her breakdown. For the purpose of the opera, science alone and the voice of reason are irrelevant—and here again the 'true' and 'false' moralities are at one. A scientifically false superstition can be poetically true: Kát'a and Dikoj are psychologically right, in the tragic world of Kalinov. And even though the engineer who speaks with the voice of science and reason survives the opera, he does so only by leaving its world to found a new life in Moscow. With the rationalism goes the amorality of his mistress Varvara; the couple are, in the final analysis, less closely bound than the other two poles which yield the true axis of the opera: Kát'a and Kabanicha, Boris and Dikoj live the lives which are truly opposed, those of true and hypocritical believers in guilt and its punishment.

But it is necessary to go beyond character, in order to near the heart of this opera; to study the unfolding of the action. Janáček, by cuts and rearrangements, frames his plot in such a way that each Act closes a few moments after a crucial advance in the psychological action; the result is a drama of radical directness. The opera opens shortly after Boris and Kát'a have fallen in love with each other; and Janáček drops the curtain on Act 1 the moment Tichon leaves Kalinov on business; for then the last external restraint on Kát'a's fulfilling her love for Boris is removed. In Act 2, their love is consummated; and the closing music portrays the intense shame which will lead in the final Act to confession and then suicide. The opera makes Kát'a's yielding seem less and less avoidable as it moves towards the centre of Act 2, the moment where she has yielded and goes out to meet Boris. There, at the mid-point of the opera, night falls; and in the darkness which dominates the scenes for the remainder of the work, the consequence of her yielding is seen to become, more and more, an equally unavoidable death.

This, however, is far in the future as the curtain rises. Here the picture is one of light and space, and the first scene presents a slow, almost static darkening of tones, in keeping with the composer's customary strategy of gaining intensity by precisely graded developments. Indeed, the opening scene is given to a pair of subsidiary characters, Gláša and Kudrjáš; and it takes time for the atmosphere of the work to become established in the action. This is why the prelude is of such trenchant power; as later in *Makropulos*, the orchestral music guarantees, before the curtain rises, that we are witnesses to events which, though initially apparently trivial, will in due course become serious. The gentle theme of the penultimate, pastoral episode of the prelude turns out to be associated, by Kudrjáš' facile celebration of the beauty of the Volga, with the river—when it is placid. And those penultimate bars are brutally crushed before the curtain rises, in a recurrence of the most stringent material of the prelude, music which will be heard again only in Act 3, when the elements rage and Kát'a's confession is at hand. After which the river finally comes into its own.

Scene i is designed merely to set up the circumstances which are to engulf the heroine: to place before us the different kinds of people who inhabit and surround the Kabanov household. Kudrjáš is only one of three visitors, each there for a moment's sight of his loved one. The others soon appear: Dikoj and Boris. Dikoj, frustrated, leaves abruptly; and his abuse of Boris then yields the opportunity to begin serious exposition. Boris's monologue takes flight from the persecution, and leads gradually, with heightened emotion, to his desire for freedom and confession of his love. So too will Kát'a's monologue to her confidante, Varvara, in the second scene; Janáček sets up a parallelism between the two which proposes a deep affinity three scenes before they meet face to face. For each, the pressure of the outside world leads, as they begin an act of recollection and introspection, to the purity of sustained chords, followed by the gentle undulation of small woodwind phrases.

But against the similarity, the difference. Kát'a's monologue is more extensive; its close will decline tragically into crazed, hysterical visions first of grandeur and then of unmixed horror. The movement is towards the revelation of what is oppressing her. Boris's is a genuine anguish, as is shown by the expectant, upward gatherings of the phrase. But it is nothing more. It is the anguish of a man who is trapped—unable to leave the town for fear of the power Dikoj can wield to ruin his sister. Boris's pain is reinforced as the people start returning from church by the pious servant Fekluša's inane praise of the meritocracy; and an outburst of real despair accompanies this.

But Boris has already found an answer, a creature who—like himself—is from a better world. The moment that he realizes that the Kabanov family are returning from church, a new theme foreshadowed in the prelude begins to enter the orchestra, and as Kát'a, Varvara, Kabanicha and Tichon come on to the stage it enters softly and proceeds to greater and greater volume and intensity.

Ex. 18 (1.i.30:6)

This has usually been described as 'Kát'a's theme'. But musical themes are not static descriptions of individuals: they are dynamic, advance the action. As the family comes near, foreshadowings of this theme underlie Boris's muted confession of his hopeless love and Kudrjáš' warning, 'You mustn't do that, you can't destroy her.' Boris retreats behind the corner of the house. And then, as the music of Example 18 develops to full intensity, we witness what is almost a formal progress. At the climax, having had his brief sight of the loved one, Boris shouts sarcastically 'and then off home'—and runs away, with a bitter laugh. What we have heard, as Example 18 moves to its climax, is the inexorable growth of Boris's love for Kát'a. This is the natural consequence of the loneliness and despair which we have already heard.

All the music of this first scene is highly episodic and polarized; but the most extreme division is to follow. Between Kabanicha and Kát'a there is no communication: their musics glare at each other across space like distorting mirrors, blocks of musical material related only in their instrumentation. And Kabanicha's implacable, gesture-like phrasing reflects Example 17, while Kát'a, in the isolated pride of her reserved orchestral sections, is apart: inward, private, radiant, her music is nearer to that of the placid river than to any other that we have heard so far. Like the river's calm, hers too—Janáček implies—is fragile. She is evidently holding herself in check; and when, in the gathering momentum of the whole opera, the unrelated blocks of sound gradually begin to become related, it will be to achieve the crushing of this music. Hence a deep, pathetic absurdity is all that the music tells us to hear, when Tichon says, 'I love you both.' Between the monolithic, impenetrable Kabanicha and the self-contained, proud Kát'a—both women determined to preserve their inner selves—his dream is impossible.

Tichon flees, to take refuge in drink. Varvara, left alone, addresses the audience. 'I pity her so much. That's it, she's pitiable. I love her. Why should I not love her?' Janáček's solo horn, prefiguring the music of Kát'a's great monologue in the second scene, makes eloquently clear the fact that the two young women, heroine and soubrette, are isolated in an oasis of true feeling and perception. But a double-edged one. 'Serious little bird, quick to take insult', was Kabanicha's comment as Kát'a left the stage; and Kabanicha is perceptive where Tichon is blind to the moral world. For the music of Kát'a's inner radiance returned in the orchestra when Kabanicha warned Tichon that he must treat Kát'a more firmly or she will take a lover—and so tells us of the source from which Kát'a has gained her inner strength. Kabanicha's fears are well placed: Kát'a wants to take flight; and there is someone able, and willing, to love her.

But does Kát'a love him? Her music in the first scene is close enough to Example 18, its reuse under Kabanicha's warnings so full of meaning, that the music has already prefigured the answer. And in giving it, the second scene also opens up the tragic dimensions of this opera. Essentially, we are offered first a monologue (Kát'a with Varvara as confidante) and then a dialogue (Kát'a with Tichon). The first explains the second—for the monologue is totally devoted to the exploration of Kát'a's mind, and by its end we have seen her both confessing her love and racked by the guilt of it. The only hope she sees of preventing herself from succumbing is to prevent Tichon's departure; in the dialogue with him she fails, and her collapse follows.

The logic of the monologue is acute. Kát'a confesses her desire for escape from Kalinov. But escape is impossible—as impossible as flying away, which is the gesture with which Kát'a begins; so confiding her thoughts to someone she thinks she can trust is Kát'a's only relief. And the course of the monologue matches, musically, the desire for escape and the physical gesture which it replaces; the music unfolds itself, with precious beauty, almost like a bird's wings, from the sustained, simple chords of the opening through the tender melancholy of the solo horn melody into more and more agitated figurations. The opening simplicity is that of Kát'a's complete unity, as a child, with nature; the beauty of the horn solo matches the sanctity of her subsequent religious experience, the agitation to follow the vertigo in which she was suspended as that worship became ecstasy.

Here the upper and lower instruments are in such tension that both Kát'a's breakdown into tears, and her sudden resurgence into terrifying visions, of religious experience and of nature at its most glorious, are only too much to be expected. The visions suddenly thrust her from the recollection of past vertigo into that in which she is suspended at this moment not by religion but by sex. And so the music of the monologue is of pointed ambiguity: the horn melody recalls Example 18, while the visions are set to figurations which anticipate the temptation scene of 2.i. So far, the movement of Kát'a's monologue has been parallel to—if far richer than—that of Boris's.

But the flying figurations of the scene's prelude return violently, expressing a desperate need for spiritual escape, when Kát'a's visions become so agitated that they terrify Varvara into asking Kát'a, 'What's wrong with you?' Kát'a has achieved flight in admitting to her feeling of being above a precipice. And now, Kát'a's tragic position becomes apparent. After this, fallen, she moves towards explicit admission of her love. And there is a contemplative calm to the scene, voice and orchestra interacting with a sensuous, almost post-coital languor. Guilt and desire blend in music of stability, calm and utter emotional commitment as Kát'a describes the temptations which constantly assail her.

Varvara is not an innocent spectator: she suggests that Kát'a should see Boris when Tichon has left. And once again—as with Boris in scene i—the music, as Kát'a reacts hysterically, anticipates that of the scene which follows. In a few moments Varvara has left, two servants enter and leave with Tichon's luggage (their comments ironically underscore the next scene: 'Is he going for long?' 'Not long'), and the man himself is before Kát'a, dressed for departure.

Here the scene echoes the movement of the first for one last time. As scene i became an acid confrontation of unrelated musical material after the arrival of the Kabanovs, so here again linear sequence is almost abolished in the conflict of unrelated blocks, to express the complete absence of communication between Tichon and Kát'a. He cannot understand why she is so desperate for him to stay; and this Janáček reinforces powerfully. By convention, Tichon is deaf to the sheer desperation which we can hear sounding out from Kát'a's orchestra. And the scene focuses its fullest tragic powers on Kát'a in her mounting desperation—even though Tichon too has his quiet misery (the circular jingle of the troika music oppresses him with the sufferings of his servile life and the journey which he must make at his mother's orders).

The musical opposition develops inexorably. Janáček is acutely aware of the way life works in such a situation: the tension between the two people increases as their argument becomes more specific. The opening of the scene merely contrasts Kát'a's agitation with Tichon's, which is expressed by the appearance of both versions of Example 17. But a new variant appears to express the impact on Kát'a, when Tichon says that rather than live this kind of life even the best of men might desert his wife:

Ex. 19 (1.ii.20:5)

This terrifies Kát'a simply because of the idea of separation; that is what she cannot bear, and as she snuggles up to Tichon and pleads with him to stay, the music—dolce, moderato for strings—recalls the dreamy languor of her description of her love at the end of the dialogue with Varvara, and so tells us exactly what she is doing: trying to channel on to Tichon her love of Boris and the emotions of the previous scene. But Tichon rejects these pleas, and a terrified, tremolo hiatus breaks the musical textures. Kát'a attempts, desperately, to fill the gap.

She does so by attempting to get Tichon to make her swear an oath to see no other man in his absence. And this introduces a final motif of the utmost trenchancy, fuel later in the opera for the storm which causes Kát'a's breakdown:

Ex. 20 (1.ii. 23:1)

and again the hiatuses and the wide separation of orchestral instruments express the desperation and the distortion of the music of love as her fear becomes almost uncontrollable.

Kabanicha is heard calling from an inner room, and as Tichon and Kát'a stand frozen, 17b plays softly. The irony is as great as the suspense: the motif has more power than any other heard in

117

the scene—but it sounds out now as a moment of peace. Janáček develops the irony and leads to the closing climax of his Act by a brilliant alteration to the original play. Kabanicha enters, and proceeds to force Tichon to tell Kát'a formally what she should and should not do in his absence—including, finally, an insistence that he should instruct her 'not to look at other men'. In Ostrovsky, this scene precedes the one between Tichon and Kát'a which Janáček has just set; and by reversing the order, Janáček achieves a hideous effect: Kabanicha forces Tichon to do to Kát'a exactly what he has just refused to do at her own request. Janáček's scene, dominated by the tritonal motif which expressed Kabanicha's severity in 1.i, is a scene of nothing but oppression; and at the end Kát'a is quite logically reduced, not merely to staring severely at Tichon (as in the original), but to breakdown.

The melody to which this happens is not painful at all. A beautiful, tender andante for flute and cor anglais over flowing string figurations, it strikes a note which is superficially unexpected—but in fact deeply expected. The theme, perfectly presented in full flower, is that of her desires, recalled from the dialogue with Varvara but now with all the instability removed from it. Under the strain, Janáček indicates, Kát'a's desires have broken free. And when Kabanicha leaves Tichon and Kát'a alone for their last words before he goes, they are curt:

TICHON: Are you angry with me?
KÁT'A: No. (*harshly*) Good-bye.

Janáček forbears to comment orchestrally, and a menacing general pause follows Kát'a's denial. There is total silence because, having recognized her failure, she is devoid of thought. And then, as the household assembles for the traditional Russian custom of sitting together before a journey, the troika bells return —now themselves menacing, dragging everyone along with them. This is the last straw. The music is now liberated, forceful; the fact of Tichon's departure is before Kát'a in all its reality. This places her plight beyond the bounds of tolerance. She clings to his neck; the flute theme returns, as it must, when she does so, and Kabanicha's vicious comment is precise:

Shameless girl!
Is he a lover you're saying farewell to?

Tichon tears himself away, and this is the curtain line. The orchestra, already infected with Kabanicha's oppression, has inserted a repeated trumpet B flat under Kát'a's music; this now disintegrates under the pressure into a trenchant climax built from Example 19 and ending on the eight timpani blows in the most strident of presentations. Kát'a collapses. The moment is as rich in meaning as it is violent: Kát'a has now broken down totally in the face of Kabanicha's pressure; but by this her love is freed—for Tichon's departure breaks the delicate balance of moral forces which has been maintained in the opera until this scene. But equally, the two women have forced his departure. And Kát'a's development throughout the scene has shown how disastrous this is bound to be. The cumulative effect is to prepare a climax of the utmost violence at a point where Ostrovsky's original play is so unconcerned that it runs on directly into the next scene. In Janáček's opera, however, the action has reached its first climax; for there is now no restraint on Kát'a's love. And for Janáček this is in itself a crucial development.

But the means to fulfilment are still lacking.

Surface calm has ostensibly been restored. As the second Act begins, two elegant, gentle themes intertwine; and the mood persists when the curtain rises on a domestic scene, Kabanicha, Varvara and Kát'a engaged in embroidery. Kát'a has evidently regained her surface self-control. Even Kabanicha's text, a querulous rebuke for Kát'a's failure to display the proper show of lamentation after Tichon's departure, fails to interrupt the placid flow of the melodies. But the mood is illusory. Tichon has gone, the women are alone; and this unleashes the moral axes of the work at their full potential. All three couples will meet. So, as Kabanicha leaves, high, forte violins blaze forth the longer of the two themes as a cry of liberation; and the next stage of the tragedy begins at once, symbolized by the abrupt descent into the lilting cadences which characterize Varvara. Kát'a's husband has deserted her—and removed the only external sanction against her love for Boris; now her closest friend provides the means. The logic of the drama is relentless: first remove the negative, then provide the positive. We now witness a temptation scene.

The two themes of such gentle interplay in the Act's prelude rapidly unmask themselves: the longer one, with its characteristic minor second leap and perfect fourth fall, becomes desperate, reflects in its transformations the developing, alternating intensities of Kát'a's moral torment, torn between passion and shame; the shorter rapidly becomes attached to the amoral temptations of Varvara. In the first part of the scene they are in conflict; but during the interruption by the offstage voices of Kabanicha and Dikoj, Kát'a comes to see herself from outside, and is astonished that the key to the garden gate should frighten her so much. With this realization the amoral theme is absorbed for the first time into Kát'a's musical world. Kát'a admits to her desire; and, after a moment of self-deception, the outcome follows inexorably: not merely the abolition of her last attempt to resist, but the positive acceptance of her fate—her love, even if it means her death—and this elevates the whole scene into a paradigm of high tragedy. In the next scene, Kát'a will succumb to Boris. So, as she leaves, an accelerated, agitated variant of the amoral theme accompanies her.

After the tragedy, the farce. The action of this Act is confined to the three couples, and their juxtaposition sets Kát'a's acceptance of her destiny in its fullest context. Kabanicha and Dikoj enter the stage; and the contrast is acute.

Ex. 21 (2.i.11:7)

The opening phrase portrays Dikoj's drunken gestures; the close Kabanicha's harsh rebuttals. And the music proceeds to develop their interplay with malicious wit. But Janáček is not merely indulging in social satire. This also is a love scene. Dikoj is a blatant masochist: when Kabanicha asks why he has come, he begs her to, 'Abuse me please, so that my heart can be calmed; you're the only person in the whole town who knows how to take me apart.' He then tells a story of his self-humiliation before a beggar whom he has beaten up; and at the end he falls at Kabanicha's feet, begging abjectly, apparently to illustrate his story. Kabanicha obliges, providing the abuse which Dikoj needs. In view of the music, there can be little doubt that we are witnessing the sado-masochistic prelude to love-making. As Varvara says to Kudrjáš in the next scene, explaining why she herself can leave the house undisturbed,

And then Dikoj is with her on a visit
such coarse people, and they understand each other!

Janáček's view of the sado-masochists shows a rare absence of compassion, and is near to hostility; the music is as unvaried as the monolithic, boring merchants whose thoughts it represents. The mirth with which Kabanicha's theme is played is completely dry, and the satire of Dikoj's maudlin gestures is full of the hollowness of his rhetoric.

The scene lasts long enough to make its point. Then Janáček dismisses it abruptly. We've had enough, and a viola tremolo establishes an authoritative pause.

Here the conductor is confronted with a choice. As printed in the vocal score, an interlude of nine bars follows before the orchestral introduction to the second scene, poignant, full of mystery and restoring the whole mood of Kát'a's tragic love as if the preceding scene had never existed. But Charles Mackerras has discovered in the Janáček archives a longer, alternative intermezzo, a lively allegretto created later by the composer in response to a producer's request for more time in which to set up the elaborate scenery for the love scene's riverside setting. The allegretto is attractive music, and continues well the burlesque atmosphere of the preceding scene; but there is little doubt that Janáček's first thoughts were better founded, dramatically. Even though the new music ends with the last five bars of the original interlude, and so ends in the same mood, it gives too much emphasis to the merchants; it is time to return to Kát'a. And the first interlude does this, evoking as it does the dusk—that of the last night to fall in the opera; for the action of Act 3, although set some weeks later, follows on psychologically from the ending of Act 2. And it is also set at night. Dusk gathers, metaphorically, around Kát'a herself.

Janáček now embarks on the largest and most masterly example of thematic transformation in all of his operas. The last scene of the Act is a double love scene. In the first part of it the music illuminates the inevitability of the consummation of Kát'a's love; and in the remainder it shows the equally inexorable growth of the guilt that follows. One group of melodies communicates, throughout the scene, the inflections of Boris's love, the way in which it overcomes Kát'a's resistance, the consummation and its aftermath. And the fullest tragic meaning is given to the scene by the contrast between the evolving melodies of the constantly developing, doomed love of Boris and Kát'a and the static, stable music given to the younger, carefree pair of lovers, Varvara and Kudrjáš. In this scene Varvara's lilting phrases come into their own, become for the first time more than mere melodic fragments; and there is also the subtle use of song: Váňa sings a song while he waits; Varvara's constant orchestral melody throughout the opera turns out, when she arrives to meet him, to be the tune of a love song; and the two lovers converse, at the start and finish of the scene, by singing alternate verses of appropriate, traditional love songs—a device that finely conveys not only that their love is conventional, follows the timeless pattern of successful affairs, but that the younger pair are the shallower—and also the more stable. For the songs have verses, and are circular, strophic, repetitive. Varvara and Kudrjáš are fixed in their love, and therefore secure in it. Kát'a and Boris are agents and victims of an inexorable evolution. And this is shown by what happens to their music (Example 22).

There are six significant stages in the development of the thematic group which illuminates the union of Kát'a and Boris. The first music printed is taken from the prelude to the scene; and in it the evolution of the scene itself, from anxious expectation to the joy of fulfilment, is prefigured by the breaking out of the lyrical (b) melody (itself related, significantly, to Example 18) from the anguished interrogation of (a). These associations are established when Boris enters: (a), separated by silences, is only gradually linked together into a continuous orchestral flow in the accompaniment when Boris tells Váňa how Varvara lured him into coming. The themes then resume their dialogue: as Boris describes his hopes, variants of (b) leap higher and higher—but as Kudrjáš comments, 'Well, now you see how hopeless it is!', (a) returns to express Boris's misery.

Ex. 22a (2.ii.0:1)

Ex. 22b (2.ii.2:1)

Ex. 22c (2.ii.15:1)

Ex. 22d (2.ii.16:5)

Ex. 22e (2.ii.17:8)

Ex. 22f (2.ii.28:7)

Varvara arrives to meet her lover, and lures Kudrjáš away with a sensuous song. But as soon as the song ends the orchestra views the scene through Boris's eyes; the dialogue between the tragic and the ecstatic themes resumes: (b) leaps higher and higher, as Varvara, leaving with Kudrjáš, promises Boris that Kát'a will soon come; fragmentary anticipations of (c) join in increasing stretto as Boris's apprehension increases; suddenly, Kát'a is there. (a) sounded alone, shows just how fraught with anguish the moment is.

Boris addresses her three times. And although she is silent, the orchestra chronicles the gradual persuasive power of his love, breaking down her overwhelming, paralysing shame. (a) is as questioning as it is agonized; and as Boris's humble plea begins to have effect, the music links up, and expresses, even as Kát'a's words reject him, that the pain is not all. When (a) flowers, despite Kát'a's rejection, not into empty words but into (c), a new, rich variant of (b), the prelude to the scene has already given musical authority to the logic of this. (a) is a question which cannot be left unanswered; so Kát'a is no longer so adamant in her rejection. She accuses Boris of wanting to ruin her; he denies it vigorously, and finds the strength for a declaration of love (d).

This is a powerful adaptation of (b). It speaks only of the overwhelming joy of love; Kát'a's resistance has virtually to be shouted against it, while the depths to which Boris is awakening her are shown by the way in which its closing semiquavers become more and more elaborated at (e). Finally, they evolve after the oboe solo to a new, upward inflection (18:4)—and the four bars of intense orchestral pressure which follow illustrate that Kát'a feels she has no choice. By the time the tremendous crescendo to the rhythmic change to $\frac{6}{4}$ has been reached, the text has been illustrated: we have heard, musically, just how Boris' will has taken power over Kát'a's. And she sings his orchestra's melody at the moment of acceptance.

But (a) recurs as she falls into his arms. This is to be a tragedy: against the inevitability expressed by the victory of (b), there is also to be the anguish of responsibility, born of Kát'a's knowledge that she has chosen freely and must suffer the consequences. This recurrence of (a) warns us in advance that that will happen; and now its occurrence is portrayed. The music which plays as they embrace is a gentle meditation, over undulating string figurations, on (d), reduced to a single line of melody given to a succession of solo instruments. This fact alone indicates the frailty, the vulnerability of their love; while the shifting harmonies of the accompaniment convey a feeling of instability; and the intervals of the recurring melody grow wider and explain why Kát'a, who is the first to break the silence of their embrace, does so with the words, 'Now might I die and die happy.' And her agony is made real as Boris tries to comfort her.

Varvara and Kudrjáš return; Boris and Kát'a go off into the darkness. And as the lighter couple gossip, and the love of the others is consummated, a vast peace—the calm of fulfilment—is spread over the scene by the orchestra. This is the emotional mid-point of the opera; a quiet in and through which the last peace Kát'a is to have is enacted. As Varvara chatters on, her music comes into its own; and the string harmonics, the chords of ever-increasing richness gradually resolve, as Boris pledges eternal love from the distance, into a fully harmonized, eloquent re-presentation of (d). The music is virtually timeless; in the kinship of this music with Varvara's, the two pairs of lovers are bound together for a few moments into one single whole.

But now Janáček begins to develop the contrast between the tragic and the simple love. Varvara has been talking about the security of the couples—the locked doors, the watchful maid servant, the fact that Kabanicha and Dikoj are closeted together. Kát'a and Boris, offstage, sing ecstatically: 'For ever I am yours.' But real time is not so generous. The music becomes animated as Varvara sings, 'And then, without danger it's nothing! If you get caught, then you're in trouble.' A xylophone intrudes on the timeless suspension of the chords—the night-watchman taps the hours as he passes—and the action moves into its final phase, even though the languor of Kát'a's post-coital ecstasy (f) holds even Varvara back for seven lento bars before she decides that, 'It's time! Call them!'

This new motif (f) infects the whole orchestra as well as the characters: Kudrjáš needs fifteen bars before he can rouse himself to answer. Then he and Varvara go slowly up the path, Varvara's melodies predominating over the restored, placid harmonics as they sing a strophic song glorying in the amorality of their love.

KUDRJÁŠ: A girl once strolled out for a time
          for a time at evening
          aj, leli, leli, leli
          for a time at evening

VARVARA: And I am a girl and young
          and I made love till the day
          aj, leli, leli, leli
          till the earliest light of day

KUDRJÁŠ: And as dawn was in the sky
          I set off for home
          aj, leli, leli, leli
          I set off for home.

The musical and dramatic polarity between the couples could not be more extreme: the bright animation of the unmarried lovers who snatch what moments they can, as joyful and lascivious as before they made love; while the others have been lost in a timeless languor, seeking eternal union. Kát'a and Boris enter 'suddenly'; the orchestra rises to an anguished, suspended sforzando; and Varvara cries out, crystallizing the significance of the conflict between time and timelessness:

I wonder if you two can part?

Janáček's orchestra reverts to Kát'a: it erupts, maestoso and with violence. Varvara's question recalls Kát'a abruptly, instantly and cruelly to reality; and the orchestra's fierce transformation of (f) shows that her ecstatic languor has turned into pain; for as she parts from Boris the music illustrates how she climbs the path to the garden gate—miserably, as the stage directions insist. The suddenness warns of the force that drove Kát'a into submission and the power of her shame; and so prepares us for the confession of Act 3.

But Janáček does not end the Act melodramatically, by leaving matters at that. To close, he achieves a precious balance, reminding us that the shame is not all, that Kát'a has gained a simple peace from her complex, tortured love. The outburst is stilled: violins and flutes enter quietly; and the Act closes in an exquisitely beautiful adagio reminder of the six demisemiquavers, twice repeated, to whose tones Kát'a left the house to meet Boris.

An enigmatic close—for this is Varvara's music, morally neutral. *Has* Kát'a gained such inner stability as Varvara?

The ambiguity is resolved at once. Act 3 sets in with relentless vigour, and the music of the storm gains increasing momentum at every stage until the heroine's confession. From now until the moment at which she commits suicide, the flow of the elements, rain, thunder and river, becomes increasingly united with Kát'a's psychological development. For this reason the music of the falling rain soon recaptures the penultimate mood of the previous scene: the orchestra gathers into a vigour as overwhelming as that of the maestoso to which Kát'a parted from Boris.

But first a now familiar Janáček dramatic pattern. As in *Jenůfa* and *Destiny*, the third Act brings the personal, private events of a second Act in which only the principals appear back before the gaze of the community in which they live. And here the context is religious, the ironies which develop almost intolerable. As the rain gathers force, two subsidiary characters, Kuligin and Kudrjáš, take refuge in the ruins of an arcade, followed by a gathering crowd. Old frescoes are just visible on the walls; one portrays the eternal fire of Gehenna. 'Every class of people fall into it.' 'Just so, my friend.' 'All the respectable ones, too.' Already, at the very opening, the idea of divine retribution is in the text; and it is backed in the orchestra by a dialogue between unpredictable, sustained sforzando entries for horns and trombones, first on A flat and finally on D flat.

Dikoj enters—appropriately, with a reprise of Example 17a— and the oppressive religious perspective develops. The paintings are ignored, having done their work; Janáček continues the dramatic argument in the orchestra, with the aid of a new, even more relevant text. Kudrjáš takes the opportunity which the storm provides to suggest to Dikoj that the town should become progressive and install lightning conductors. Dikoj's incredulity increasingly animates the orchestra, and the figurations culminate in a maestoso declaration (Example 23). As their argument finishes, the weather apparently clears, and the characters leave the stage. But the next music is puzzling on first hearing: Example 23 returns pianissimo and flows serenely on until Varvara enters with Boris.

This is not accidental. The storm music is unusual: it is mild,

Ex. 23 (3.i.5:8)

and above all authoritative. With the stage empty, we contemplate for a few moments a natural phenomenon, the river. Even in this scene the music is circular, beckoning: it anticipates the power of the elements to lure Kát'a, in the final scene, to her death. Dikoj's claim is to be taken seriously. For when Kát'a enters the same theme sounds out, even though the weather has temporarily abated. Kát'a has already been through, and put behind her, hysterical panic such as Boris shows, when Varvara tells him of Kát'a's anguish and near-madness since Tichon's return. When she comes on, clasps Varvara's hand tightly, and sings, 'Oh Varvara! This is my death', it is already with calm acceptance. For here again Example 23 recurs. She has absorbed her anguish; but the peace attained at the end of Act 2 is illusory. The guilt has penetrated her soul. And it only needs the sight of Boris to lead her to confession.

But the music lends a surprising additional dimension to the confession scene. Janáček secures psychological continuity by running directly from Varvara's description of Kát'a's agony into Kát'a's own experience and her movement to confession; his libretto thus expresses Kát'a's moral disintegration after her husband's return in an extremely short space of time. And this enables him to create a remarkable parallel. Kát'a's movement to confession is parallel to Dikoj's gradual loss of his temper; and both are caused by their superstitious belief in the storm's religious power.

The parallel would be absurd if it were achieved by a full reprise of Dikoj's music. In actual fact the second half of the scene develops two entirely new motifs:

Ex. 24a (3.i.8:7)

Ex. 24b (3. i.11:19)

but they evolve naturally out of a familiar environment. As Varvara begins to tell Boris what has happened, tremolo strings continue the main melodic line of Example 23, played there by the harp—though at over double the speed. 24a is created out of these tremolos as her two friends begin to fear that Kát'a will confess; and its gathering, upward inflections lead into a full, calm—but accelerando—reprise of Example 23 on celesta and harp as Kát'a enters—just as the opening rain music led smoothly into the same accompaniment for the equally superstitious Dikoj. But in both cases Example 23 gives birth to faster, more intense music as the characters' religious beliefs lead them to heightened emotion. 24a continues to intensify its gathering, upward inflections as the weather worsens again and the crowd, gathering again under the galleries, start to notice Kát'a's distracted state; and the reassurances of Varvara and Kudrjáš are not enough to prevent it from breeding 24b when the basses

E

comment that, 'Nobody can escape from that which afflicts them.'
And this is the music which leads to Kát'a's confession—when
Dikoj and Kabanicha observe her carefully, and 17a, added as a
culmination to the other motifs, illuminates the effect on her of
their accusing stares.

The dialogue between the themes continues. After the admission of sin, the orchestra is calmed back into Example 23; but
gathering outlines of the same melody accompany the details and
erupt finally into a dissonant climax as Kát'a confesses the name
of her lover. Ferociously suspended chords for woodwind and
brass are added to a timpani reprise of 17a, and Kát'a falls sense-
less into her husband's arms. But the musical tension shows that
this collapse is an insufficient release; when the suspensions have
become almost intolerable they break, and the upward inflections
of the strings, threatened ever since Dikoj's argument with
Kudrjáš, gather and drive the entire orchestra into a massive
tutti which works out all the variants of the storm music and is
underpinned by reiterations of 17a. Kát'a tears herself from
Tichon's arms and rushes out into the storm—embracing at last
the force which has been beckoning to her throughout the scene.
This stage direction is Janáček's own; and to it he adds another:
everyone rushes out in confusion. Kát'a's agony has been trans-
mitted, as mass hysteria, to the crowd.

But the tutti, which plays on after the curtain has fallen, is
complex. Extremely loud and vigorous, it none the less has in it
an overall feeling of rest. The storm is both violent, as Kát'a is
agonized now, and nobly calm, as she will become later.

All the energies of scene i have been discharged by the tutti, and
the embers of the themes come to rest on a fermata. The world of
Kát'a Kabanová is at peace, as the heroine has found once again
the union with nature of her childhood. But this is tragedy, and
one thing remains: the culmination of this union, the realization
that her true place now is death. Kát'a's monologue does not,
however, stand in isolation. Janáček frames it, places it in the
perspective of two vignettes: first a dialogue between Tichon and
Gláša, which tells us that Kabanicha thinks Kát'a should be
buried alive as punishment; second a scene between Varvara and
Kudrjáš, in which they resolve to flee to Moscow and begin a
new, happy life together. On the one side the harshest morality,

on the other the escape of the couple whose gay, superficial love allows them to remain alive, and even to escape from Kalinov. What will Kát'a's place be?

The answer emerges gradually in her great monologue. This opera is the reverse of *Jenůfa*; here the heroine matures to an understanding which leads her to her death and her lover to Siberian exile, while it is the light couple whose values enable them to stay alive and escape from the community.

The monologue is violent in its changes of mood. And Kát'a reacts not only to her own inner thoughts but also to three interruptions, as first Kuligin, then a drunkard pass across the stage, and Boris himself finally encounters her. And there is one more element—the wordless call of distant voices.

As Kát'a comes onstage, the love music of the second Act is momentarily recalled (19:4-5; cf. Example 22d). She is alone, and a calm appears to be spread over the scene by the orchestra. But it is illusory and impermanent—Kát'a is recalling her affair with Boris 'as if in a dream'; and although at first it appears as if she and the world are at one, the impression is rapidly undermined during the first part of the monologue. 'If I saw him, said good-bye, then even die.' The music is caressing and indulgent—25a—but the falling scale at the end of the flute phrase moves to an unstable close, and this intensifies; 25b is repeated; a peaceful death is not to be attained so easily. Kát'a changes her mood, meditates increasingly on her guilt; 25b therefore persists as Kuligin enters, singing wordlessly and looking piercingly at Kát'a. He leaves without speaking to her, but his appearance has only intensified this mood; the repeated eruptions of 25b chronicle her growing awareness of her guilt. Her memory fails, and she becomes more and more terrified of the darkness. The repeated disturbances finally flow abruptly downwards and come to rest in 25c. The distant voices, chanting like a funeral procession, beckon Kát'a like the music of God's storm in the previous scene—to which their melody is related. But after the storm, the calm is natural; and they are no less cogent. They too have the power of a call of nature, wordless—and ambiguous. But it is only later that we realize exactly what they are.

For Kát'a resists the call. A drunken man passes, stares at her; she feels she knows that he does so because she is guilty; but she is racked by the need to go on living:

They say that they used to kill women like me!
If only they'd take me and throw me in the Volga!
But to live like this, and torture myself for my sin!

Ex. 25a (3.ii.19:13)

Ex. 25b (3.ii.19:18)

Ex. 25c.(3.ii.21:9)

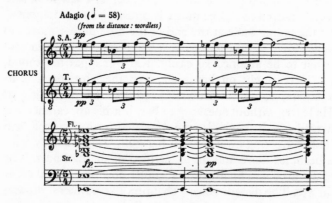

The thought gives her increasing pain: agitated scales run up and
down in the orchestra. 'Nothing can make me happy.' And the
motif which has dominated the score since the appearance of the
drunken man surges once more before falling to a crushing, final
defeat (Example 26).

This is the end of the monologue's first part: all human
pleasures have deserted Kát'a, and the world is nothing but pain,

Ex. 26 (3.ii.24:14)

as death refuses to come to her. The music presents this as a full, mature understanding of death and desire to accept it.

But Kát'a regresses. Astonishingly, a variant of 22d begins to form in the orchestra, and Kát'a calls out desperately for Boris to hear her. With the appropriateness of the deeply expected, Boris finds her, answers her call; and an extended love scene follows. Kát'a dominates it from the beginning (the contrast with Act 2 is acute). Her mind is volatile: warm, tender, absent-minded, realistic, violent. Tortured by the knowledge of her guilt and of Boris's helplessness she reverts to tender meditation on her longing for him. And her mood becomes a childlike innocence; confused, she needs to concentrate desperately on what she wants to tell Boris. And finally she is capable of doing so:

> As you go on your way, give alms to every beggar,
> don't forget any!
> And now let me look at you for the last time!

133

As Kát'a embarks on the second phrase of the text, the stage grows dark and the offstage voices return, still soft but now with a menacing figure sounded, like a summons, in horns, flutes and violas. After all she learnt in the monologue, and absorbed after Boris came, by sharing it with him, Kát'a knows beyond doubt that she is being called inexorably to self-destruction. The voices, we are now told in the directions, sound 'like a sigh of the Volga'. Kát'a tells Boris to go; and the moral authority which she has regained is evident in her voice as she dismisses him, accepts the sound which summons her to beyond our world. So there is no question of elopement: Boris leaves alone because he has reverted to dependence. Kát'a's authority over him is that of one committed to death. An outcry of guilt and shame, the voices are at once forces within and outside Kát'a's mind: they are not to be resisted. So they draw her to the edge of the river.

The music makes us hear Kát'a mesmerized by the waters:

Birds will fly over my tomb
bring their young ones
and flowers will bloom there
red flowers
blue flowers
yellow flowers.
(*she creeps towards the river*)
So quiet
so lovely
so lovely
and I must die!

Woodwind and violas repeat the same delicate phrase over an increasingly ominous pedal; the repetition of 'so lovely' marks the moment at which Kát'a is mesmerized; and she jumps into the river. The orchestra erupts in savage, turbulent protest.

The remaining pages of the opera are almost beyond description; Janáček works out the consequences with ruthless logic. Even the flowers are denied Kát'a; her death-leap has been observed, and the body is recovered. The heroine is turned from a person into a thing, as the community in general—and Kabanicha in particular—reassert their power. Tichon accuses Kabanicha of killing Kát'a, and as she retorts angrily, 17b, in a strident trumpet version, chronicles the return of the dominance of the merchants. Dikoj retrieves the body; and the close is implacable. Tichon collapses, weeping, over the corpse, and there is a brief moment of peace as a solo oboe adopts the melody of his grief and pronounces Kát'a's elegy—three phrases, eloquent, but desperate and inconclusive. And the opera does not end with this attempt to endow the death of one woman with significance. The oboe phrase dies out; the orchestra gradually alters its inflection; and the stage action ends in the obscene resumption of the merchants' power.

> KABANICHA (*bowing in all directions*): Thank you, I thank you good people for your kindness!

The crowd stares in horror at the corpse. But any attempt by the audience to share this emotion is barred: the music has not yet ended. A macabre ostinato, prestissimo, hastens the drama to a baffling, vicious end. And all that remains is based on the oppressive Example 17. A tentative rising phrase for the brass does not develop, achieves nothing; and the music halts only when the voices of the Volga, now strident in their triumph, are joined by the timpani in the final moments. The end is abrupt and brutal. We have heard first the triumph of Kabanicha, then that of the river which has possessed Kát'a's mind and body, then a sudden, empty silence. Kát'a has been gradually swept away from us in the victorious assertion of the ostinato, a violence which closes off the opera completely by its reprise of the two related main themes of the prelude. There has been no advance—as the almost arbitrary conclusion insists. Normality has been restored. And the world of the opera withdraws from us with grim finality.

Only to haunt our minds. This opera offers no redemption, no hope, little but the brutality of its pessimistic outcome. Kát'a is the only character in the opera who develops, but her deep spiritual beauty is set in the focus of hypocritical holders of her own beliefs, distorting mirrors which parody it; and it leads her to destruction, while the social order of the merchants reconstructs itself as if she had never existed. Here Janáček's objectivity is at its most frightening: he makes no judgement on anybody—and so leaves us without moral guidance in the baffling pity and terror of the ending. Kát'a's richness of life gives her nothing but an ignominious death; Varvara survives, but has to leave Kalinov to do so, and is completely superficial; Kabanicha is understood, but is seen to be filled with nothing but hypocrisy, pride and hatred. The male characters are all, to a lesser or a greater extent, worthless. Janáček wrote no more savage tragedy; and it is a fierce irony that his most negative and pessimistic drama should also be his richest, in its beauty of sound and its lyric invention.

Adventures of the Vixen Bystrouška

This is the original title. The conventional German and English versions ('Das schlaue Füchslein' and 'The cunning little vixen') are sadly symptomatic: the West has shown too little ability to interpret an opera whose vision is as far from Disney as it is from the clumsy symbolism of Max Brod's 'arrangement for the German stage'. Janáček's animals are not patronized or sentimentalized by the attribution of human features: human singers and dancers, taking on the masks and skins of insect, bird or animal, find themselves for the duration of this opera members of an order nobler, by its deep humour and its simple, amoral enjoyment of life, than that of humanity. The particular moments where animals assume the manners of men satirize human rather than animal behaviour: no animal is portrayed ironically, except the dog and hens who have succumbed self-righteously to exploitation by mankind.

Man himself is viewed in double focus, as a wayward creature: at times noble, sharing the great forest of Adamov on equal terms with its other inhabitants—when he lives, like the animals who are his kin, by his instincts and in harmony with nature; at others cruel or stupid, in his attempts to dominate and oppress creatures which he does not understand. Janáček reinforces his vision by a striking convention: both humans and animals speak the same local dialect of Czech—and are thus equally comprehensible in the privileged vision of the audience; but neither can understand the language of the other. The libretto thus insists upon the gulf between animal and human, at the same time as its delicate tissue of parallels between individual characters, half-made and half-understood, reinforces the similarities. But the balance of the opera as a whole is acute: if the libretto predominantly divides the worlds of man and beast (and sets two of its scenes in Pásek's inn, the retreat where man is alone, protected by its walls and by alcohol from the vibrant life of the world outside which the animals dominate), the music gradually comes to unite them. The moments of man's most wanton cruelty are chronicled remorselessly, in such a way as to make us feel and understand the sufferings of the oppressed animal; but at many other times the orchestra includes men and beasts together in the framework of an instrumental music rich and expansive on a scale unmatched elsewhere in these operas, the music of the great forest within which they all walk the ground; of its trees and of its insects, amphibians and birds, creatures whose silent dance or near-incoherent speech enclose and punctuate the action, in eloquent choric comment.

Despite the title, that action is far from episodic. Janáček selected from, rewrote and extensively rearranged Těsnohlídek's original story so as to achieve a clear pattern: Act 1 presents Bystrouška's adventures in youth, Act 2 those of her maturity and Act 3 those of the evening of her life. The pattern is that of developing life, leading—by a crucial alteration to the original, in which she lives on—to Bystrouška's death and beyond it into the closing vision of renewal.

The dramaturgy is very different from that of Janáček's earlier tragic operas. The pattern disclosed by the action is not, as before, a complex interaction between psychological and material pressures, with cause and effect studied in tightly knit, unfolding detail: here and in the two last music-dramas, the action is set in the framework of a natural, recurrent pattern of life; little force is therefore needed to establish its inevitability. Full, permanent personal relationships are no longer worked out thoroughly; they are taken for granted, expressed in elliptical, shorthand statements. Instead, we are shown the manner in which, in actual life, the processes of nature work.

The effect is to alter the balance through which meaning is communicated. The characters now stand in abruptly etched, near-symbolic attitudes to each other; they are set, in all three operas, within an evocative (and precisely evoked) milieu—the forest, the transitory but atmospheric Prague settings of the three Acts of *Makropulos* and the oppressive prison camp of *From the*

House of the Dead; and in the *Adventures* and in *Makropulos* they are also grouped in relation to a single, dominant but enigmatic central character. It is impossible to penetrate the soul of Bystrouška or of Emilia Marty; indeed, the ultimate futility of the attempt, made by male characters in both operas, is mirrored in the music. Where the meaning of *Jenůfa, Destiny* and *Kát'a Kabanová* was to be grasped by ever-closer understanding of the inner depths of the heroine, this is now useless; the meaning of this opera and of its closely related successor radiates outwards to the other characters, and to the audience, from the influence of the opaque amorality of the central figure who is its catalyst.

But this meaning is, as before, embodied in the unfolding of the action. In Bystrouška's adventures two strands, allegory and parable, are intertwined: on the one hand, Janáček illuminates the course of the vixen's life, allegory not only for the eternal cycle of growth, love, death and renewal in the animal world but for that of all life, whether animal or human; on the other he expounds a parable, a series of almost ritual confrontations between man and beast through which one man, the forester, is finally led under the growing influence of the vixen from the cruelty and exploitation of Act 1 to the wisdom and ecstasy of the final, visionary harmony with nature. In the road to this achievement lies a precarious but exultant final optimism. Elsewhere the work's tone is often dark; Bystrouška's influence over men is never total, and in Act 3 of Janáček's opera she dies at their hands. But Janáček relieves the terror of the moment—Harašta himself is portrayed with compassion, shoots Bystrouška only out of dire need at the moment of sharpest conflict between the concerns of men and those of animals. Nor is Bystrouška's fierce amorality exalted naïvely. As the opera unfolds, the audience is initiated into a higher degree of wisdom: they are led to a complex understanding of our world through which they may share in the profound union of powers expressed by the closing pages.

The episodes bear titles. The first is 'How they caught the vixen Bystrouška'. And the emphasis is from the start on the contrast between man and animal. And on a mild paradox: Bystrouška's name means 'sharp ears', but it is not until the second scene that she displays the intelligence implied by her name. In the first, she is truly 'Malá Bystrouška', a little vixen; innocent, she is captured by the forester, and taken away as a pet for his children. Man begins the opera with an act of gratuitous harshness, for which he pays in the second scene, as soon as the vixen has begun to mature.

The opening action is simple, almost stylized in comparison with the complex patterns of the later scenes. The forester is tired, the vixen inarticulate. And this is deliberate; their first confrontation has in itself a simplicity which responds both to her young innocence and to his lack of vision. But it is set in the frame of the teeming life of the forest, unfolded in the expansive orchestral music which plays before and after the forester's approach, and while he is asleep. This musical action presents a full picture of the world within which man and animal must mature as the opera unfolds.

The portrait of the forest is not static: Janáček's dramatic world, even here, is far from meditation or impressionism. The music begins in a leisurely way, mysteriously, almost inarticulately (and very much in the manner by which Vaughan Williams's *Pastoral Symphony* introduces its world); and the forest gradually takes shape through ever-clearer orchestral forms, the disclosure of the stage-picture (a precisely described forest scene), and the use first of choric and later of solo dance. The three media evoke in detail the life of the forest, its languor and its vigour, its gaiety and its melancholy; the extended portrayal establishes before the forester even appears the homogeneity of the world which he will disturb, as the opening music flows on continuously, embracing without effort the frequent changes of rhythm, harmony and dynamics which narrate the events of natural life. After this, the music when he appears establishes the central point of the scene: at this stage of the opera, man is an alien intruder in the animals' world. But—surprisingly—so too is the vixen.

The opening presents two themes, in sharp contrast (Ex. 27), and as the action begins their associations become clear: 27a is the gentle, melancholy music of the forest itself—the ravine, black and dry but yet with the sun shining down; against it (b) is the music of the flies, first, lightest and most insubstantial creatures which we are to encounter. The subsequent dialogue between these themes is extraordinary: the urgency of (b), now in the bass, soon imparts an almost painful intensity to the sixth

Ex. 27 (1.i.0:1)

reprise of (a), violas doubling flutes high on the treble clef;
while by an equal contrast a savage, octave violin reprise of (b)
forces the glorious and luxuriant, but immobile climax of figure
2; after which, without rest, a delicate return of (b) leads seamlessly into the very different music of the blue dragon-fly's solo
dance. This subsides, after taking its course; and the final reprise
of 27a is plaintive, pathetic in cor anglais and violas. We hear the
forest quelled into apprehensive listening.

Already the logic of the music has been other than human: the
range of emotions, the variety of guises for each theme—from
delicate to savage, stately to grotesque—are both wider than
those normally bestowed by Janáček on human affairs, and also
more closely knit. The world of the insects is unified, calm even
in its most violent moments. The forester disrupts this unity
completely.

He enters sweating, ill-at-ease with the world around him. He
is tired, expects a storm—but despite that proposes (with a lack
of concern for self-interest contrasted to that of the animals) to
take a short nap. Immoral rather than amoral, he is prepared to
deceive his wife; he remembers the morning after his wedding as

141

one of tiredness—in the opera's final perspective, it was an ecstatic communion between the young couple and nature; and he hails his gun as his closest friend.

Long before his gesture of renunciation at the end of the opera, it will become the emblem of human oppression. But the forester's inadequate perceptions are here only undermined gently. His music is indecisive and colourless, almost borrowed from the threatened storm which is occupying his mind as he enters. The orchestra struggles to find a grander gesture for his mention of the dawn after his wedding—but this attempt collapses abruptly. And there is a further indignity: much of his text is not even accompanied by music of his own, but by that of a cricket and a grasshopper, who are busily bringing on a small barrel-organ in preparation for a dance and concert. This burlesque is the final touch: the mockery points up the relative triviality of humans in the wider life of the forest—which the insects re-establish, cautiously but firmly, as soon as the forester has fallen into the dreamless sleep which in his lack of imagination he deserves.

Here a new pattern begins. Cricket and grasshopper share their waltz in amiable co-operation; but the forest rapidly assumes the larger rhythms of the chase. A mosquito dances drunkenly; he is eagerly pursued by a young frog. In the orchestra, all is ecstatic, luxuriant, amoral glory. But the chain is abruptly broken. Bystrouška enters, and is expected to pursue the sequence of chases—the frog is frightened to death by her entrance. But the little vixen (alone for the first time?) is dependent; she halts and hesitates:

Mummy! Mummy!
What is it?
Can I eat it?

The mistake breaks the forest's natural patterns of action and reaction. The frog leaps in fright on to the forester's nose, awakens him; and in his annoyance the forester 'thrusts his predatory face through the thicket and snatches Bystrouška like a beast' (Example 28).

Bystrouška's innocence is that of a creature alien, through her youth, to the other life of the forest. And—skilful animal though she will become—she is captured now, because of her

Ex. 28 (1.i.14:1)

innocence, by one more skilful and more cruel. For these reasons 28a and b are both evolved from the music which had accompanied Bystrouška's naïve, faltering entrance; the transformation shows both how Bystrouška's innocence has led to her captivity (lifted up 'like a dog by the collar', she is treated like a domestic animal), and the fundamental kinship, yet to be fully revealed, between mankind and this most cunning of wild animals.

The forester takes Bystrouška away in cruel triumph. And now, after the violence, the forest takes longer to resume the threads of life; its life as a whole has been diminished by the

143

vixen's mistake and its consequences. There is a general pause; and the music resumes slowly, tentatively, on solo flute and violin. The dragon-fly reappears, searching in vain for the vixen; and, as in her first appearance—an anticipation of her role here, as choric commentator on the action—the dragon-fly's extended dance evokes at its close the music of the highest pathos yet heard, setting up a frame for the remainder of the opera's action. The silent dance is now more eloquent than words: the improvisatory beginning, the gradual gaining of momentum, the length and the dignity of her dance all stand in poignant counterbalance to the violence done by man. And as it proceeds, the motion, the depth, the rich, strange life of the forest seem to gather once more around the pirouetting, anxious and beautiful insect; the sonorous, wide spacing of the chords which accompany the melody speak now of a finer, deeper movement than her first, a dance imbued with passion and purpose. And when the dragon-fly, exhausted by failure, sinks to the ground and folds her wings, the forest assumes an awesome peace. Man's violence is absorbed and tamed, and the woods return slowly and majestically to their original repose. Rich, deep textures absorb Example 28c, contemplated by solo instruments, into the world of Example 27; and the closing orchestral image of the forest at peace is profound; gravity and passion, resolution and ecstasy, motion and rest. This final, complex image stands out and underlies the vigorous action of the rest of the opera.

The forester's cottage is by the shore of a lake. But the season is autumn, and the pastoral image is belied. The courtyard is a world of sadness, and Janáček's music takes flight from the fact that here the vixen is a captive. The motif first heard when Bystrouška appeared has evolved now into a new melody for muted upper strings, a melody of deep pathos (Example 29); and the vigorous variant forms of this new theme which hold dialogue during the interlude while the scene is changed speak first of a desperate gaiety and then of a harsh oppression. The vigour is not brutal, but its gaiety is deceptive—that of indifference rather than of any real joy. And this impression is confirmed by the way the interlude ends: Example 29 returns in the original, sad form, only to be crushed—gradually but totally—by ironic, sharp interjections derived from the central section:

144

Ex. 29 (1.ii.0:1)

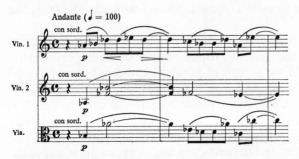

In the next scene, Bystrouška grows to adolescence and liberation. But the contrast expressed here is not merely between this intelligent, sensitive animal and the cruel indifference of the human characters: domestic and exploited animals now make their appearance. And the distinction is acute. Bystrouška's meows are integrated into the last notes of Example 29—and despite the sadness of the orchestral phrase of which they are part, they are upward-facing and expectant; of a wider range than her cries in 1.i. Captivity has not tamed her spirit, and her sadness is maturing, capable of development. By comparison, Lapák's extended lament is set to circular, self-indulgent music; the dog has no independence, and even Bystrouška needs time to dispel the melancholy which he creates. But her reply shows that she can develop: it removes Bystrouška from childhood. Although she has no personal experience of making love, the young vixen glories in the free, amoral amorous activity of the forest's birds; her sheer joy in the telling of story after story lends the orchestral music greater and greater lightness and animation—and when Bystrouška achieves the unwanted effect of exciting Lapák to an amorous attempt on her she strikes down the oppression without hesitation. Bystrouška is mature enough to defend herself.

This she has to do at once. The forester's son and his friend, Frantík, appear suddenly and torment her for amusement. Here the convention of the opera is at its most powerful: we can understand both the animal and the humans, know the sounds which to the two boys are just growls for the desperate pleas of a proud animal; while Janáček's orchestra chronicles remorselessly the savage, irregular flow of unprovoked violence to the moment at which Bystrouška is provoked into biting back—and beyond, to the forester's reprisal. She is leashed by the neck, like a dog.

The violence goes no further (indeed, it is hard to imagine how it could: the stabbing, triplet ostinato of the upper orchestra is painful to the ear as little of Janáček's music is before *From the House of the Dead*). And after the oppression, Janáček places the scene of cruelty, and all for which it stands, in deep perspective. Example 29 returns from the prelude, again with Bystrouška's questioning, as yet uncomprehending cry of apprehension as its close; dusk falls; and the orchestra builds up, in the music of the night, an extended meditation on this theme, an elegy which is central to Act 1. The music is slow, measured, rich and warm: in it we hear the young animal mature from under the impact of her suffering. When Bystrouška cries again—from her sleep, just before the coming of dawn—the cries are an 'a——' of anticipation, and the tumultuous, ecstatic leaping of the dawn music is that of the expected fulfilment of a desired awakening.

But we are not merely made to hear the maturing of the suffering animal from inside; Janáček seizes on the cruelty of what we have just witnessed and points up man's outrage, his inability to comprehend and accept the inner freedom of the creatures among whom he moves. As Bystrouška is heard to mature, and to absorb her suffering, she is transformed into the form of a girl, and it is in this apparition that she moves from suffering to her anticipation of the dawn. The simple device speaks eloquently: nobody who has heard and seen this can forget the fundamental kinship of human and animal, the bond forged here between woman and this most intelligent of female creatures by their equal capacity to feel and absorb suffering. And when, at figure 14, the vixen resumes her animal form, the orchestra, after suffering six bars of extreme tension (sustained, hammered xylophone B flats creating the utmost agitation) launches into a climactic consummation.

There is no doubt that the musical and stage imagery here is sexual: the music of the dawn is that of eros and its triumphant fulfilment. Bystrouška is ready for the adventures of maturity, the world of Act 2. But first a pleasing irony. Her spiritual liberation is in sharp contrast to the self-righteous rebukes of Lapák and the rooster—for which they now suffer. Bystrouška's first employment of her new maturity gives her redress for the cruelty of uncomprehending man: her developed wit, sophistication and complete amorality gain her freedom. In a delicious scene entitled 'Bystrouška in politics', and surely intended as a direct satire of pseudo-marxist revolution, Bystrouška subverts the capitalist, exploitative economy of the arrogant, chauvinist rooster and his contentedly subservient hens, totally satisfied that their work justifies their existence. Both their shallowness and the rooster's monotonous vanity are, in the opera's terms, direct acceptances of the worst of human values; the fine wit of the scene lies in the way in which, to gain her own truly animal ends, Bystrouška adopts the mask of an equally false human veneer—that of the revolutionary who has no one's interests at heart but his own. The text, deftly cut from Těsnohlídek's original, is a masterpiece of ingenuousness; the music surrounds it with a glittering web of melodies, ever more complex as Bystrouška's sophistry becomes more and more outrageous:

Look, sisters, what kind of leader you have!
He wants you for his own lust,
and takes pay from man for it.
Comrades! Sisters!
Abolish the old order!
Create a new world,
where you will have an equal share
of joy and happiness!

Bystrouška's cunning is that of a true animal. The rooster and the hens fall her victims through two human vices, stupidity and pride. Their neglect of their own self-preservation, the most elementary of an animal's interests, leads to catastrophe. And when Bystrouška abandons her mask of disdain, and systematically kills off every hen in the yard, Janáček crystallizes the destruction of its economy in a short, agitated finale in which running scales and reiterated notes convey vividly the impotence of the hens and the forester's wife in the face of events. The forester himself is no more adequate at this stage; he confronts Bystrouška again, for the third time in the opera, and this time determined to beat the animal with a club. But too late: with her new maturity, Bystrouška has also learnt defiance and strength. She bites through her leash, hurls the forester to the ground and runs off into the forest. The orchestra is fearfully agitated in the penultimate moments, forcing us to share in the terror when a further outbreak of successful human cruelty seems possible; but it gathers into a joyful, playful tutti the moment Bystrouška gains her freedom. Janáček has by now succeeded totally in making us see the action through the amoral eyes of nature; for the slaughtered chickens are forgotten as the curtain falls. No audience can fail to share, at this moment, Bystrouška's exultant ridicule of human clumsiness and inadequacy.

Act 2 begins abruptly and with vigour. The energy is that of liberation: Bystrouška, having destroyed the complacent economy of the forester's yard, is no longer captive, and now free she can assert her maturity. In this Act Bystrouška has an adult female's self-confidence and the strength of young adulthood, which makes her capable of marriage. And the music reflects this immediately. Furthermore, the adult, confident and amoral vixen now has the support of the rest of the forest, is in a real sense in harmony with its life; for this reason she has the constant support, throughout 2.i, of a chorus of forest insects, at one with her in her successful efforts to undermine the badger's pomposity. But not all in the forest is joy. At the fourth reprise, the exultant opening melody is overlaid with a sadness in the flute line which almost recalls Example 29, and which is certainly at one with the meditative close of 1.i (30a). The power of Bystrouška's liberated energy is so great that it can contain this sadness; the violin melody soon reaches complete ecstasy and the flute melody develops from this to a triumphal new tutti assertion as the curtain rises. At the fourth reprise of this phrase, Bystrouška's new, developed cry is heard (30b), the full life-assertion of maturity and freedom.

A badger seems feeble opposition; and this impression is compounded by the fact that his hostility, robust to the point of intemperate rudeness in the text, is ironically given no further support in the orchestra than the delicate downward flourish which appears in the violins as Example 30c. But his pompous, bourgeois behaviour is an important stage in the unfolding of the opera's constantly shifting perspectives. Bystrouška has already broken free from a life subject to human control, and shown the difference between wild and tame animals; but Janáček now ex-

Ex. 30a (2.i.1:1)

Ex. 30b & c (2.i.3:1)

plores the parallel which he has set up, the implication of the
night-music that between vixen and human female there lies a
deep affinity. In the dramaturgy of Act 2, this idea is developed
further, as Bystrouška's influence begins to be strong enough to
affect humans. Ironic light is thrown on human foibles by en-
dowing wild animals with them—the badger here (like the owl
and woodpecker of the end of the Act) exhibits petit bourgeois
morality, while the vixen herself and the fox who woos her in
2.iv display every absurdity—as well as every depth—of the
human in love; and the contrasts set up in this scene are taken
back to the world of the humans. For in 2.ii the parson, whose
part is doubled with that of the badger, exhibits all his limitations
—and is equally undermined by Bystrouška, first through the
forester, who has by 2.ii begun to learn amorality and a wider
approach to life from Bystrouška, secondly by her direct influence
on his own thoughts as he returns home through the forest in
2.iii. The close of 2.iii, central in the running time of the opera,

149

is emblematic: there forester and vixen, united in the forest's rhythm of the chase, terrify the two men who will remain, in the longer perspective of the whole opera, stubbornly immune to the liberating influence of the forest and of the vixen.

The badger, then, is the nearest element the forest offers to the narrow-minded male humanity of the next scene: in Bystrouška's direct triumph over him we see foreshadowed her indirect influence over the inhabitants of the inn; in the forest's rejection of his legalism a premonition of the deep victory at the close of the whole opera, a victory in which all sadness, even that of Bystrouška's own death, is placed in a perspective so wide that it becomes, miraculously, part of the joy of renewal. Hence the sheer strength of Bystrouška's music now; the scene at the inn, with the forest shut out, will be musically subdued. And indeed, as the badger departs self-righteously, his orchestral phrase of rejection finally gains the heavy orchestration, and the pompous sforzando close, which it so obviously deserves—and then proceeds to generate the transformation music.

The dramatic transition from the badger to the over-assertive, noisy and constricted humanity of the crowded inn is a natural one; and the parson's thoughts in the next scene echo the badger's. He too desires to leave for a better neighbourhood—and the orchestra again repeats the repressive gesture. But the musical transition is illogical: ungainly, angular melodies with piquant accompaniment, each phrase open-ended and unsatisfying. Fussy repetitions of the music of the inn's empty activity bury the few graceful variants; and they are terminated quite arbitrarily for the rise of the curtain.

Affairs are little better when we reach the parlour and the orchestral noise is shut out. The text is dominated by false hopes —the parson believes that his transfer to a new parish will bring him a better life; the schoolmaster has an ill-concealed, hopeless crush on a girl named Terynka; the music responds with introversion and dry, empty figurations. The schoolmaster's nerves are on edge, while the parson broods, silent except when moralizing monotonously 'non des mulieri corpus tuum'—a theme which turns out in the next scene to be as related to his own problems as to the schoolmaster's. But there is a redeeming contrast. The forester's encounters with Bystrouška have begun to give him access to a wisdom higher than that of these notables;

and his apparently unpleasant, malicious personal humour should not be taken at the face value of the text.

As the scene proceeds he enters gradually on the road to the knowledge of nature's patterns which he will attain by the close of the opera. His humour is designed to expose the falsity and self-deception of the withered schoolmaster's hopes; and the first music in the scene to give any intimation of joy or real depth is his song, 'Bývalo, bývalo . . .', where the text is a recognition of the natural ageing of everything, women and love along with the larch tree (and with it, by implication, the rest of nature). When the schoolmaster mentions the vixen, the deeper, mysterious music of the forest tentatively begins to enter the orchestra; when he leaves to go home through the woods, it calls with a powerful horn solo; and when the parson, distracted by the demands of the human world, goes too, the axis of the work between morality and amorality emerges at full strength.

The forester launches into a monologue, assisted only by that most natural, liberating of aids, alcohol. For him the disturbances have only led to a deeper peace: first, a finer understanding of the schoolmaster and his needs than he shows himself, then a richly hedonist defence of the consumption of alcohol against the claims of scripture, aimed *in absentia* at the parson's moralizing, and couched in sophistry which begins to align him with the glorious self-interest of Bystrouška herself. And the music is miraculous. As the forester proceeds, Bystrouška's motifs gradually return, filling the spaces of orchestral silence in the glorious, ecstatic forms from the start of the Act: open, upward-facing music which points forward to the close of the opera as a whole. In rejecting the restraints of the parson and the fantasies of the schoolmaster, the forester starts on the road to true wisdom.

But he fails the final test. Pásek reminds him about the vixen, and he breaks out again in angry reproach as the curtain falls. Bystrouška herself is still too much for him to accept. The orchestra conveys his failure eloquently: despite his protests, the forest's music intrudes with a wholly new power when Pásek mentions Bystrouška, and it overwhelms the forester the moment he stops speaking. This is the climax of the Act which displays the height of Bystrouška's powers, the moment at which she makes the forester recognize the forces of life and of sexual attraction. The tutti as the scene changes is therefore the richest of all, its orchestration the lushest.

The forest and the vixen assert both their overwhelming authority and their magic. And in the next scene both are demonstrated. The musical balances of the inn scene, and the parallelism between parson and badger, have already foreshadowed a world in which the ability to be at one with the forest—and so with nature—is given only to a few. Now, in the forest itself, we learn not only how, but why, the schoolmaster and the parson are inadequate. And with them most of male humanity; the two voices, high tenor and deep bass, are chosen to embrace as wide a spectrum of character-types as possible.

The forester has begun to learn wisdom in two ways: untouched by false ideals of womanhood, he is developing towards the true amorality of Bystrouška. Both are bound up with the recognition, which humans can attain, of the great cycles of change in the world. The schoolmaster and the parson typify the two attitudes which prevent such wisdom—excessive passion and excessive restraint. The schoolmaster, we now see, is obsessed with his crush on Terynka, the parson oppressed by guilt about his unsuccessful encounter with a woman. Both attitudes have already been seen as ludicrous; and their failure is now brought out in an extraordinary scene. Encountering Bystrouška, the embodiment of unrestrained femininity, their repressed desires emerge. But the enlightenment which they receive is illusory because of their lack of real awareness; and any pathos we might feel for their miserable, static lives is swept away (as totally as sympathy for the hens at the end of Act I) by the glory of the close, where forester and vixen are seen united in the amoral energies of the chase. And this is necessary, as the focus of the opera widens yet again in the final scene of the Act.

The forest is from the first moments alien to the schoolmaster; alcohol has not liberated him but clouded his wits: he can hardly walk along the path, and the music vividly chronicles his hesitant, inadequate movements. As he curses the natural pitfalls of the path—and the rain, equally natural, which has made it so hard to walk in the darkness—the rich music from the previous interlude returns, now transformed into more and more oppressive figurations as the forest overwhelms him.

The schoolmaster began his monologue with attempts at self-awareness; but his failure is rapid. Overcome by his anger at the path and by alcohol, he falls to the ground. Pedantry fails him; and now that his self-sufficiency has been undermined, the forest exercises its full power. Again, as the vixen runs behind the sunflowers, the music of ecstasy sounds out in the orchestra, and the animal world calls to the human with the same instruments, harp and horn, that conveyed its influence in 2.ii. But the textures dissolve; the schoolmaster's wonder at the mysteries of the night, the vixen and the sunflowers are translated not into insight but into a bizarre fantasy. The spectacle elicits a complex response: the man's misdirected passions are at once absurd and pitiful. And Janáček sets the scene with delicate, detached objectivity, forcing us neither to laugh nor to cry, merely to observe and wonder at the indignity of man.

The parson receives the same dramatic treatment. Though he does not succumb to the illusion that Bystrouška actually *is* his loved one, her influence pervades his thoughts no less than the schoolmaster's. The orchestral motif which is heard prompting the memories on which he meditates is a barely developed variant of Example 30; while Bystrouška's eyes glow through the bush as the parson recalls the miscarried sexual encounter which, as a young priest, made him incapable of an honest approach to women. For him also, to meditate under the influence of the forest and the vixen is to be forced to expand his vision, and the quotation whose source the parson cannot remember, 'Think of your duty to be a good man' elicits, in this environment, not a theological meditation but reminiscences of his own failure to do so in an encounter with an innocent-looking girl.

But again—as with the schoolmaster—the enlightenment which follows is illusory. Recognizing his own failure and uselessness, the parson comes not to self-recognition but simply back to pedantry. He remembers the Greek original of his quotation—with Bystrouška's help, since the celesta chord which marks the moment of revelation is generated yet again from a variant of Example 30; but suddenly all the absurd structure of the schoolmaster's fantasies and the parson's false, belated illumination is swept away. The rhythms of the forest disrupt the scene in their usual arbitrary yet natural way, and humiliate the two notables; the forester catches sight of the vixen and, in their fourth and

153

final personal encounter, takes two wild shots at her. And this is more than high comedy. A fierce ecstasy transforms the orchestra as the second shot misses the vixen: 30b sounds out with the utmost force, translated into the sphere of romance in violins and clarinets and restored to the absolute form of the start of the Act; and the forester emerges from the woods, gun in hand:

I'll bet you anything, that was our vixen!

The forester has reached understanding of Bystrouška's intelligence and cunning. He is therefore not drowned by the tutti; the orchestra carries his words along with it, and the curtain music tumbles over itself with all the wit and joy of her escape, a joy in which the forester is now able to share.

The work is now unified in its progression, unswerving in the line which leads directly from this moment, the mid-point in its running time, towards the inspired union between worlds at the close. Here the opera broadens its emotional and intellectual range, preparing us for the astonishing, cumulative expansions of focus in Act 3.

With the return to the life of Bystrouška herself, the extensive desertion of the human world, love enters the drama for the first time; and in a scene so extended, so accomplished, that it becomes a paradigm of all loves, both animal and human, from their hesitant inception to the mingled, exultant joy and sadness of their consummation. To achieve this in presenting the love of the vixen and the fox, Janáček interweaves animal manners and human as closely as emotional seriousness and a penetrating humour. And since the affinities of animal and human have already been established (1.ii), so now Janáček—having also made us see both worlds in their solemnity and their absurdity—can blend at full strength two kinds of music, the lightest (though always with a touch of almost ritual fervour which preserves the dignity of the animals) and the most tender and contemplative. The composer demands that his audience accept, in this first encounter of Bystrouška's sexuality with that of a male animal, almost lightning shifts of tone from solemnity to high comedy, illumination to parody. The vision is inclusive: we are offered a scene in which humour, logic, sophistication, desire, nobility and beauty overlap in an almost incredible but totally convincing *mélange*—which at its close establishes the unity of the entire

forest in support of the marriage. The effect is that all moral
restriction, both animal and human, is confronted and overcome
in the course of this Act by Bystrouška and by her maturity in
love. Hence the appearance at the close—and the absurdity—of
the sententious owl who is a reminder both of the badger and of
the parson.

Here, in the summer of the vixen's life, the forest celebrates
her sexuality in anticipation, by the stark interplay of two related
themes, vigorous and ecstatic (Example 31)—but the splendours
of this introduction are abandoned as soon as the curtain rises,
and the whole of the first, hesitant courting of Bystrouška is
accompanied by delicate, frequently staccato variants whose
purpose is to show up the sophistication, the nonchalant ease
of the conversation in which the two animals disguise their
desire for each other.

Bystrouška is the heroine of this opera: the fox appears only
briefly. And though Janáček's couple observe social convention
to the extent that the fox must do the wooing, his inclination to
give predominance to the female subtly overshadows it. The
bond between Bystrouška and Zlatohřbítek is created in the
central section of the scene, the monologue in which Bystrouška
tells of her captivity and her defiance of the forester. Critics have
observed that the events described here do not correspond with
those of 1.ii, and that the narration has in fact been taken from a
section of Těsnohlídek's book which relates another encounter
between Bystrouška and the forester, an episode otherwise
omitted from Janáček's opera. Carelessness in Janáček's adaptation has even been implied. But the effect achieved is perfectly
apt: the earlier part of the scene has already shown that Bystrouška is quite prepared to descend to 'white lies' in pursuit of
her man. Janáček's hearers are bound, in the opera, to take this
monologue as an account of the events of Act 1; and so the effect
of using it is to show Bystrouška as amorally prepared to exag-
gerate her own adventures in order to gain the fox's admiration.

But Janáček, having gained this effect, characteristically oversets it with another one still, as the monologue develops. Example
28c returns, placed now in an angry, furious context as Bystrouška's narrative builds up, musically, into a remorseless
tirade against oppression. And Janáček throws himself so
earnestly into the setting that Bystrouška's self-dramatizing be-

Ex. 31 (2.iv.44:9)

comes forgotten in the truthfulness of the evocation of human cruelty; the sophistry and joy of her original response to the real events of Act I are put behind us, and a wider perspective gained in which the social protest of this text becomes real and the heroic defiance almost unbearable:

'Strike, if you want!
But then . . .'
And he struck me!

156

'Tyrant, You've got what you asked for!'
He staggered like a cut-down tree.
I escaped . . . and since then I'm a wild animal again.

In the closing moments of her story all the threads are gathered
together: text and music show the animal and the forest transcending human oppression, absorbing it into their wider, wiser
world in a manner now more profound, because more emotionally full, than that of the close of Act 1:

Ex. 32 (2.iv.59:5)

After this, all tension is spent, and the love of vixen and fox can develop with a return to the courtly grace with which it began. But the emotional undertones of Bystrouška's final rejection of human *mores* remain, and the drama is soon ready for the portrayal of the growth of her love, first in the andante while the fox leaves to seek an offering for her, secondly, after their delicate communion, in the perfect symmetry of the rise and fall of the tutti to which she accepts his simple, universal declaration:

> Truly, Bystrouška, it's you, you!
> I've fallen in love with you
> because you are just like the one
> I've wanted all my life!

And the closing moments, the vixen's humble admission that she too wants the fox whom she has moved to tears of joy, are set with piercing tenderness.

It is poetically right that at this point the blue dragon-fly should return; for once again, as in 1.i, Bystrouška has been abducted from the midst of her fellow-creatures. But this time a very different outcome: Janáček seeks to celebrate not merely Bystrouška's wedding but also her pregnancy, and so compresses real time more boldly than anywhere else in the tragic operas. The return of the couple from their den presents a stark dramatic contrast: sunrise and happy activity among the other animals, while Bystrouška is sobbing. But the pain is removed: in the opera's last moment of high comedy, the fox undertakes to make an honest vixen of her; and at last, after the constant alternation of styles which has marked the path to their marriage, reflecting all the changes of mood which precede that harmony, Example 31 returns overtly in voices and orchestra, bringing with it unity and continuity, nobility and release. So deep is the harmony achieved by this, the total fulfilment of Bystrouška's life, that an extended choral finale, danced by the animals of the forest, celebrates her marriage; so all-embracing is the ecstasy of the celebration that even the music of Bystrouška's sobs is transformed into a joyous part of the energy discharged in this finale.

The ecstasy is precisely placed. The total unity of the forest marks the climax of Bystrouška's life; it is also so complete that it cannot be exceeded. Thus there is logic in the sharp contrast of the angular music with which Act 3 begins—insisting again on the relative limitation of humans (one human reaches these heights at the close, but only in a dream), and preparing us for the pathos of Bystrouška's death at their hands.

The contrast is acute. Act 3 is introduced by disturbed, unsatisfying music over a rigorous, over-controlled and staccato basis. And almost all the music of the first scene, between Harašta and the forester, is dry, abrupt to the point of gesture when not overtly violent. After the ending of Act 2, the principal point is clear: human music, like the human mind, is introverted, preoccupied with outside concerns, wistful where not barren in comparison with the rich life of the forest, ever-anchored in the present. Harašta has won a woman, as the fox has won a vixen—and is the only human to gain one in the course of the opera; but to draw the parallel is to point the contrast. Harašta's song is far from joyful, he accepts marriage with the human's characteristic reservations; and the hint in the orchestra at a mystery like Bystrouška's, when the girl is named, dissolves rapidly. Harašta is neither fulfilled nor happy, and there is little true humour in his attempt to gain verbally at the forester's expense.

Only one man will find fulfilment in this opera, and then only in reminiscence and dream. It is the evening of Bystrouška's life, and—since the whole opera reflects her life—the limitations of humans as they grow older are shown up too. The atmosphere is already autumnal, heavy with premonition. The forester is alive to the mood: finding a dead hare left by Bystrouška, he performs his duty of setting a trap for her heavily, with reluctance, and perhaps with the knowledge that he can no longer outwit her; a new transformation of Example 30 conveys both the sadness of the moment and the regret.

She still gives me no rest!

The humans are depressed. But the animals remain as joyful as ever. And Bystrouška is now far too clever to be trapped—as are her cubs. In the last scene of Bystrouška's life, we see her fulfilment at full strength. The music of the cubs develops Bystrouška's melodies from the first two Acts to a circular, self-fulfilling form, while their song celebrates the joy and pride of this most intelligent of animals.

Janáček now takes an extreme risk. Recalling and developing

the music of fulfilled love from 2.iv, he writes just before Bystrouška's death a delicate, tender scene for vixen and fox. But the death scene avoids sentimentality by the power with which it presents the final confrontation between the two logics, moral and amoral, and the two lives, burdened and unburdened. To the end there is a vigour and energy, both of which are generated in the moment when Bystrouška heroically disregards normal animal prudence and so evokes the worst hunting instincts in Harašta; the music opposes two motifs directly, Bystrouška's delicate figuration against Harašta's lumbering one, as the animal outwits the human, brings him to the ground. But this is not the end: Bystrouška is not shot out of cruel rage. She and her cubs devour the chickens which Harašta is taking as a present to his bride, and there is a real if comic pathos as the human, lamenting his predicament, comes near to being a tragic figure for the only time in the opera. But Bystrouška cannot understand: to her, Harašta's human emotion is inexplicable—that she should take the chickens if she can is both normal and natural: why lament the law of the forest? So the vixen's last moments are set as a triumph: the cub-cry blazes out in the orchestra as she defies him, for the whole of her life has been fulfilled in the training of her cubs to an amorality as successful as her own. And the music makes us hear this, the intolerable pressure which this successful amorality places on his human concerns, as the force which makes Harašta, 'filled with anger and sorrow', shoot her.

The entire orchestral fabric collapses instantly: the wanton destruction of all dialogue between the two worlds, the emptiness of the power man wields by the force of arms in comparison with the magnetism of Bystrouška's triumphant cunning, leave nothing to be said. And out of the silence Bystrouška's motif sounds in this final version, at once question and lament, capturing her like a photograph in the moment both of her fulfilment and of her death.

Ex. 33 (3.i.31:8)

The curtain falls, and the orchestra slowly makes this melody into an elegy for Bystrouška as if the whole forest were gradually united in mourning. But there is no release: in eighteen adagio bars the pathos simply becomes more and more desperate until the assembled tutti plummets to a heartbroken, unresolved close. In the immediate aftermath, no sense can be made of the drastic, sudden death of the creature around whom the whole opera has revolved.

But Janáček's instinct, here as always, is to attempt understanding of the experience he presents. And it is the measure of how difficult he sees this task as being here, that two further, extended scenes are needed before the end. In the music played while the scene is changed, the orchestra makes attempt after attempt to comprehend, to find a melody adequate to what we have seen; but each collapses in failure, undermined by renewed emotional agony, and when the curtain rises on the garden of Pásek's inn, it does so after a sudden outburst of repetitive, violent sforzandi has marked the interlude's failure to come to terms with Bystrouška's death.

The failure reflects that of the forest's inhabitants. Bystrouška's death, like everything else that has happened in the opera, is natural, part of the great, inexorable cycle of life which Janáček is exhibiting to us; but now the forest has been diminished, and before the movement to the shattering surprise of renewal may begin, its people must attempt to understand their place in the autumn of life. The forester has now begun to learn such understanding from Bystrouška.

Her den was empty when he sought it out, and the unnatural stillness which he found there is matched in the atmosphere of the pub garden; many delicate touches in text and music establish the altered, autumnal world. In this world, the beginnings of renewal come through the recognition of truth, the loss of illusion which such an emptiness confers. The forester is denied his wife's ambition to have Bystrouška as a muff; the schoolmaster's illusions are assailed by the buoyant vigour of the forester's banter about sunflowers, and even more cogently by the violence of the music with which the forester forces him to realize that a woman like Terynka is not for him. And with the news that the parson, too, has failed to realize his dreams—the new parish has brought him only loneliness—the phrase which has risen twice in the orchestra since Bystrouška's death ascends for the third and final time, and now has the strength to shift the opera into its closing movement (Example 34).

Without Bystrouška, old age enters the scene. The forester decides to drink no more that day, for he has gained a deeper wisdom than that which alcohol confers:

THE FORESTER (*suddenly*:) My bill—I'm going.
THE SCHOOLMASTER (*astonished, softly*): And where, so early?
THE FORESTER: Where?
 To the woods, and home.
 I didn't bring Lapák with me.
 He's got a sore foot, he's resting.
 He's old, schoolmaster, like us.
 How long ago it is,
 that we behaved stupidly.
 And now a man is glad
 if he can sit down somewhere
 and doesn't even feel like moving!

The music gently develops the closing phrase of Example 34 into a spiritually approving accompaniment; the forest surrounds with warmth the forester's acceptance of his mortality and of his old age; the path to wisdom.

But this is not all. After the cruelties of misunderstanding, the progressive confinement of true joy to animals alone, Janáček redeems the opera's picture of man by showing the immense rewards which nature confers on those who can accept it. An interlude of unrestrained vigour, leading at its close to a deeper grace than ever before, takes us back to the black ravine which was the setting of 1.i. Again the weather matches the phase to which nature has led us, anticipates the mood of the final scene: sunshine after a drizzle. This time the forester is in harmony with nature, first admiring the perfect shape of the mushroom he has picked, then led by it into reminiscences; and now his wife is no longer a shrew, and his bridal morning was no day of tiredness, but the ecstatic, careless communion with nature of two young gatherers of mushrooms:

162

Ex. 34 (3.ii.43:10)

she like a young fir,
he like a dark pine,

the true, amoral ecstasy in which they—like the animals of the
forest—were truly careless:

Some they crushed, trampled down, because . . .
because in their love they didn't see them.

In return, the forester is embraced throughout this reminiscence
by the overflowing, upward-facing music of the forest as no
human character has yet been. And this gives him the authority
to achieve the ever-rising, ever-broadening perspectives of the
closing meditation. For the first time the forester can hail
nature, look forward, celebrate and welcome to himself the
glories of the forest; he has now proved his unity with it. And he
is rewarded with the heightening of his consciousness to a miraculous degree. The orchestra takes on a new richness, building
up as the moderato begins (51:3) massive, ecstatic patterns
which already anticipate the end; and as the forester's vision
embraces the spring, the return to the forest of its nymphs, an
indescribable animation infects the orchestra, assured and
generated totally from the vision which he has been granted of
nature in the act of fulfilling itself. And man's place? To *grave*
music of the utmost mystery, the forester is initiated into our
true role in the forest:

And people will go past with bowed heads
and they will know
that they are experiencing superhuman bliss.

The violas gather the forester into the orchestral music, and he
falls into the sleep through which he may experience the opera's
final vision. The inverted triads which endow this moment with
all its solemnity and tenderness rise higher and higher over profoundly calm figurations, leading the music on to the closing
gesture in which, in the forester's dream, all the animal life of 1.i
returns for him to relive and remake that moment. The dream-
world quells the orchestra to scattered, isolated phrases; and
from the circling triplets of the flutes, which themselves re-create
with a new richness the music of Bystrouška's elegy, the cub-song
emerges, and with it a new vixen, identical to its mother. And the

forester—for this is a dream—attempts to catch the new vixen
as he did the old, and refashion the story

> . . . but I'll bring you up better
> so that people don't write stories about
> you and me in newspapers.

But he fails, catches the little frog instead; and the forest's
triumph—precisely that of a dream, for it transcends the forester's
attempt to bend the order of the original moment which it recalls
—instantly animates the orchestra with fierce, rising carillons of
perfect fourths and fifths, building up an almost intolerable need
for the end:

> THE FORESTER: Eh, you horrible cold beast,
>   where do you come from?
> THE LITTLE FROG: This isn't me
>   This was my old grandfather!
>   He used to . . . used to . . .
>   tell me about you!

The renewal is complete: the forester recognizes the justice of
his failure to catch the new vixen when he sees the justice of the
renewal even of the frog, senses that the harmony of nature is,
and results from, a process of eternal re-creation. This the complement to all that he has learnt in the course of the opera; and
so, in the final and culminating gesture of the work, he lets his
gun fall to the ground—abandoning man's weapon against
nature and so achieving total harmony with the forest: acceptance
and understanding. The musical tension breaks, and the opera
concludes in a pavan of solemn ecstasy, final expression of concord. Circling around itself in glorious perfection, Bystrouška's
motif finds the form which, in retrospect, it has been seeking
throughout the opera, and her triumph—albeit after death—is
complete (Example 35).

This opera makes no concession to popular ideas of entertainment. Behind all the refinement of its wit, *Adventures of the
Vixen Bystrouška* is a deeply serious, finely conceived tragedy: a
drama of fierce reality, which as it unfolds calls into more and
more anguished question the bases of human existence. Like its
austere, daunting companion-piece this opera grants tribute to

Ex. 35 (3.iii.58:13)

human mortality only late, and with qualification; for as the forester himself asks of the closing vision of concord, is it fairy-tale or reality?

In this work, Janáček accepted the pessimistic vision of mankind which makes *Kát'a Kabanová* the bleakest of the tragic operas, and found the strength of vision to envelop that world in a wider surround—that of nature in all its glory. Here, as in *Kát'a Kabanová*, mankind is again harshly viewed; and our cruelty, ignorance and petty concerns are ruthlessly exposed by the wider context of the animal world. But there is more to the piece than a discourse on man's cruelty. Holding up to us, in Bystrouška's life-story, an amorality which is glorious in comparison with the constrictions of human morality, Janáček also expounds to us the ideal of a life we should lead. The affinity of the vixen with human femininity is a pointer, shows that the musical insight lavished on the depiction of each successive stage of her life is intended to have deep meaning for us. Human beings, like vixens, are born, grow, marry and die; those seen in the opera live lives poor in comparison with Bystrouška's—

166

except for the forester, whose road to wisdom is carefully charted and on whose closing vision Janáček lavished some of his most inspired music. Janáček's restraint, his gradual revelation of that transcending possibility, show a superb control, even in an opera so filled with detailed events of life that its meaning echoes far beyond the forest of Adamov, fills in some way the place of every man as he stands on this earth, set apart from its other inhabitants by his arrogance and his technology. Janáček illuminates for us the cycles of life and of nature; and at the same time he shows us archetypes of the morality of the humans who cannot accept those cycles—and the road by which one human eventually can. By so doing he has enabled us, his audience, to share in his own all-embracing, natural perspective.

Makropulos

English fails before the enormity conveyed by Čapek's original title: *věc Makropulos*, the *thing* whose mystery and terror are so great that it cannot be described. To term it a secret or an elixir, to speak of an affair or case are to evade, to emphasize the complexity and legalism of the stage plot at the expense of the human depths which are its source. Despite the initial, surface elegance, *Makropulos* is the least merciful of operas. The text is cruel and ironic, the music turbulent, passionate and strange.

Like Bystrouška, Emilia Marty is a creature beyond morality, set down in the world of men both for what her own life has to tell us and for the light in which she places the actions of other, normal human beings. But in this opera the focus in which our lives are set is not the overwhelming richness of nature, comforting to those who have the power to embrace it. Marty is the creation of science, of an invention terrible precisely because of its inhumanity: in prolonging the life of Elina Makropulos by over three hundred years, the *věc* has stripped an intelligent, sensitive girl of her natural, developing beauty and left her as an artificial object of love, condemned to an eternal emptiness in which life is meaningless. It is for this reason that glacial stretches of silence seem constantly to surround Janáček's sparse, dissonant score.

The premiss on which Čapek's drama is founded was—and still is—scientifically impossible; and the playwright uses the idea of indefinitely renewable life more as a philosophical possibility, an hypothesis whose dimensions are elegantly argued in the closing scenes, than as a matter close to the tissues of life. The drama is sophisticated, intellectual, ironic. Janáček, on the

168

other hand, was fired by the imaginative possibilities of the play on first viewing; and he rightly saw that Marty's predicament is in itself tragic. At some points the play is so harsh as to be almost anti-human; Janáček tones down its cynicism and hardness, and takes every opportunity to make us feel compassion for the heroine despite the wounds which she inflicts on others; by the end of his extensively rewritten third Act our sympathy is given totally to her. Janáček makes the superhuman suffering of the victim real to us as she nears the end of her life. In Marty's torment he gives us a portrait of what it can mean even for a mortal to be utterly weary. And her closing monologue, shaped by Janáček from fragments of Čapek's final scene of ironic comedy, transforms the play into tragedy.

But her extraordinary fate is not designed to stand alone. In Janáček's drama, it exists not solely for its own value but for the light which Marty sheds on the other characters: they are no less important. Through Marty's existence they are placed in a harsh light (to her they are so often 'stupid'); and by their confrontations with her we are illuminated as directly as by a myth. For here Čapek is at his finest; the principal characters who surround Marty, each of them precisely and economically drawn, represent and invest with believable human characteristics six different, widely typical aspects of ordinary, mortal humanity: three faces of youth (Krista, Gregor, Janek) and three of age (Vítek, Kolenatý, Prus). Janáček responds with music of sharp characterization; and all are shown up, during the main body of the action, by their encounters with Marty as by a catalyst.

Or, more precisely, as by a distorting mirror. For Marty is a perversion of the course of nature—a terrible mistake, in her own words—created by human weakness and greed. And she has the same effect on those who surround her. The other characters of the libretto are apparently trivial, their lives monotonous, their ambitions petty. All are engrossed, in very different ways, in the pursuit of the great Marty. She fires each according to his interest, evoking Vítek's love of history and Kolenatý's delight in deciphering a legal tangle no less than Janek's hopeless love and his father's complex, Bohemian intrigues.

But the music redeems their humanity long before the end. Janáček never lets us forget that ordinary human pursuits are no less full of meaning because of their monotony—for each of these

limited characters is filled with worth by the intensity of the
music in which they are re-created; and we are equally conscious
of the strangeness of the focus in which this drama places them.
Janáček constantly reminds us that the magnetism which Marty
imposes is a superhuman one, that of three hundred years of
experience; that the demands which she makes are beyond
human attainment, the penetration of her soul impossible; and
that for this reason her existence distorts and stretches the other
characters. Their ambitions reach beyond normal ambition and
appear ludicrous; their attempts to achieve them become pathetic
or immoral—for the 'ideal' which Marty has attained cannot be
reached without hideous cost. The most central instances are
Gregor's love and Prus's desire for her: both emotions begin in
a manner recognizably akin to normal human feelings, but they
have degenerated by the closing stages of Act 2 to such an extent
that the music portrays each man as reduced to a subhuman
state. Gregor whines and threatens like a caricature of a raging
beast, while Prus throws away the honour and aristocratic re-
serve of generations to gain one night in bed with Marty; and the
music hears his surrender as that of a creature overwhelmed,
reduced to a hoarse, barely animal demand.

The plot is completely generated by the most inexorable of
natural processes, death, and Marty's quest to evade it. Until the
centre of the opera, her superior power over the other characters
(none of whom she has met until just before the stage action
begins) increases; but against the increase in her influence is set
the gradual onset of greater and greater weariness. And this
leads to a third Act of extreme tension, since Marty's success in
recovering the object for which she has intervened in their lives
has been achieved only at the price of enough mistakes on her
part and wounds to the other characters for them to force a confession. With her confession and narration of the truth about
herself a clarity long aimed for by the music is finally achieved,
and Elina Makropulos recognizes her place in nature, decides to
renounce both the *věc* and her life. The decision is on the surface
surprising, but on reflection deeply expected. Act 2 is an in-
human comedy, in which the other characters become Emilia's
playthings; but as the drama progresses humanity begins to return
with her growing weakness, and in her great closing scena Marty
herself recognizes the value of humanity in all its brevity of life.

But the close is complex, shot through with ironies. Speaking almost with the authority of a *deus ex machina*, she terms us fools —because we do not recognize how lucky we are. It is not merely one woman who confronts humanity here—the whole suffocating weight of the past, the centuries of misery through which she has lived infects these pages, and Janáček does no more than give us our due when he has a male-voice chorus, in the orchestra pit, accept and echo these words on our behalf with hollow enthusiasm. Marty expiates her life and gains her freedom: another woman, Krista, redeems mankind by destroying the monstrous thing which has distorted Marty's natural life; but the ending is severe. The music concentrates remorselessly on the crushing out into death of Marty and the destruction of the *věc*. Janáček remains fiercely objective to the close: the hope for man is of the most tenuous, the reinstatement doubtful of outcome.

We have seen both mortal and immortal weariness; have learnt that our lives' meaning rests on their brevity, our mortality; that our most cherished values would be lost if life were prolonged. But the opera is more than a refutation of utopias of scientific progress, more even than a definition of the limits of human existence. Remembering, as we leave the theatre, the shattering distortions suffered not merely by Marty but by every character in this tragedy, we hear beyond them to the essential humanity and worth which even the most ordinary of men retain throughout: there is already, in the agonies and the integrity of all those who are here tainted by the *věc*, that 'spark of God' which Janáček was to discern and portray in the Siberian prisoners of his last opera. But the focus here is different. *Makropulos*'s settings are urban and ordinary; the milieu is at first sight a strange locale for this composer's music, especially as his first choice of subject after the rural vigour of the *Adventures*. Here for the first time since *Destiny* Janáček's cast must put on suits, ties and elegant city clothes. But the effect is precise. The music is passionately intrusive, constantly reminds us (like the heroine) of the raw animal needs which lie beneath the veneer of a great city's sophistication and manners. The play and the music combine to unique effect, the harsh wit of Čapek's 'comedy' being surrounded by Janáček's tense, agonized music in which the emotions which generate it are revealed. And in the outcome even we, so like the ordinary characters of this opera, are ultimately sent forth from this most demanding of Janáček's operas with some hope: that minimal hope, snatched from the jaws of superhuman suffering, which is the emblem of the very highest tragedy.

The music is from the first moments strange, yet full of meaning. It begins violently, almost incoherently—but with the entry of the upper strings bearing the extended, utterly weary first theme it is rapidly clear that Janáček is about to present the gravest opening argument of any in these operas. Nor are we merely treated to the longest prelude yet heard before a Janáček opera: it is wide in range and offers constantly shifting perspectives. Hectic activity alternates with weariness, violence with serenity, the continual motion of an endless quest with the heraldic fanfares of a world centuries old. At figure 8 a halt is called and the implications are drawn out, in trenchant notes of mounting desperation. The release after figure 14 is no true release: the opening theme plays in echoing imitation of itself, and the extended use of counterpoint is so rare in Janáček that it speaks for a few moments of humanity and warmth; but all is lost in the brass-dominated, tutti reassertion of the fanfares and their powerful counter-subject. A few tenuous moments of ecstasy are bitterly dissolved as the curtain rises.

This prelude achieves an effect beyond the powers of the spoken theatre. Even before Emilia Marty has come onstage— and long before the music has been obliged to declare her identity and find a vocabulary large enough to encompass all her suffering—we have already been involved in her superhuman quest. For this is the music of world-weariness, of endless travel, boredom and agony; the dialogue between a real, ceremonial past and its terrible, continuing consequences—bitterly bound together by the musical relationship between the opening theme and the fanfares, and by the prelude's constant undercurrent of violence. There is a strong, fruitful contrast with the mood of the first scenes, the clarity and calmness of musical gesture in the conversation of Vítek, Gregor and Krista. In the original play, we have no basis on which to judge Vítek's meditations, Gregor's ambitions or Krista's despair; in the opera all are already set against the large, severe context of the prelude, music which speaks a language we will hear only rarely before the

172

closing pages. The true past and true weariness have unfolded themselves before us in their glory and their superhuman futility; in this context, the emotions of the opening stage action seem muted but not—as in the play—ludicrous. Vítek's vision is limited, and we hear in his weary historical reflections more of an attempt to penetrate the mists of time than a true sense of the pressure of the past:

Ex. 36 (I.24:1)

But his apparent triviality is redeemed by the musical contrast with the appalling, monstrous genius of what we have just heard. Here are true human reminiscences, true hopes and fears. The same will be true of Gregor and Krista.

And a similar effect recurs when Vítek launches into a violent social protest, borrowed from Danton. The text may invite amusement by its incongruity; but the orchestral support, exaggerated but not mocking, does not allow you to forget that, in comparison with the prelude, all here is stable and genuine. And if tedious, it is genuine precisely because of that tedium. It is the stuff of life. Vítek's gesture of tiredness gains for a moment an upward inflection in the trumpets, as he assumes his heroic, revolutionary pose; but this is lost, as Gregor, entering and over-hearing, pricks the balloon of his rhetoric. So with all truly human emotions. Marty will, in Act 1, be invulnerable.

Gregor's hopes are no less fragile, easily wounded by Vítek's cynicism; but there is still reality to his concern. His thoughts of suicide are not mere rhetoric. And Krista completes the atmosphere of delicate, preoccupied mortality which prepares the road for Marty. The tender, muted string triads which pervade her scene in gentle motion speak of a true girlish beauty; while by contrast, the figurations which convey her despair in the face of Marty's greatness are impossibly delicate and tentative, their fragility that of one reaching after an unattainable ideal.

Idealism, despair, infatuation. Past three people in the thrall of real, present emotions (all apparently trivial, but all rooted in their feeling for the immediacies of the past and future), Emilia Marty steps into Kolenatý's office, to an unearthly light, an equally mysterious chord-cluster, and a theme for viola d'amore which is as intangible, timeless and enigmatic as the person herself.

The preparation is precise, for the same axes remain dominant as the main action begins. This is Marty's first encounter with the other characters, and—though it begins in studiously elegant politeness—her opening exchanges with Kolenatý continue the contrast established at her entry. The formality, the determined factuality of the lawyer are at once opposed by a larger, more arresting mode of musical gesture: Marty's orchestra skirmishes round Kolenatý's earthbound motif, by turns arrogant and mysterious, always with a timeless disdain. And these preliminaries do not issue in stability: the exposition of the 'facts' which Marty demands merely increases her conflict with him and forces her to begin to show her true self.

Just as we are asked to register a contrast between the prelude and the prologue in which three minor characters set the scene for Marty, so too the longer span of Act 1 contains an equal contrast; the turning-point, marked by a triumphant flourish in the orchestra, is Kolenatý's departure. In Act 1, Marty's powers over the other characters are in the ascendant; her conflict with the lawyer rapidly becomes violent, since Kolenatý (alone among the male characters in being untouched by her sexual attraction) represents all in civilization that is resistant to Marty: a man precise, formal, and immune to the touch of anything outside the sphere of normal experience. Only after persuading Gregor that her story is true can she succeed, by using him, in breaking down Kolenatý's resistance. The way is then clear to the winning of Gregor himself—and, apparently, to her repossession of the *věc*. Before Kolenatý leaves, the orchestral conflict is between the matter-of-fact (and false) perception of the past which Kolenatý offers and the mysterious warmth of the truths which Marty summons from her reminiscences; afterwards, the roles are almost reversed, Marty's becoming the opaque music as she retreats into guarded privacy, while Gregor's becomes more and more ornate in his increasingly frustrated attempts to express the emotions which she has stirred in him.

The conflict between Marty and Kolenatý unfolds only gradually. At first, Marty's abrupt, totally assured gestures co-exist in the orchestra with Kolenatý's confident pedantry: each character is equally adept at irony, and in their early exchanges the lawyer's flow is hardly disturbed by Marty's interruptions. But they have a cumulative effect. The orchestra gradually begins to take its cue from Marty's animation, and its dutifully bored accompaniment to Kolenatý's pomposity (he enjoys incorporating the German legal jargon of the Austro-Hungarian empire into his otherwise Czech exposition) becomes increasingly playful. And finally Kolenatý is brought up against a real mystery, the alleged deathbed testament of Pepi Prus (figure 69), and his own words, sung with solemnity over an opaque chord-cluster, force Marty to intervene and recall the strangeness and mystery which have engendered the whole case (Example 37). Marty can object no longer: the real past breaks in and she must speak herself. For she, her immortality and her masked identity, are the roots of the entire lawsuit. The deep, mysterious chord which recalls that to which she entered grows in its influence, forcing the tiny rising figure in quavers to flower into the beginnings of a passionate intervention. 'That must be a mistake, a mistake! Pepi must have been thinking of Gregor, Ferdi Gregor!'

And now Marty dispels the mists of time. Her viola d'amore

Ex. 37 (1.70:6)

theme, buried beneath the textures when she entered the stage, flowers unfettered as she explains who Ferdi really was, remembers her son by the only man she ever really liked. Kolenatý's disbelief leads to increasing violence and impatience: he concludes the courtroom version of the story to aggressively descending flourishes in the woodwind, and relieves his tension by scribbling irritably on a scrap of paper. Again the mystery recurs, and there is one more obstacle; to clear it, Marty takes the initiative, and the contrast becomes acute between Kolenatý's cynical incredulity and the seductive, romantic flow of her persuasion:

her words are to be enunciated 'mysteriously, with burning haste', and the elusive association of Elian Macgregor with Pepi Prus generates a seductive clarinet melody. This dominates the next pages, competing successfully against the motifs which express Kolenatý's scoffing contempt. Gregor is converted, and the scene ends in the utmost agitation, all the motifs being dissolved in the empty, prestissimo figurations which dramatize the conflict through which Gregor forces Kolenatý to do Marty's will. The tension between 'fact' and 'fairy-tale' (between falsehood and truth) is now so severe, the music has become so hollow in its violence, that there is nothing but relief when Kolenatý goes—even though the passion to follow is far more intense.

All that he has heard, the reminiscences and buried warmth of Marty, have stirred a wonder in Gregor which can now find expression; and the music acquires a strained but definite beauty as their dialogue begins. Kolenatý's departure releases a confrontation implicit ever since Krista's banter with Gregor; and in the scene which follows Gregor comes to stand for all the men who have encountered Elina before the opera's beginning. This is a first encounter, and Gregor is a sensitive man; as Marty's weariness begins to overtake her for the first time in the opera, she rebuffs him and Gregor, not yet totally maddened by her rejection, is spurred to deep insight into what she is. Because Gregor's sensitivity, and the fact that this is the first sexual confrontation between Marty and any man which we see, make this scene the strategic climax of Act 1, Janáček studies the stages of Gregor's decline with care: his fall from anxious humanity to stunned subservience is the first indication that the 'miracle' of Marty has powers more dangerous than that of dazzling young starlets and overcoming legal pomposity—and it therefore prepares us for the more naked cruelties of Act 2. Marty's increasing implacability drives Gregor from real humanity to hysteria, for while each stage of the conversation is apparently initiated by Marty, she has in her weariness no desire to develop them, and in this way Gregor, love-struck and desperately anxious to impress, is driven by her near-silence into more and more flamboyant emotional gestures, which are chronicled vividly by the orchestra.

Gregor believes in fairy-tales. And his gratitude for his

rescue is sounded in music of a warmth which reflects his humanity and his imaginativeness. But his first attempt to describe Marty (figure 106) takes the orchestra's figuration, as well as his own vocal line, to a height at which both sound strained to the point of absurdity. She laughs—not unjustly—but by doing so provokes the second stage of the scene; Gregor's repeated questions, his unbearable desire for enlightenment press more and more:

A miracle.
But every miracle must be explained.
Or else it is intolerable.
Why have you come here?

—but the pressure is not on her, for she is unmoved; when the musical tension breaks (figure 109), the rest of his questions are set to an ironic clarinet figuration which suggests that his pursuit is useless as well as absurd: the music is circular, ugly and empty. Only when Gregor reveals that he is an orphan does the orchestra relent from its constant implication that he is stupid; Emilia is moved to contemplate the brevity of life seriously for the first time in the opera:

GREGOR: . . . You see, my mother is dead.
MARTY: Bah! Bah! All of them just die.

This moment establishes an affinity between them, and Gregor gains the courage to probe the identity of Elian Macgregor. Both Marty and the music respond to this, the strings soaring with impassioned grandeur as Marty tells about her—but the orchestra retreats into mysterious privacy as Marty is inspired by this to give a response of full, personal honesty (Example 38).

Marty is exhausted, asks him to end his questions. But the insight has only spurred Gregor on, and in the final section of the scene he renews his attack. The music gleams with a spurious, fearful magic: extraordinary figures of increasing agitation measure his decline from warmth, through pleading, to reckless acknowledgement of his own infatuation. Marty has wished to give nothing away, to use Gregor simply for what he can do for her; but she has failed. His ardour forces the mocking glitter of her viola d'amore theme to return to the orchestra; and under its

178

Ex. 38 (1.116:1)

magnetism, embracing his own near-insanity, Gregor is able to find words to describe Emilia:

You stir a man, like a summons to battle.
Have you seen flowing blood?
It inflames a man to the point of madness
And you, I knew at the first glance—
in you there's something terrible.

His insight now evokes at full force the timpani cross-rhythms of the prelude. And having forced *this* penetration of her soul, Gregor—knowing that he has lost his mind and that her coldness only drives him further—has the strength to attain a gruesome insight. Glacial chordal patterns of external weariness suddenly appear (figure 124); and the climax is reached, as Gregor's glimpse of eternity, his realization of her searing, superhuman attraction spur him to such heights of eloquence and his music to such rhythmic power that even Marty is moved to beg for rest. A light shines; and Gregor's persistence has its reward, for its gleam illuminates her soul to the depths—but by a supreme irony Gregor is so crazed that he can see nothing but her beauty. It has dazzled his mind to the point of blindness. The whole musical structure of the scene therefore crashes to a devastating stop.

But, being beyond human stature, Marty still has strength left. The colossal energies which the scene has aroused discharge themselves on to a slender violin tremolo; but this has only to dissolve and in a moment, to stark, ugly music, she attempts to force a numbed and truly exhausted Gregor into giving her 'the Greek document'. He hasn't got it; she explodes into incoherent fury. The contrast is total between the hollow emptiness of her music—rubato scales reiterated wildly and violently until he retreats into silence—and the richness and warmth of emotion with which Gregor's convoluted, distorted but real, growing love was imbued.

The situation is deadlocked, and conveniently saved by Kolenatý's rapid return; though this is no real salvation, since no advance in the action or psychological revelation occurs in the remainder of the Act. The 'miracle' has pricked the bubble of the lawyer's authority, and he behaves and sounds just like the bumbling old fool he says he is. The nervous, scurrying accompaniment does nothing to contradict this impression. Marty and Prus converse over his head, ignoring his music, as superior beings—for the action is now in their hands. But there is as yet no need for a direct confrontation: Marty believes she has the power to win the case for Gregor and so acquire that which she seeks. And no one yet has any good reason to contradict her. So the action ends in pure comedy. Marty's flourishes finally generate an exhilarating dance vividly expressive of her sharp delight in victory over the law and lawyers, a waltz pompous and playful by turns. But ironic in its triumph. The melody is that of Marty's coldness and cruelty, thinly adapted from the climax of the scene with Gregor; and the final bars are dominated by two echoes of the prelude, strident cross-rhythms in the timpani and flourishes in the brass, vivid reminders that her triumph is not a natural, human one. Marty has left the office confident and amused; but in Act 2 the joke goes sour on her. Death will begin to overtake her; Prus is not the man to accept defeat inertly; and not even Kolenatý is the figure of farce he now appears. Surely it is at his request that Vítek gets Marty to sign the incriminating photograph?

In the second Act Marty is at the apex of her powers, in particular in her power of sexual attraction. She needs to be, for this Act is also the turning-point of the opera's action. Throughout its second half she intrigues in order to recover the formula, struggling against increasing weariness towards her eventual triumph. The first part of the Act shows Marty holding court, mercilessly trampling over the ordinary human emotions of all the other characters, and in the second she successively reduces three of the principal men to degradation. But the moral depths plumbed in the Act are partly counterbalanced: with the onset of deeper weariness come greater revelations of Marty's misery. In this process the Hauk scene, the first moment at which we are given real insight into Marty's past life, is central. But still, Janáček is too fine a strategist to give our sympathies totally to her at this point in the drama: there are many moments of cruelty, and the final moments of the Act exhibit Marty at her worst, glacial in her empty triumph over Prus.

There are few places more empty and illusory in spirit than Čapek's chosen setting—the stage of a large theatre, in the early morning after a performance; and Janáček matches this by the sparse economy of the music, which sets in with a high, tired sadness, alternates constantly between a dry staccato and a desperate lyricism, and proceeds to a conclusion of barren, almost bestial horror.

Ex. 39 (2.0:1)

This is the opening. The music is not that of the two minor characters who begin the action, but of the empty, seductive woman who dominates their conversation and their thoughts. (a) is a new transformation, a subtle unmasking of the Act I prelude music in the new form which dominates this Act—and hindsight will make sense both of the unexpected clarity of the C major triad on which the melody comes to rest and of the fiercely strained, glacial after-echo; while (b), the apparently minimal decoration, becomes in the course of the Act the musical token of the rising power of Marty's barren sexuality.

The cleaning woman and the stage technician are only indirectly influenced by Marty; they are therefore rapidly succeeded by Krista and Janek. This is their only scene alone (or almost alone; the Act's atmosphere of corruption is set at once, since Janek's father observes them from the wings, a hidden voyeur). Krista's innocence has been destroyed: she is now infatuated with Marty to the point of absurdity, and torn between the ambition of devoting herself to singing in order to emulate her and her own inability to stop thinking about Janek; while

182

Janek is the only man not yet touched by Marty (whom he has not yet seen), and therefore shows, in his tender, utterly sincere love for Krista, the only undistorted emotion to be found in the whole opera after Krista's entry in Act 1—only to be rebuffed.

The effects of Krista's infatuation are tragic; Janek's emotions are shown as so hesitant and delicate that after Krista's half-rejection he will become besotted, fall as Marty's easiest and most complete victim. In the orchestra, Janáček contrasts three styles: a staccato, 'col legno' accompaniment to bring out the inanity of Krista's distorted ambition, and two other musics, a long, lustrous melody in the strings when each expresses their love for the other, and a delicate descending phrase in the woodwind when Krista, encouraging Janek to come and sit beside her, expresses irritation at his 'stupidity'. The implications of this music are not pleasant: the second and third themes are barely adapted variants of music from the Gregor-Marty scene of Act 1, the music of Gregor's floundering love and that to which Marty mocked his stupidity. Krista, it is implied, has it in her power to be a second Marty: in her feminine capacity to reject and encourage by turns, shown here, are the seeds of an affinity with Marty which is developed to the end of the opera, where it becomes central in the tension of the close.

The speed of the dramaturgy is not relaxed. Another moment, and Marty herself is before us—desperately strained, fending off her admirers, Example 39a sounding over an empty, monotonous patter to convey the agony. And now a remarkable scene builds up, in which every major character except Kolenatý is finally involved. A scene in which Marty's merciless superiority to humanity is revealed; and also the complete emptiness of her life.

First reducing Janek to silence by a brutally audible combination of charm and angry indifference, she is confronted by Prus—whose strength some instinct warns her not to test yet. In his place she is offered three victims in succession: Gregor, Vítek and Krista. Gregor's encounter with her is set with directness and deadly irony: in the orchestra, a single phrase conveys his aspiration, his striving to please; while a downward flurry and trill counter it each time, conveying Marty's rejection and contempt. But Vítek's love of history turns the pressure for a few moments on her; he has the power to stir the *prima donna* to the depths:

MARTY: Did you like my performance?
VÍTEK: My goodness, oh yes. Quite a Strada.
MARTY: So you heard Strada? Strada whistled. Corona had a lump in her throat. Agujari was a goose!
VÍTEK: Oh please, she died over a hundred years ago. . . .
MARTY: So much the worse. Perhaps I know that!

—and the music is suddenly free, detached from the stage events and admitting us by its novel, utter strangeness to the Makropulean power of Marty's separateness and misery, even as Krista tries to escape from Marty, who proceeds with brittle animation to humiliate her completely. The subject of course is sex, and a new, espressivo theme chronicles Krista's misery and shame. Marty terminates the inquisition abruptly ('Shut up, stupid, if you haven't then you will'), and the two new themes are brought together in a moment of total revelation (Example 40). Prus peers into the depths of Marty's soul, and hears in it not only the misery that even Marty shares with Krista's human wretchedness (and so with mortal suffering) (b), but also the icy, superhuman agony that is hers alone (a), which is heard, like her entry in this Act, over a meaningless, recurrent patter. The *věc*, the miraculous element that lies submerged beneath this drama, now emerges openly for the first time in the music (till now, even Gregor's extreme pressure on Marty in Act I revealed only its effects). And before the insights of this powerful man, whose knowledge entitles him to probe with such penetration that he may share her music, albeit in the darkest, questioning registers of the lowest instruments, Marty is forced to confess her total indifference.

There is no more chilling moment in the Act or the opera than this brief, fragile passage of rare calm. And it is the turning-point. Marty has now insulted all the characters: until this moment, she has been in the ascendant. But now her tiredness, the inhumanity that has been laid upon her, and her terrifying amorality, have been fully revealed; from now, as her powers begin to wane and she no longer makes the running in the case, sympathy for her can begin to grow. And the next scene, a self-contained episode in ternary form, at once offers a contradiction of the thesis of Makropulean indifference and a counter to the total victory over the human characters which Marty has

achieved by reducing even Prus to silence. With characteristic perversity Čapek embodies the counter in a senile madman, living only on his memories. But even memories have worth, provided they are human ones; and the Hauk scene affirms warmly that life *is* worth it to ordinary mortals. The attack is pitched on Marty's own chosen ground: sexual love. Hauk's devotion to the memory of a girl he loved over fifty years ago directly opposes Marty's strained, whispered assurance that, 'Really, I assure you, it's not worth it.' Strangulated, tremulous and grotesque though the music of Hauk's admiration is, there is also in it the fragmented outline of a real feeling which begins to make up for the stunned impotence to which the other characters have been reduced. And the pathos of his devotion even brings animation to Marty; enough to make her give emotional support to another being for the first time in the opera. Hauk leaves, still broken but with the glorious memory of his days in Spain now re-created for him, so deeply that he is moved to tears.

But the reign of the *věc* over Marty's soul is yet far from over, and the harshness returns immediately. The orchestra erupts violently, expressing the moral confusion of the moments in

186

which the main action resumes. Which side of Marty will predominate? In a moment of tenderness which confirms her affinity with Krista, Marty relaxes and signs the photograph which will incriminate her; but this is for Krista as much a moment of loss, since Janek, infatuated, does not leave with her. And Marty's superhuman weariness overtakes her again. Violent, immense orchestral gestures show the effort involved even in ridding herself of Janek; and Marty can only summon by a supreme effort the power to feign a feeling of affection warm enough to persuade Gregor to leave. The beginnings of death are now beginning to overtake her in earnest, and the music of her weariness here anticipates that of full self-revelation in the opera's final scene: cf. figure 69 with Example 44. Only now, when the orchestra has revealed the extremities to which Marty's emotions can be forced by the effort needed for simple persuasion, is the stage emptied for the first of the four grim confrontations which conclude the Act: Marty and Prus.

Here the plot begins to turn against her, as nature has already. The strongest man in the drama confronts her, and he has possession both of the *věc* and of her real name. Being but mortal, he does not realize that he has either; but being the possessor of wide experience and powerful self-confidence, he comes as near as a man can to penetrating her secrets. Marty fascinates him not for her mystery but because she seems to embody all experience: Prus's music in this scene is that of a man seeking to penetrate an abyss. And the depths are not those of her character—Emilia Marty has none—but those which her immortality has given her. So a flash of sense is made when the grace-notes of Marty's seductive power (39b) grow from the music of mystery which illuminates Prus's mention of 'the sealed envelope'; we are reminded intuitively that her power is not a natural possession but the *věc*'s gift. As the dialogue unfolds, and the baron tells of the letters of Elian Macgregor, a terrible empathy grows in the orchestral music: Prus, sexually experienced and as near to amorality as any normal human may reach, strives to penetrate the erotic secrets of a supernatural being; and the music shows the cold tendrils of decoration proliferating, surrounding his words as if they were tentacles, probing the depths of time and reaching out for the woman to whom he is speaking and whom he senses, but cannot know, he is also describing. This elaborate

187

music also evokes, with piercing originality, both the decorative postures and the essential sterility of Marty's sexual performance. Beneath all the decoration the timeless, weary motion of the music of the 'sealed envelope' persists: we are never allowed to forget that this glacial sexuality was and is conferred by the *věc*'s bestowal of eternal life.

Prus cannot penetrate this secret. In the second part of the scene, his researches have brought him so near to Marty that 40a, again heard against the dry patter of drums, conveys her impenetrable fury; but his threats evoke from her only a rich, elegant faith; and when she asks his price for the document, the references of the music leave little doubt of what she is offering. Prus's departure is momentarily halted by a simple, descending orchestral phrase that will not be forgotten; he has been fascinated, but he has not yet fallen completely. The stage, and the exhausted, motionless Marty, are left to Gregor.

He has fallen totally. His text has the brashness of one who has nothing to lose; his music now has no elaborate structure: it is a dislocated montage of gestures, reflecting his unrestrained, abrupt and extravagant emotions. He shouts, he abuses; and is now rebuffed not out of caprice but by a woman who is beginning to feel the cold of death. His passion has descended from the nobility of Act 1 to an inane violence. But even in this there is perception; he senses the horror of his position, the perversity of being impelled to bestow his love on one so cold to him. And he succeeds in arousing her emotions.

GREGOR: You're evil, base, terrible. A beast without feelings.
MARTY: I'm not, Albert—
GREGOR: You are.
MARTY: I'm not.

Wide separations and a terrible, throttling control over the melody thrust it into the lowest registers as Gregor, as if gazing into a pit, sees despite his madness what she is—'cold as ice. As if you'd risen from the grave.' And so the music fearfully conveys the paradox which is the truth: she both is, and is not, without feelings. The tension of this moment means that the end is soon near: such intensity demands a fuller revelation still. And it is soon provoked. Marty bends her powers to get him to save their

188

case by fraud; but after this vision Gregor is ready to ask the one question he has not yet had the courage to ask:

And will you love me?

And 40a lowers in the trombones to explain the devastating reply.

Never, do you understand? Never!

This releases all the energies which the scene has built up. Again Gregor threatens to kill her, and for the first time Emilia rouses herself to accept the impulse of his music and reply.

> Do you see this scar on my throat? That was another one who wanted to kill me. And if I stripped myself naked before you, then you could see how many other souvenirs of yours I have! Why am I always something you want to kill?

Once again, at this tremendous climax in which Marty has been forced to self-expression, and Gregor becomes aware of the distortion into violence which he has suffered, Gregor stands for all the men who have known her; and now, in the moment of understanding forged by his becoming helpless and aware, as so many have before, the two tragedies of lover and loved one are for a moment bound together in the pathos of the viola d'amore melody: the tragedy of the mortal and of the immortal who, for the first time, desperate but unheard, utters her own real name (Example 41).

This poignant passage of introspection is the climax of the Act, a moment of deep pathos which is the only one at which the two worlds come together. From now on they are driven apart by the onset of death, until the end of Act 3 when the choice between them must be made. Gregor cannot understand her, and the scene dissolves in farce and frustration. Marty is left alone once more, and the Act winds down to its terrible conclusion. She seduces Janek, first in words and music which reveal the *věc* in all its mystery and then, when his terror of his father makes him hesitate, with an abject, begging desperation which totally belies her claim that, 'It's just a keepsake of no value', and whose pressure is so intolerable that Janek assents, completely resigned.

Prus emerges from the shadows to drain the dregs of his earlier intoxication with Marty, and dismisses Janek. The

Ex. 41 (2.118:1)

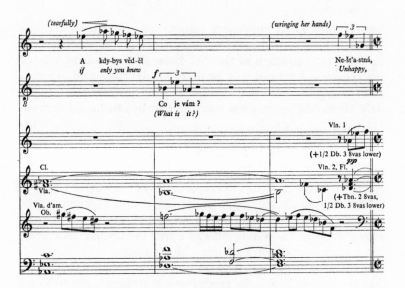

(tearfully)   *(wringing her hands)*

A   kdy-bys věd-ěl   Ne-šť'a-stná,
if   only you knew   *Unhappy,*

Co   je vám ?
(What is   it ?)

Cl.

Vla.

Vla. d'am.
Ob.

Vln. 1

(+1/2 Db. 3 8vas lower)
Vln. 2, Fl.

(+Tbn. 2 8vas,
1/2 Db. 3 8vas lower)

un poco più mosso ($\downarrow = 80$)

ne – šť'astná   E - li - na !
unhappy   E - li - na!)

+Fl.

Vln. 2
Vla.

Harp   Tamb. di bambini

B. Cl.

Vc.

Vc., Db., Bsn.

melody rises to an impetuous climax—for, though he does not know it, Prus is trampling over his son's grave. And now the strident, final triumph of the *věc*. Even after admitting why he has returned, Prus can only be overcome by the naked use of all Marty's powers. And that is what we hear now, for the first and only time. She approaches so close that he can hardly breathe.

MARTY: Well then, give me the envelope.
PRUS: Not mine to give you.
MARTY: Bring it to me!

After the direct challenge to his scruples, her summons rings out three times, in electrifying, monstrous gestures of trumpets and cymbals. At the third command he breaks, and a whiplash of semiquavers in the woodwind and upper strings, last and cruellest transformation of Example 39b, is hurled into silence. It tells us the intolerable force of the desire which she has generated. As Prus succumbs and the rendezvous is arranged, the orchestra gathers maestoso, in mounting dissonance of protest at the sordid, futile outrage to which Marty has reduced him. And the close is terrible. The tutti finally falls, by bizarre modulations, on to a triad of C major, most neutral and—in this context—most hollow of keys; and this in its turn is overshadowed by the icy, metallic gleam of the cymbals. The closing scene is the meaningless triumph of inhumanity, emptiness and the quest for the *věc*, whose glacial victory confronts us in this curtain music with stark, unswerving horror.

The horror is not yet over. Until Marty is cornered and forced by Kolenatý to begin to reveal the truth, her merciless amorality continues. Only after that do humanity and sympathy for the suffering heroine begin to invade the music of Act 3; and the central portion of the Act contains lightning contrasts of mood, drawing out to the full the conflict between the savage, dehumanizing powers of the *věc* in its last moments of influence and the increasingly revealed, underlying humanity of Elina Makropulos. This conflict makes sense in retrospect of all that Marty has done in Act 2 to the other characters, and also prepares the way for her recognition of her humanity, her final renunciation of the artificial renewal which the formula confers.

But its reign is not done. Indeed, the first matters to be ex-

192

plored in Act 3 are the consequences of her triumph at the end of
Act 2. So the Act opens with a strident perversion of Example
39: the curtain rises to this new, harsher flourish as Prus and
Marty put on their clothes. While they are dressing the orchestral
instruments play an empty, staccato game, a game which vividly
parallels the emptiness of their night together, and which degenerates into inane gestures of violence as the two characters
emerge from the boudoir. Violence frequently erupts in the dialogue and the orchestra in the scene between them, and indeed
only Hauk's appearance prevents it from being transferred to the
stage action. This is because Marty is at the height of her inhumanity (the music of her triumph is empty, when she finally
regains the document for which she has been intriguing since the
action began). Prus is degraded, and his self-disgust at being
reduced to theft for so treacherous a reward is so great that the
orchestra becomes grotesque in response: trombones and trumpets play alone on mocking phrases. And these phrases remain
to underlie Marty's intolerance in the next scene, as the chambermaid attempts to do her hair; they convey the brutal inhumanity
of her indifference as much as the mounting agony of the response which it has created.

Prus's final humiliation is postponed by the scene between
Marty and the chambermaid. In this the gulf between Marty's
world and that of normal humanity is developed still further,
partly by the almost surrealistic flavour given to the conversation
by Janáček's heavy cuts in the text, partly by the orchestral
music, which is a grotesque collage: again Marty's contemp-
tuous, staccato phrases echo each of her interjections, while
between them the violin and viola melodies of real, human
pain illuminate the girl's innocent agitation—melodies which
flower, when Prus returns, into a fierce, full expression of the
grief which his servant's appalling condition presages. The girl's
role is that of a messenger, preparing the way by her music and
her story for Prus trapped, forced finally to feel human emotion
by the death of his son; and the most extreme conflict in the
opera ensues. Marty is now too weary to respond, and devotes
herself imperturbably to the arrangement of her hair. 'Oh, so
many people kill themselves,' she replies; and the vocal line reflects not the contemplative emotion with which she reflected on
human mortality in the first Act, but a simple, cold indifference

against which even Janáček, otherwise chronicling as objectively as always, is moved to protest, sounding against her the orchestral melody which expresses the pathos and nausea of Janek's death: it has moved even Prus to agony.

The conflict is so extreme that only Hauk's arrival rescues Marty from another onset of violence. But the respite which the madman—again affirming the value of natural mortality even in his senility—provides is short-lived. Just as Marty is moved by reminiscence to accept his appeal, Kolenatý and his party arrive, and Hauk's promised rescue is overwhelmed. Repeated, suspended discords gradually undermine his melody until he is led away to an asylum, another victim.

Kolenatý's interrogation begins to orchestral silence, occasionally interrupted by a flourish in the darkest register of trombones and double-basses. And by the repetition of the same implacable phrase, gradually extended into the silence, Kolenatý's logical deductions drive Marty from her indifference, and she is forced into an anguished response (Example 42). From Example 40a, the music of the *věc* itself, a new phrase of real feeling begins to flower in Example 42a: a melody which will play a crucial role in the remainder of the opera. This is the turning-point of Act 3: the persecutor has become persecuted, the victor a victim. Emilia Marty must strip the veneer from her mask, renounce her aliases: this phrase begins her road back to accepting that she is Elina Makropulos.

The contest is that of male factuality and female intuition; on this plane Kolenatý is bound to lose, as he lost in Act 1. But Marty is now more desperate; and her actions have poisoned the conduct of other characters beside Prus. Here again, Example 40a, when transferred to basses and timpani, conveys graphically the force of a fierce male attempt to probe the mysteries of the *věc*: Gregor resolves to search Marty's luggage. Marty leaves the men to do it, with music of ambiguous contempt—is she too weary to oppose them? And the orchestra accompanies their search with music of empty, sharp ugliness to illustrate the complete unscrupulousness to which they have descended. Kolenatý falls lowest: he behaves at one moment like a circus clown, in the next demands his gown pompously, and descends to brutal abuse when Krista weeps in misery at what the men are doing to Marty.

Ex. 42 (3.39:13)

There is no deep truth to be gained from such a quest. Marty is trapped, and must return. She does so drunk, clutching a bottle of whisky with which she staves off, desperately, the onset of death; and the orchestra rouses itself to a ferocious new flute theme (Example 43).

Here the power of the *věc* has become a consuming energy, a force which animates Marty to nothing but contempt; this is the voice of the sheer horror and desperate mockery to which it has reduced her as she declines and its powers come to an end. From now until her final collapse, the music is an alternation of moods as the *věc* fights nature for her body: the outbursts of hysteria to which Example 43 is the constant, repetitive accompaniment slowly become subdued as Example 42a and cognate inventions

195

Ex. 43 (3.58:1)

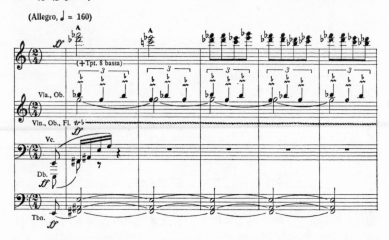

enter the musical fabric and Marty, moving towards acceptance of the natural order, illuminates for us on a superhuman scale the necessary processes of coming to terms with death.

The movement is gradual: her empathy with Josef Prus at first calls forth only a few brief moments of yearning lyricism, and her real name, Elina Makropulos, is thrown off petulantly; only when her anguish is such that she feels as if on fire, and the power of her feelings subdues Example 43 in the orchestra into querulous fragments (figure 77), does the music take on stability and real feeling. But it all dissolves with the mention of the *věc*. Vicious terror invades the textures, and Elina is led to the strangled admission

> but then he left it with his will!
> He thought that I'd come back for it
> and . . . and . . .
> and I came back at last!
> I had to get that thing,
> which gives a man three hundred years' life!
> Three hundred years' youth!

The revelation is total. Elina begins to declaim the last three lines over chords so chilling that we hear, as the mystery is dispelled and we near the truth, the horror, the coldness, the superhuman danger and also the terrible compulsion of her quest. And the

196

open declaration of the nature of the *věc* that shares its name with her precipitates its last, most terrible assertion, a reckless dance of triumph in its recovery in which Example 43 sounds relentlessly to convey the sheer outrage to nature of her joy. Exhaustion then overtakes her; and in the telling of the truth, all begins to be purged. The thematic material of the Act I prelude returns, transformed to evoke first the stark reality of Rudolf's court and then, ever more whispered by the woodwind, the delicacy of the girl of sixteen on whom the *věc* was inflicted. In the maestoso chords of figure 97, we hear the transformation of Elina Makropulos from life to a living death; and as the rest of the story unfolds, relived in spirit by the victim both of the *věc* and of endless wanderings, it gains absolute poetic authority. Example 42a steals back into the textures, and dragging chords return as she begs Gregor, in an almost ritual gesture, to feel the coldness of her hands. But Kolenatý interrupts insistently, standing for incredulity, making a final, futile defence of the natural order against the implacable facts which have now been revealed; and Marty is forced to acceptance of who she is. With that acceptance she can carry conviction to the others (and with it the authority to speak to us from a position of privilege) and so gain insight into her own place in the world.

The acceptance is painful. Elina's last agonies begin—now almost truly Elina's, for she falls back into her mother tongue and an awareness that she is near to death, as she utters the first words of the Lord's Prayer in desperate piety. Here Example 42a is strained to a point where the language of music is almost broken, by the double tension: both that of the appalling, bitter conflict within her body as she still resists death, and that between her and Kolenatý's remorseless insistence on his beliefs.

Don't lie!
You are Emilia Marty,
you stole that medallion from Eugenia Montez!
We know everything . . .

He repeats the last line four times, gibbering like a madman— for he is deaf to the orchestra which we can hear gathering itself in expression of her inner conflict—and asks for the last time:

What is your name?

In the orchestra the *věc* joins him in its last, most ferocious attack. And they lose; for as she sinks to the ground in the first phases of death, she utters the truth, for the first time with total acceptance; and in the tenderness with which, after all the strain, Example 42a points the line, we hear that she has become herself at last:

Elina
Makro—pulos

She is carried into an inner room, where she loses for ever the form and romantic appearance of Emilia Marty. Example 43 bursts out viciously in the orchestra, celebrating with final savagery the cruel joke which life has played on her and on her world; but it is abruptly stilled. And now a solo violin gradually gathers the whole orchestra into maestoso contemplation of Example 42a. We hear the return, after all the deception, intrigue and turbulence, of calm and assurance with the emergence of truth. An adolescent girl, buried for three hundred years by science, is reborn in this interlude. And as the triumphal close is reached, Elina Makropulos stands before us, like a shade or phantom, but unmistakably herself; for in succumbing to age she has regained her youth. Her first words embrace her fate.

I knew, that death was reaching out for me.
It has not been so terrible.

She speaks not merely to, or for, the stage audience. At the moment of acceptance in which Elina begins her *apologia*, Janáček instructs that both stage and auditorium be flooded with green light. We are all to share unblenching in the closing moments of this opera: the harsh wisdom which Elina has learnt and which lends her authority is not to be thrust on us from outside. The four male characters who remain onstage are reduced to a purely choric function, standing for us no less than the chorus (in the pit) which will echo her harshest truths on our behalf. Of the characters who have played parts in Čapek's intricate plot, only Krista remains real in Janáček's finale. And now even she sings only a token line of knowingly inadequate apology, attempting like the men to find words for that which cannot be spoken, the depth of wrong done in ignorance by mortals to the suffering Marty. But Krista is entitled to express a sympathy with Elina which the men who have persecuted her cannot; and it is the empathy established here which informs the final, agonized moments of the opera.

The remainder is in three parts. In the first, a mood of deeper penetration sets in, and Elina describes us all, elaborating the contrast which separates her, in her superhuman anguish, from mankind—with whom she yet feels an affinity which can enable her to understand. She propounds the paradox at the root of all human existence:

> Here you all are
> and it's as if you did not exist,
> you're just things and shadows
> dying or living
> it's all one, it's the same thing!

Mortality has laid its hand on her, and the music conveys both her spiritual agony and the difficulty with which she speaks, as if through the veils of time. The voice is that of authority: these are words whose ruthless truth we cannot challenge. But her agony leads to a wholly new animation as she propounds the other half of the paradox, that which divides her from us.

> Oh, if only you knew how easy it is for you to live!
> You are so near to everything!
> For you, everything has sense!
> Fools, you are so lucky!
> Because of the idiotic chance
> that you die so soon!
> You believe in humanity, achievement, love!
> There's nothing more you can want!

The music moves here with ever-increasing harshness; each statement sounds as if forced out by a paralysed effort from a will suffering, bitterly conscious of the gulf that is being opened. And Janáček adds a central irony, paving the way for the ambiguity of the close. His chorus, acting for us in the orchestra pit, accept humbly her first verdict, that we are mere shadows, transient mortals; but in this passage they join her with hideous animation: 'Fools,' they proclaim complacently, 'We are so lucky'; 'We can want no more.'

The polarity is complete. There can be no greater separation than that between this accepted self-satisfaction and Elina's torment. The music therefore comes to an abrupt, bitter halt, and the chorus are heard no more. But now, in the second part of the finale, Elina's insights have brought her to a point where she may come to terms at last with the *věc* and with her own fate. The fierce music of the *věc* is reduced to a breathless pathos in the first three bars of Example 44, and it falls on to a dolce, stable form of a figure which has been striving to emerge at moments since the start of the scene. And this music continues, with the calm but inert motion of this phrase of empty peace (44a) gradually overtaken by the yearning cadence of 44b, as the apologia concludes in words terrible in their assault on humanity:

> That dreadful loneliness!
> They're just as useless, Kristina, singing and silence.
> I've grown tired of good things,
> I've grown tired of evil things.
> Tired of the earth,
> tired of the heavens!
> And then one knows, that the soul has died in him.

Elina confesses, in full knowledge of mortality and of immortality; in this appalling final line she recognizes the death of the spirit. And with this, now, her physical death is fully congruent. A firm cadence, therefore, with the closing words; for they elicit an obvious question, asked in cowed chorus by the men on the stage:

> Why then did you come for the *věc Makropulos*?

And with her decision the drama enters its final phase. A phase of terror, for in renouncing the paper Elina offers it to us, and its strangeness and powerful glory sound in the orchestra, beckoning, as she holds it out; while her music of renunciation is transmuted into figures of mounting stridency and desperation as, failing to persuade any of the shadows of men who stand on the stage to accept the *věc*, she turns to the girl with whom she has felt an affinity throughout the opera:

> Nobody wants it?
> You're here, Kristina,
> I took your lover from you

Ex. 44 (3.121:1)

you're beautiful
you take it!
You'll be famous
you will sing like Elian Marty!
Take it girl, take it girl!

The pressure is extreme, the moment a ghastly parody of the last moments of the *Vixen*. Here again we are offered, before the eyes of men, the possibility of a feminine renewal; but not now the renewal of nature, but the outrage, the threat that Krista will succumb. The opera could begin once more: the beauty of Krista, so natural and movingly presented in the first scene, could be frozen and corrupted like Elina's. In her own destruction, Elina turns the whole weight of the opera, of her own tragedy, back on us, threatening to bring Krista down and to continue the perversion of nature.

'Don't take it,' the men shout, not as a rational decision but, in Janáček's setting, almost as a purely emotional reaction. The choice which Krista must make is absolute, and leaves no room for compromise. But here Janáček is at his most enigmatic; for the men speak so much for us in our new knowledge of the limits of mortality, so much in instantaneous reaction, that it is impossible to claim that they influence her choice. And nothing but a general pause of one bar ensues, before she acts. Krista chooses mortality, true renewal; she sets aside Marty's last plea and recognizes the deeper truth of all that has been said and done before. But we never know *why* Krista makes this choice, unless simply because it does renew and redeem, because the spurious gleam of the words of Elina's final appeal is belied by the underlying orchestral music, which threatens her with eternal agony by its fearful development of both elements of Example 44.

And the end is of unparalleled grimness: objective, repressive and harsh, shattering in the pity and terror which its truth evokes. As Elina collapses and Krista burns the document, we all share in the cleansing holocaust of renewal as we have in the apologia—for red light floods the theatre. Like those on stage, we in the audience are crushed into 'overwhelmed silence'; for the fire music, cold and harsh as nothing since the opening scene of this Act, leads without pause into the *grave* final bars in which Elina's abnormal life is crushed into death and the *věc* which was its cause into extinction. At Janáček's most chilling curtain, human mortality and wisdom are restored and nature resumes its course—but brings no joy. Searing, dissonant and rigorously controlled, this music draws its close conclusively from Elina's death, drawing out the most severe implications of Example 44. Krista's choice has redeemed human existence—our own as well as hers: but to what end? The comfort is so late, so transitory as to be minimal. Yet we must live with it, for it is all with which we are left, at the close of Janáček's most profound and shattering drama.

From the House of the Dead

Makropulos was in every way a *tour de force*, the culmination of the direction in which Janáček's operatic energies had been moving since *Jenůfa*. The concentration of the drama on and around a single, central figure of suffering womanhood; the compressed musical argument of abrupt emotional contrasts; the gripping, theatrical and highly effective plot: it is hard to imagine how any of these elements could have been taken further, or used to create another drama so unswerving in its contemplation of the fundamental conditions of life. A regrouping of powers was needed, and Janáček did not begin to write the new opera for over a year—the longest break since the Prague success of *Jenůfa* in 1916.

The result is, on the surface, a complete inversion of all the most successful modes of Janáček's dramaturgy. The last opera is without plot or central figure; and the music, while rivalling *Makropulos* in austerity, dissonance and novelty of texture, is far more episodic; laconic and on occasions bizarre, but less complex and above all slower-paced. The hectic animation and driving quest for the end are gone; in their place *From the House of the Dead* and its companion-piece, the Second String Quartet, exhibit the profound simplicity and spaciousness of a master's last works.

But the surface differences should not be allowed to mask the fundamental similarity of concern. Janáček's last opera is the logical conclusion of his theatre work, a final exploration of the question posed with increasing anguish, and answered with increasing difficulty, in each of its three predecessors: what is the value of humanity, the purpose of existence? Janáček now places his quest among the lowest of men, the criminals in the Siberian prison which is a monstrous perversion of human society, a deprivation of all that makes life worth living and therefore, truly, the house of the dead; and sets beneath his title the answer which justifies all the misery seen in the opera: *V každém tvoru jiskra boží*—in every creature a spark of God.

This truth is demonstrated gradually, elliptically. Dostoevsky's 'Notes' or 'Diary'—the Russian title is ambiguous—are, in the original, an objective record, a chronicle of the sufferings of a world other than our own and the extremes of behaviour to which its unfortunate inhabitants must resort in order to survive. The libretto treats the extended canvas of the novel as if it were a dream; Janáček's opera is a synthesis of fragments. Names, places, events and details of incident are fused together, altered, and merge to form a concise, passionate mosaic, a pattern of action which is no mere documentary. The work is an offering, an emotional gift and a testament to the underlying goodness of man, *from* the house of the dead.

The arrangement of incidents is not haphazard. The orchestral music which precedes the rise of the curtain is neither an overture nor a prelude: it is termed, precisely, an introduction; for by it we are led into the house of the dead, just as in the closing scene we are abruptly and suddenly withdrawn from it. And once within the gates, we learn that prison, although an isolated world, has its own cycles—the rhythms of living death. The prison is a catalyst which brings out the worst of humanity; the ordered patterns of its work, torture and play, by which this is achieved, unfold like the seasons of nature itself. Except for one highly necessary indication, Janáček is vague as to the time of year at which each Act takes place; the effect is that natural rhythms are overshadowed by those of the camp, and these dominate the action in the same way as the patterns of nature which ordered the action of the *Adventures of the Vixen Bystrouška* and *Makropulos*. Act 1, metaphorically, is an autumn and a winter: an introduction to the camp, and a first vision of its violence and cruelty. Act 2, set outside the camp (and with a distant hut on the steppe affording a glimpse of normal human habitation), is a spring and a summer: it includes the Easter celebrations of the convicts, the summer of their entertainment by the play and mime—and the sudden, mocking return at the end of the prison's underlying violence, along with the dusk.

This is an autumnal gesture. And so, as the gates lock behind the prisoners at the close of Act 2, we are thrust indoors for the darkest moments of the opera. The prelude to Act 3 foreshadows both the lowest depths and the ultimate hope of freedom; and in the darkness of night in the hospital, we face the lowest degradation of the whole opera, Šiškov's story: the winter, the purgatory and the night after which 3.ii is a new spring, daylight, and for one convict resurrection, for the others a brief but real vision of the outside world and of freedom.

By these means the narrative structure mirrors, in less than two hours of music, the meaning of a sentence to years inside the prison, and creates a perverted metaphor for our normal life. And this organization is complemented in other ways. Petrovič stands in uneasy, shifting relation to the central energies of the opera; his initial terror, his joy and grief in Act 2, and his freedom in Act 3 are emblematic: we see him as he enters the prison, as a settled prisoner serving his sentence, and at its end. But he is also set apart, both by his aristocratic birth and by his subdued, almost choric function in the action. The effect is that interest in him as a person is blurred to the extent needed to enable his prison career, together with the fate of the wounded eagle— tortured and unable to escape in Act 1, freed from the prison like Petrovič at the close—to stand as the axis round which we apprehend the cycles of the prison's life.

And one more device completes the opera's organization, throwing the routines and torment of prison life into a focus which gives them wider meaning and sharp authority over the most innocent among us. Janáček's increasing preoccupation with the setting of narratives of past events is evident in every previous opera, from Kostelnička's confession to the final scene of *Makropulos*. In this work it is taken even further. Janáček seizes from Dostoevsky's record the stories of the crimes which brought three prisoners to prison, sets them with little alteration, and employs them (together with a fourth, subsidiary narrative in Act 3) as the focal points of each Act. These meditations are related to, and so order, the activities and the prison routine of the remainder of each Act; they both counterbalance the real, violent energies of the prison's life and offer a wider mirror in which they are reflected.

206

Luka's story is one of naked violence, set to music of abrupt gesture, and placed in a military setting little removed from the oppression of the camp itself; it mirrors the tortured world of Act 1, the physical pain which even at that moment Petrovič is undergoing. Skuratov's tale, the focal point of Act 2, is by contrast a romance, broader and more wistful in its musical material, and admitting—like the festive occasion on which it is told—a wider world than that of Luka's army barracks. The story is set among civilians, and is concerned with a crime of passion. And in it heterosexual love, prison's most obvious deprivation, enters the world of the opera, albeit at less than full strength. But in Act 3 the process is completed. In Šiškov's story, the musical treatment is no longer monothematic: Janáček's fullest energies are pressed into the realization of every stage of the narrative, while a wide range of materials captures in action each of the characters whom Šiškov describes. And the story itself is the most extensive of the civilian world's invasions, a complete drama of sexual passion, in which Russian life is summoned before us in its tragic, absolute blend of savagery and sentimentality. As we are told of the death of Akulka, we peer into an abyss. And at the end, the recognition by Šiškov of Filka, Janáček's own invention, completes the chain.

We began with a sense of the otherness of the camp. But it has been undermined. In Act 2, the camp shares simple joys, which we can recognize as the stuff of life; in Act 3, the pain of the wounded prisoners in the hospital merges indissolubly with the sufferings of the characters from the outside world of whom Šiškov speaks; and in the moment of recognition, the two worlds are fused by the meeting, at the point of death, of two who had been men and enemies in the world outside the prison. As the stories have brought 'freedom' more and more near to us, we have been made to realize that brutality and tragic compulsion are not merely the stuff of prison, are not merely due to its deprivation and the intolerable absence of women; that they dominate our world no less. And the fusion of worlds makes the token freeing of Petrovič and the eagle into the outcome which is poetically right. Commandant and convict are equal, dream becomes reality; the prisoners receive a vision of freedom as the eagle comes into his own as 'Tsar of the forests'. Camp and outside world are, for a few moments, one—before the savage dissolution of this unity by the closing march, in which the routines of oppression re-establish their eternal pattern.

But by this time Janáček has vindicated his motto. We have seen the men of the camp at large, and in each successive story we have stared into the depths of a morally more worthless individual; but Janáček illuminates their compulsions, and so elicits our understanding and our compassion even for the unthinking, brutal Šiškov. While at the same time, because of the same music, we now know what is at first sight of the prison so strange. These men are not alien creatures; their world is not merely a perversion of ours, but also a mirror: we are they. In *every* creature a spark of God.

A strangled march emerges out of silence in the most tenuous instrumentation: two powerful restatements, identical with the first but for the completion of the harmony and the addition of the whole of the violin section, insist on the pathos, the intensity of a prisoner's endurance; but in a moment the introduction has turned to mocking, macabre games in which a solo violin, grotesquely inappropriate, leads a desperate search for gaiety. The search is without success: the continuing dialogue between the march and the play leads to increasing tension, and only later—just before figure 6—to a tentative attempt at calm and at true emotion. This is undermined at once, by the lengthy, ugly but rigorously logical quest for the fanfares which finally emerge in the horns at figure 7. They speak of joy and freedom, but their development brings only a desperate dissonance, which counters the power of their most strident, maestoso assertion, and then a delirious, violent presto. This leads to the climax of the introduction, a new maestoso in which the fanfares return, now enunciated purely by the trumpets under gentle figurations which speak for a few brief moments of a glimpse of freedom, a vision of joy arching above the sorrow and desperate aspirations of all we have heard so far. But this vision is cruelly undermined. In the closing allegro, the march returns at full force; the clatter of chains recurs, literal reminder of the confinement of human aspirations which is at the centre of the opera, now allied for the first time to the march. The effect is to subdue the fanfare, transform its energies into bitterness. The close is crushing: it removes all hope.

Our journey is complete; for we could not be introduced more completely to the world of the prison than by the manner in which the march recurs, more ominous and more crushing at each reappearance, successfully obliterating playfulness, delirium and finally hope as if none of them had any chance of permanence in the world of the opera. This is the house of living death; and at the end of the opera, though we escape and are sent out the wiser, it remains intact, persisting as savagely in the strident, perverted march of the opera's closing moments as in the dragging, hysterical struggles of this march at the end of the introduction. And now we are not released; on the contrary, the curtain rises at once on the courtyard of the prison, to an apocalyptic outcry of pain:

Ex. 45 (1.0:1)

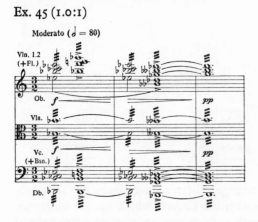

—a drastic gesture expressive both of anguish and of the plea for relief, which recurs like a signature of the violence which dominates the opera. And entering the house of the dead, acknowledging in this first instant the absolute nature of its horror, Janáček intones a prayer. A solo oboe quotes, with only minute alteration, the melody to which, in his *Glagolitic Mass*, he had recently set the words 'Gospodi pomiluj'—'Lord, have mercy on us.' The sun rises, and Janáček snatches from this fact also a kind of consolation; the melody rises higher and higher. But it is dissolved. A side-drum sounds—its dry, neutral texture speaks at once for the inhumanity of the camp; and the prisoners emerge for the day.

Ex. 46 (1.1:1)

As they come out, a strange, bitter phrase (Example 46) alternates in the orchestra with the prayer, which sounds out twice
more, at each appearance with greater compassion—before it is
crushed. Example 46 soon predominates, and is then succeeded
by grotesque presto figurations of grating dissonance which
vividly convey the violence and the distortion of personality
which are the burden of the camp. Most of the prisoners, we are
reminded in a stage direction, are silent and brooding. And the
implication is brought out at once: the constant undertone of
violence erupts into a quarrel between two convicts. This is no
real fight—Dostoevsky records that such quarrels served as
entertainment, and rarely ended in serious violence; and the
stylization of orchestral and vocal gesture shows that the composer has taken Dostoevsky's point. But there is more to the
music: a remorseless insistence and edge convey that the quarrel

is an attempt to release the prison's otherwise intolerable tensions.

Act I proceeds by alternation: Janáček constructs a dialogue between contemplation of the camp and illumination of what it does to its inmates. This incident stands at the start of the opera, containing in itself all the aggressiveness and strain which the prison imposes. And now Janáček develops his dramatic argument by making Petrovič enter. The orchestra gathers suddenly on a maestoso stab of pain; and we see the prison for a few moments through his emotions, those of one contemplating this eternally repeated scene for the first time. Time seems to stand still, as a solo violin, joined tentatively by flutes and cor anglais, meditates on the prison, helps us to absorb what we have seen. With absorption comes compassion, and a soaring meditation by the violin, vastly separated from the darkest colours of trombones, celli and basses—as if we, like Petrovič, were gazing into a bottomless pit. But the spell is broken; as the small convict comments, the angular, dissonant figurations of the first presto intrude, now slow but insidious, and break the flight of the violin. The enormity of imprisonment is yet too large for us to grasp; the reality of the prison's activities obtrudes on Petrovič; and the orchestra descends once more to the sinister neutrality of a side-drum.

This heralds the resumption of routine. And as this is Act I, our introduction to the cruelty of the prison, Janáček has Petrovič bear the force of the commandant's worst brutality. The implications of the orchestral introduction, the dialogue between hope and oppression are now drawn out. We see a man reduced, all traces of human dignity removed by a gratuitous sadist who has absolute power over him. The orchestra assumes a hideous, distorted gaiety, menacing where it is not simply stark in abrupt, descriptive gesture as the commandant's abuse gains its own momentum. Towards the end, as the commandant pulls Petrovič's beard, strained elements of increasing contempt enter the upper orchestra; the hiatus between the emotional intensity of the upper lines and the perpetual tension in the bass becomes more and more extreme, and the tenuous threads of humanity which bind even a commandant to a convict suddenly break.

A hundred lashes! Right this moment.

The orchestra spares us nothing when Petrovič is led away.

Example 46 returns over a disturbing viola tremolo, as if to tell us that even this extreme torment is part of the normal routine of the prison; excruciatingly protracted trills prepare us for the moment at which his cries of pain are heard; and at the moment when his agony begins Example 45 returns in the upper orchestra, completing the fierce, bitter purpose of the scene. By this gesture Petrovič is initiated into the house of the dead: the musical outrage which we were forced to experience as the rise of the curtain joined us to the prison has now been turned to dramatic reality. After which the closing phrase of Example 46 returns, limping, crippled, under a chillingly strained chord. Gently repeated, and echoed softly by the drums, it closes the episode with a desperate, fragile peace.

Except for Aljeja—whose affinity for Petrovič is established by his anxiety during the flogging—the prisoners are indifferent to his suffering. But the return of Example 46, to which they themselves hobbled on to the stage, has already shown his kinship to them, the way in which his sufferings stand for those which they have each endured here already; and this is pointed up by the parallel which is now formed between him and the eagle. For a few minutes a real animation enters the yard, as the eagle's freedom, the independence which birds have and men have not, gives some spirit to the prisoners; but the irony is, in this first Act of the opera, too strong for this mood to survive. Even as they cry out, 'Eagle, tsar of the forests', the eagle struggles with his broken wing, and the music limps with him. It is not because they are 'just people' that the eagle is different from the prisoners, but because they are trapped. So too, now, is this eagle. He embodies all the pathos of their situation. Men—even convicts—*are* like eagles, capable of soaring high at least in imagination. We have now seen the suffering of the convicts—Petrovič's flogging is as emblematic of this as the initial quarrel was of their violence. And the eagle's wound embraces all that we have seen; the torments which some prisoners inflicted on him as the opera opened remind us that cruelty is endemic in all humanity, by echoing in miniature the remorseless brutality of the commandant. He now returns, harrying them off to work; and this cements the link between the harassed, suffering convicts—all of them—and the wounded eagle.

And now that all this has been established, the true peace

which is so desperately needed can come, a more profound contemplation than has been possible before Petrovič and the eagle have revealed, literally and metaphorically, the extent of their suffering. Example 45 is developed at length, in spacious, open dialogue between the calm, resigned acceptance by the chorus of prisoners of their fate, and the orchestra's increasingly anguished interventions, which draw out the pathos of their situation. By the time that the outside working party has faded into the far distance, their suffering has been totally absorbed.

Here the dramaturgy becomes more complex. From the facts of prison life Janáček turns for the first time to the reasons for the convicts' suffering. But to do so he does not proceed directly, even now, to the first of the opera's narratives. Twice the recurrences of Example 45 swell back to their original violence, and each time Skuratov breaks into a fragment of song. For him, the pain of his imprisonment has led to madness. Skuratov has become mad because he is the only prisoner who admits to and feels the desperate failure of his life, and the pathos of his loss of freedom. But the power of the next episode is not generated merely from the pathos of his fate. Snatches of song alternate, in his exchanges with Luka, with moments of sanity. And in them there is a true desire to be kind, and a true warmth.

Luka rebuffs them roughly—as he has to, for to accept such feeling is to court the danger of sharing Skuratov's own fate. But the madman's humanity is still a real humanity, and when the prison finally overwhelms Skuratov (Example 45 again rising in agonized crescendo) there is an emptiness to the scene, a sense of loss. Although apparently ignoring Skuratov's collapse, Luka gradually fills the silence, being drawn by introversion into giving the first of the opera's extended monologues. Spaces of emptiness left by the departure of the working party and the end of Skuratov's animation evoke yearning orchestral phrases which gradually, gently mature into a narrative. The nearness to a sense of loss makes him compassionate: he recalls first, not merely his own imprisonment, but the sufferings of an old man, weeping in court for his innocence and his lost children; and the orchestral phrasing recalls, now muted and sympathetic, the violent maestoso forces which overcame Skuratov. Convicts are driven either to madness or to violence by their sentence.

Luka himself is a man of violence. The brutal indifference of

213

the judge, endlessly scribbling, is heard to break the rising phrases of the old man's yearning; the downward flourishes of the orchestra show his scribbling as a rejection, a literal condemnation which unites the old man, near to madness, with Luka, driven to violence. Example 45 therefore returns, plangent and muted. 'So too fell my own head.' And his narrative begins. It is an attempt to explain his fall. But as it unfolds it becomes far more, a precise statement of the way in which violence breeds more violence; and through this, at its close, a union between all the energies of Act 1.

The abrupt melody (little more than an obsessive pattern) which expresses the major's confident persecution generates aggressive, falling fragments in major seconds which simply alter their inflection as the narrative unfolds: they turn upwards and gather continuous force as we hear how Luka resolved to approach him, a concealed knife in his hand, and fragment again with the major's arrogant attempts to repress his subordinate. Then they gather again in sinuous upward movement to express the consequences. The music shows the two men as bound directly and indissolubly in action and reaction. With the description of the murder, Example 45 sounds out with the fullest force, and then again, more muted. This gesture prefigures the implication of the entire opera: violence is not merely the prerogative of the camp, men drive their fellow-men to desperation in the world outside, and so lead the perpetrators to the house of the dead.

The music captures this point directly, and impresses it on us; for as soon as the murder is described and the major has fallen, the march from the introduction sounds out twice, plaintive and incomplete. This is its only recurrence in the body of the opera; and it tells how his crime has led Luka to the prison. The remainder of the Act now, after this moment of sharp crystallization, gathers all the threads of violence together, establishing a complete congruence between narrative and stage action. Luka's own act bred immediate retaliation; the scene dissolves in increasing anguish as he describes his own flogging. And this too ends in the renewed onset of Example 45, now in an almost unbearable, heightened reinforcement which pirouettes in triumph round the narrative of agony, Luka's extreme torture as the executioner's sadism reaches the heights already achieved on

stage by the commandant. The tutti swells to a gigantic fortissimo.

But Luka survived.

LUKA: I thought I was dying.
A VERY OLD CONVICT: And did you?

The irony is precise. Literally, of course, Luka is alive; but only
literally, for he is in the house of the dead; and in the final
moments of the Act it closes in. Guards return bringing Petrovič,
crippled by his flogging as was Luka. The violence has now
become so appalling, so extensive and unmitigated, that at this
stage of the opera there can be no release. A protracted tutti
counsels despair, suggests that the only adequate reaction is
madness—for the old convict's comment evokes the melody of
Skuratov's brief, lunatic vision of freedom, and it gradually turns
sour, infecting the entire orchestra and closing the Act in total,
desperate ferocity.

 Ex. 47 (2.0:1)

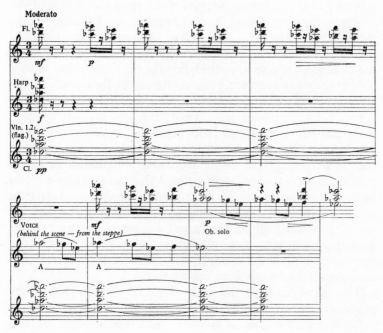

The opening calls us immediately to a new, different attention. These bars establish a clarity that is no longer harsh, and as the voice from the steppe is gradually doubled by caressing tones of violins and clarinets the audience is called to a wider world than that of the prison. The voice is that of freedom—but it is right that it should be supported so tenuously, and should fade away long before the curtain rises. Sunshine and blue sky appear then, together with the endless perspective of the steppe; but the contact of the prison with the outside world can only be a fragile, delicate one. The steppe offers a glimpse of freedom, and the voice is its call; but the scene is also daunting because of its vastness, which is the safest guarantee that no serious attempt at escape can be made. And the wordless song is as much a pastoral of melancholy as of freedom: it is sad and inconclusive. Ironically, there is almost a relief, a fruitful development when the same melody returns in harsher transformations, accompanied by the clatter of tools, the sound of a saw and busy figurations of repetitive activity in the strings. The yearning is transmuted into the practical vigour of the prisoners' labour; and a real, simple gaiety is achieved in the gathering energies of the prelude's closing phase.

The contrast in this orchestral introduction foreshadows the mood of the whole Act. Here, with an outdoor setting, guests and even a prostitute mingling with the prisoners, the world is at its most physically present, surrounding the convicts in their chains. And every scene contrasts yearning for life in the outside world, attempts to share its delights and joys, with the realities of the convicts' Easter celebrations. Their true pleasures are simpler, more harshly etched and more limited. Janáček implies that prisoners are bound to a world in which memory stirs the most painful longings, but here we are shown by contrast that even prison has its own joys, and in these themselves there is some value. None the less all this is gradually overshadowed, and the power of the coda finally submerges it. After the play and the mime, dusk gradually closes in and a series of precisely drawn vignettes bring out all the undertones of violence which confinement can never fail to imply, and which have not been buried far beneath the surface even during this Act.

The first episode is the most direct illustration of how the prisoners are trapped by the setting; the festive atmosphere provokes recall of life in freedom, and this in itself leads to heightened emotion. Petrovič's affectionate questions induce Aljeja to speak of his sister, and the warmth of the music becomes gradually infected with strain as he recalls her beauty. This makes him think also of his mother, and again the stabs of pain are heard in the orchestra, immediate counter to the warmth of the horn melody underlying Petrovič's kindly attempt to draw him out. Reminiscence generates more reminiscence, and under the pressure of real emotion the orchestra shows Aljeja's pain as becoming ever more intense, more fragile and vulnerable:

> By now she must surely have died of grief.
> She used to love me even more than she loved my sister. . . .
> Last night she came to me, and wept over me.

Intensity is, in prison, no guarantee of permanence. The emotions collapse as abruptly as they came, and the sounds of the other convicts at work break in more and more forcibly. There is ironic contrast; futile though their task is, the music for their work becomes more and more vigorous and joyful as they succeed at it; and this music ends with cries of anticipation of the holiday which temporarily remove from our minds (as from theirs) all thought of the pathos of imprisonment, through the intensity of their relief.

Now a wholly new dimension intrudes. Janáček proceeds to build up an introduction to the Easter holiday; and in it, the degree of meaning which these few moments of relief have to the prisoners becomes apparent. Words are useless to convey such feelings; the cook's passing remark is simply a cue on which to hang the extensive orchestral illumination. And this is conveyed by a dialogue between ecstasies, spiritual and temporal. Deep bells from the distance, accompanied only by a delicate oscillation in the violas, establish a mood of Orthodox piety; against them a soaring figure, first carried by the violins in their highest register, is tossed between the upper instruments. This being Janáček, there is no tension between the two musics: their coexistence soon leads to amalgamation, smaller bells sounding out from the fortress until the whole orchestra is united in a raucous, festive march as the commandant arrives. And after the march, a deeper joy. All is stilled as the priest blesses the feast and the river; the lowest bells return, in hushed, sacred dialogue with double-bass harmonics which gradually rise to almost unplayable heights.

217

PRIEST: I greet you on this holiday!
CONVICTS (*crossing themselves*): And we too give you greetings!

The energies of the musical dialogue are released; the orchestra tumbles over itself as prisoners and guests set to their feast. The accompaniment goes out of its way to expose the degree to which the occasion inverts the prison's normal values: fragments of the commandant's processional march are repeated over and over, without any incongruity; a side-drum, elsewhere in the opera the most sinister of instruments, now conveys merely the feverish excitement of this unique joy; and on this day of celebration even Skuratov is near to sanity. As the passionate flow of the first moments of the feast dies down, we are given a story whose simplicity and romance blend well with the atmosphere, the true festivity which has now come about; but which, equally, returns us to higher consciousness of the convicts' plight, bringing with it as it unfolds deeper insight into human calamity.

With one exception, the convicts listen fascinated: they demand the story from Skuratov, assist in restraining the drunken convict who feels compelled to interrupt, and are so involved by the end that they need to release the tension by breaking into desperately gay songs. Skuratov's story brings with it humanity: the compassion which he elicits from us is given equally by the convicts, and in this way *their* essential humanity is shown. Here they are not under the intense pressures of the camp's normal régime; and this, together with his humanity, is why they show an interest in Skuratov which contrasts with their indifference, in the two outer Acts, to Luka and Šiškov. Even the drunken convict's interjections, apparently born of an obsessive need to deny, aid this picture—none but a drunkard would oppose the truths which lie behind Skuratov's imprisonment and his bursts of madness; and the drunkard's opposition, the music implies, is that of one who finds these truths too hard to bear.

Ex. 48 (2.13:1)

This melody dominates the greater part of the monologue. Its simplicity and purity are absolute; and as the story unfolds it comes to define the limits of the happiness which Skuratov is able to attain, gradually gaining an association with Luise, the simple girl who would, in a juster world, have been ideal for him.

Ours is less generous. At first the melody flows placidly on, showing the normality and sanity of Skuratov's emotions. At moments a part of it indicates completely, by its inflection, the feelings of the characters in the story: (a) aspiring upward as Skuratov describes how he sought, found and fell in love with Luise; the same phrase reaching the heights as he aspired to take her physically, turning downward as she gently rejected this, gathering again in placid upward inflections as she asked him to marry her. (b) has other implications. Janáček makes Skuratov exclaim ironically, rejecting Luise's proposal as absurd; and a renewed attack of the drunkard's incredulity is allied to repeated recurrences of (b), which colour the music darkly as the story begins to oppress Skuratov and his hearers.

The central section of the story evokes new material. Sinister figurations chronicle Skuratov's disturbance, his anxiety when Luise did not come to him; and their endless descents take us to the point of tragedy. Weeping, Luise confesses that she has been promised to another; Example 48 sounds as a whole, high in the strings and doubled at the octave, to express the extreme of this anguish. For a moment, man and woman were united in the misery of the need to separate. And with cruel irony the orchestra falls from the heights, angular and defeated, at the very moment when Skuratov tells of the last time at which Luise embraced him. An emptier mystery is all that is left, as Skuratov goes on to describe his growing wonderment at the ugliness of the man to whom he had lost his girl.

Reliving his experience, he is moved to tears—which the drunken convict feels provoked to ridicule. The violence and impotence of Skuratov's predicament in the story invade the stage action, and he subdues the drunkard. Then the narrative resumes its course—but now the peace of the return of Example 48 is short-lived. The last note of the phrase is protracted, conveying the endless time as Skuratov learnt that he could see Luise no more; with his decision to go, and take a gun, this endlessness becomes strain; the motif sounds out ironically, in the highest register of the violins. Its self-parody conveys the destruction of illusions. And now there is no smooth flow. The rest is illuminated in gestures, first identically repeated, violent sforzandi to illustrate the paralysis imposed on the wedding guests by Skuratov's arrival, and then an angular march (Example 49) supported by strangely harmonized and orchestrated chords which undermine the apparent reasonableness of Skuratov's words of greeting and of his melody: they illustrate the mounting desperation with which Skuratov attempted to control his anger.

Ex. 49 (2.20:1)

Provocation by the bridegroom leads to further sforzandi, again indicating the tension; and as Skuratov tells how he shot his rival, Example 49 sounds out stridently in the orchestra, now with full clarity. Janáček has shown how Skuratov threw off his mask, released his tension.

—And lost Luise. The composer now illuminates the intolerable pathos of this forced, desperate *crime passionel* by reminding us of the essential simplicity of the man whom we have heard driven to such bizarre extremes. Example 48 recurs, in its purest form. Skuratov was condemned. 'And Luise?' 'O, Luise!' The melody breaks, Skuratov goes crazy with grief, and the convicts break out into wild songs, oblique, strange snatches of melody in

220

which they attempt to sublimate the impact of his story. Only with the beginning of the play are they set back in order; and this provides us with what appears to be relief.

The intrusion of the outside world in Skuratov's story has turned to tragedy, and by contrast we are now given a 'comic' treatment, an ironic parallel to the tragic drama of sexual love which has just been narrated to us. But the entertainment focuses centrally on the prison's deprivations. As prisoners in their chains enact the adventures of Don Juan and the story of the miller's beautiful wife, we are made acutely aware of their constriction and of the absence of women from their world; and although the other prisoners are seen to enjoy the play and mime, their underlying tensions are brought out in the coda to the Act, where these 'plays within a play' have a direct influence on the convicts. Furthermore, both stories are pathetic, and their outcomes end in failure or delusory triumph for the Don; and the music does more than match this mood. That for the play is fussy, busy and with an undertone of hysteria even in the few moments of grace; while the only melody of real feeling, that to which the Don finally defies the devils, is undermined by Kedril's mocking laughter, which becomes shared by the convicts in the stage audience.

The pantomime is more elevated. An elegant clarinet melody undergoes ingenious transformations as the miller's wife engages in her series of constantly frustrated liaisons; and at the end Don Juan's defiance, when he is finally discovered and forced to abandon his disguise, is more protracted than in the play: it becomes the heroic waltz of a man determined on defiance in the face of damnation.

There is thus considerable point when the alternation of chords which closes this waltz (and with it the prisoners' entertainment) is transmuted to become a gentle undulation of flutes and violins, expressive of the nature of the dusk which now concludes the day. And the transformation is not to be forgotten. As Aljeja expresses his enjoyment of the show, a tentative grace is achieved in the orchestra; but it is undermined immediately. The tensions which the play and mime have created find release in various ways. One young convict goes off into the shadows with a very ugly prostitute, to grotesque, graceless music: a parody of love. Others sublimate. Sighs are heard from the barracks—and the orchestral accompaniment is that of Juan's failed defiance, now transformed to despair: the misery of the camp begins to return, in these wordless cries of yearning for freedom; and the sighs become the underlay to a tiny vignette scene, half-paradox, half-truth, almost a summary of all the sadness of the prison:

ŠAPKIN: Old Antonič, God save you! God save you!
A VERY OLD CONVICT: If you're not joking, sit down!
ŠAPKIN: I thought that you were dead!
VERY OLD CONVICT: You'll die first, and I will follow you.

As Antonič utters the last line, the phrase of aspiration from the Juan music which lies beneath the prisoners' sighs reaches a cadence at last; with Antonič's wisdom we hear that one prisoner at least is totally reconciled to the pain and the strangeness of the camp. But as Antonič's rejoinder to Šapkin implies, other convicts, not so old, are not so reconciled.

The mood of yearning and aspiration develops further, as Luka's sad song puts into eloquent words the pain and longing of the chorus's inarticulate sighs; and in the small convict, yearning becomes resentment. Three parallel orchestral lines of protracted notes, menacing in their strained, wide separation, gather into a continuous motion which refuses to let us go, is fed by the momentary approval of some other prisoners, and cannot be calmed by Petrovič's true, humane generosity. Once again the sad song of longing is heard, now sung from the barracks by Čekunov—and this, the call of confinement twice reiterated with the highest pathos, generates the end. The orchestra is united in a strained fortissimo: two sustained semibreve chords force us to hear how the small convict's resentment gathers new menace, and new precision. The parallel motion now spurs him to increasing self-assertion, as his mind circles in mounting anger round the aristocratic luxury of drinking tea; and the end can only be the return of violence. Aljeja is desperately wounded; the orchestra explodes; the guards drive the prisoners back into the camp; and the melody to which the convicts hail Aljeja's deliverance from death twice struggles to rise—but is forced back by the ferocious, neutral hatred expressed in the dominating timbre of the solitary side-drum to which the curtain falls.

Act 3 begins with a sinister murmur, in the lowest strings. And the melody which the upper instruments begin in the third bar is tenuous in the extreme, easily undermined by violence, which soon forces it to lead to figurations of increasing anguish. This is the dark night of the opera, both metaphorically and literally: here in the hospital, Janáček's quest for the 'spark of God' is at its most acute, following the failure in which the Easter celebrations ended. There, it is implied, the hope of joy was too easy, and the attainment so shot through with the bitter alienation of prison from the real world that a disastrous close was unavoidable. Janáček must go deeper; and the opera is now locked not merely into the prison but into its hospital. Here, against a background of intermittent cries of agony from the patients, we hear two stories, each of which takes its narrator to the limits of psychological suffering. Šapkin's is a straightforward chronicle of physical persecution, a textual counterpoint to the agonies we see on the stage and which culminate in the ferocious outburst of Example 45 as Skuratov is subdued. And with this further intense penetration of human misery, our picture of the camp is complete: the lights are put down, and Janáček contemplates the scene in a plangent quartet for violin, clarinet, flute and bass clarinet.

But the prelude to this Act has not promised only suffering. The strangled, urgent tones of the opening yielded rapidly to soaring outbursts, fanfares and animated woodwind figurations which recall the most vigorous sections of the introduction to the opera as a whole; a promise of freedom which is redeemed. After the lights have faded, the quartet breaks out into a powerful plea, in octave violins: a new dawn seems to be breaking. 'Lord, have mercy on us,' the old convict intones; and the spacious setting in which Šiškov's story opens comes as if in answer to his prayer.

That story is of course the most extensive, and the most finely realized, of Janáček's operatic narratives. And its role is to bring the outside world back before us; without it, and the shattering intensity in which it closes, the return to light and air, and the freeing even of one token convict would be an illogical, undeservedly joyful ending to Janáček's posthumous tragedy. In Šiškov's account of the circumstances in which he murdered Akulka, all the threads of the opera are gathered together and

FROM THE HOUSE OF THE DEAD

fuse, in his recognition of Filka Morozov, into the central knot after which we may be released. In him, we confront the most worthless and wanton of murderers, a man whom we find, if we consult Dostoevsky, to have been among the most despised and hated of the prisoners. But his actions are invested with understanding by this music: Janáček makes sense even of Šiškov, and by doing so gives our sympathy even to a thoughtless, impulsive man of extreme violence. But more. In this story, prison and outside world become truly united. The sighs and moans of the prisoners, turning in their sleep, come to represent the sufferings of the characters in Šiškov's story; and by this simple musical device a profound point is established, the kinship of convict and 'free' man. Again we are prepared for the finale, the temporary union of worlds which is 3.ii—a union prefigured by the climactic scene of recognition, in which for the first time two who have been linked in the world beyond are linked together in the house of the dead.

That link is forged in hatred. And this fact leads to the third, most devastating contribution of Šiškov's story. It is a tragedy of men and women who inhabit separate worlds, people who are in the deepest sense unable to communicate. The near-incoherence —in the libretto—of its psychology is a pointer; even Šiškov himself can hardly interpret his own actions and those of the other protagonists in his story. Their musics glare at each other, developing under the influence of opposition in such a way as to make the outcome inexorable but at the same time framed so as to make completely plain that theirs is a world of irreconcilable divisions. It is for this reason, I believe, that the music of *From the House of the Dead* comes here nearest to breakdown; that there is in this story a feeling that Janáček is at the very limits of his resources. To confront truth, without harshness or sentimentality; to avoid any element of escapism or fantasy: all this is enough, given the chosen setting of the opera, to confirm finally —if this were needed—the height of Janáček's achievement. But to dramatize this story, to attempt to make sense of a series of experiences which, in the ultimate reckoning, do not make sense: this is the composer's most far-reaching achievement. And it is necessary.

From the chilling reality with which Janáček confronts this almost inexplicable disaster comes the power of the ending to

224

the entire opera. There, Janáček is armed with the strength
which he has extracted from this story—and in particular from
his unswerving contemplation of the murder of Akulka, surely
the most revolting event chronicled in these operas—and with
this armour he confronts the realities of separation. 3.ii rebuffs
Forster's 'only connect' as a trivial inadequacy. No opera has
attempted to establish human communication in more extreme
circumstances than this one; at moments, Janáček has even
abnegated his customary objectivity in almost desperate attempts
to bear the fate of each man on to other men. The opera's motto
is vindicated: moral strength is to be seen in the simple facts of
existence—humanity, harmony with nature, acceptance of
mortality. But this meaning is circumscribed as in no previous
drama. In the ending of this opera, the act of renewal—Petrovič's
freedom, the eagle's escape—is bound indissolubly with the pain
of separation. We have our *jiskra boží*; but the freedom for
which the prisoners cry is as far beyond our grasp as beyond
theirs. Connection is impossible. Ultimately, we must part. All
are alone: if not now, at the moment of death.

Aljeja has learnt to read. Feverish, he remembers the words of
Jesus:

Forgive, do no harm, love!

but this ideal is as far from his grasp as the flight of a bird.
Reading has brought him nothing but the heightened realization
of what cannot be attained; the anguished figurations of the
Act's prelude mount higher and higher, in increasing torment—
and then collapse, in hopeless, fading ambition. The vignette is
succeeded by another cameo: again one of humanity and rejection, Luka against Čekunov. The argument appears futile; but
we are now worlds away from the sparring of the large and the
small convict in Act 1. Luka is dying, Čekunov offering a simple
service to two other convicts; and in their dialogue truth becomes
revealed. Čekunov forces Luka to abandon his illusions. 'Since
God has laid you low, lie there and die!' This is not the rejection
of callousness: Čekunov has already shown his own humanity in
the delicate orchestration of his ministration to Aljeja; and the
futility of Luka's defiance is complete. Fierce sforzandi show his
words of anger crushed by the pain of his coughing; the old

convict's call for the Lord's mercy on him seems nothing but appropriate. Defiance is useless in the face of death.

Indeed, it brings pain throughout the world. Janáček chooses to make Šapkin take his cue from Luka's sufferings to tell his story, final illustration of the sadism which is at the root of all the suffering that men can impose on other men. Before we are to be released, we must hear once more a story of meticulous detail of torture. In its accompaniment, reality and fantasy, extreme and normality are mingled, blending eventually in the path to the most hideous suffering. From the tentative, compassionate joys of Šapkin and his fellow-tramps we are transported through the self-feeding brutalities of interrogation to the near-madness with which the chief of police tugged relentlessly at Šapkin's ear. Janáček offers us the explanation of the violence in the text only when the torture has become so extreme that variants of Example 45, albeit muted, have returned under the rising motif of anguish.

And the lunacy of which he speaks now spreads elsewhere in the hospital. In this most nightmarish of Acts, Skuratov is mad: the eternal pressure of Example 45 generates an abrupt, savage recall of the phrases which illuminated his madness in Act 1, and the climax of his deed now obsesses him to such an extent that even Luise's name evokes none of the gentler material of his narrative from Act 2. The most predominant element of these figurations persists in the xylophone even after he has been subdued, and for the first time since Act 1 the tutti bursts out in naked, uncompromising outcry: Example 45 at fullest strength in the original form, totally embracing the madness and misery which have infected the hospital at this darkest moment of the opera.

The agony seems relentless, beyond all redemption. But the sick convicts are exhausted; and as the lights go down and they settle down to sleep, peace descends on the scene. The peace brings not further despair but a new dawn: Janáček's orchestral meditation passes from compassion to vigour. When the peace returns at the close of the interlude, with the old convict's despairing prayer and his knowledge that he will never see his children again, this darkness has already been overset: the central section of the interlude has prefigured a new radiance. And as the fullest visual darkness surrounds the characters, and gently falling phrases of violas and harp transport us musically into the world of Šiškov's story, the effect is to take us away from the house of the dead. The darkness of the stage enables the music to focus the fullest light on Šiškov's story, and on the comments of Čerevin. Here there is virtually no dramatic counterpoint between story and stage action: there is no stage action, and the sleeping convicts become, except at one moment, absorbed into the musical devices of the narrative.

This has two purposes. Firstly, we do indeed seem to be entering a spacious, open world as Šiškov's narrative begins. With the introduction of Akulka's father, Akulka herself and Filka Morozov three rich, highly contrasted characters enter the opera's dramaturgy. And therefore we can be said to have truly left the prison for the first time, to be entering our own outside world in a complete realization. But the story ends in almost unspeakable agony, and at the climax stage action resumes with vengeance, in the moment of recognition; our escape has been delusory not merely in the sense that the story turns from light to dark, but that the darkness leads us back into the world of the camp. And there is the final irony which completes the opera's meaning. The story's violence is as savage as that of the camp: we are no better than they. Indeed, we are the same: the reasons for the story's tragic outcome are exactly the same as those for each of the appalling events which we have seen inside the camp.

It is a tragedy of inability to communicate. This is evident at once, in the opening scene. The rich old merchant, Akulka's father, moves among his contemporaries with confident, expansive ease—disregarding their penury even as they hang on his every word. The orchestra chronicles his progress with the grace he would doubtless have felt it deserved, and the respectful greetings of his inferiors have to be squeezed as best they can into the breathing-spaces of the melody. His sons are of no importance—and the music clearly tells us that they are cast in the same image as their father. Akulka, however, is very different. The music halts abruptly before she is introduced (Example 50). The implications of this music cannot be misconstrued. Akulka is unutterably, tenderly beautiful—but, equally, she is an impenetrable mystery, a woman so vulnerable and so determined to guard her inward privacy that she shields the sources of the aspiration, the longing and the tragic delicacy implied by this

Ex. 50 (3.11:20)

phrase from all except herself until her life is ruined and concealment has lost its purpose.

There is one more central character—besides the narrator, who takes no immediate part in the action, and indeed is not fully involved until his mother spurs him from rest. Filka Morozov, Šiškov tells us with bitterness, was after Akulka. And the impenetrable chords continue their flow as Luka, dying in a nearby bed, sighs in recognition of his own true name and of his own past life. He too must listen to this story. But his reactions now are not the central focus. His reactions then, however, as Filka, are of the essence. Akulka's chords return for the third time—surely they are by now impressed on our souls as deeply as her personal mystery was impressed on Šiškov's and on Filka; and this time they precipitate the beginning of the action.

Ex. 51 (3.12:11)

228

This melody does nothing to show Filka's character—for that is not revealed to us until the honest, direct confession with which, at the end of the story, he admits to Akulka all the slander which he has heaped on her, and begs her forgiveness. The third protagonist of this drama is, for the bulk of its unfolding, hardly a character at all. Example 51 is directly generated from a penetrating presentation of Akulka's chords; it is cruel, harsh and mocking. The implication is clear: her impenetrability has turned Filka—whoever he was, and we know from Luka's monologue in Act I that he is not a man of peace—to the violence and contempt of attempts to relieve unbearable frustration. And it is that frustration which is expressed by Example 51: its ingenious variants and extensions now chronicle the slanders with which he drove Akulka's father to breakdown; surely, Akulka's music implies, because he has taken her enigmatic impenetrability to be a refusal of him.

Against this, the music has increasingly argued her purity; and when Filka and his friends finally provoke the parents to beat Akulka, Janáček weds the sighs of the sleeping chorus to a muted, tremulous orchestra in the attempt to penetrate the depths of her suffering. Theirs also: the convicts, like the woman, are passive victims.

Šiškov himself enters the story at last—but hardly as an independent agent, since he simply joins in Filka's abuse. Akulka, however, has only to turn her eyes on him—such wide eyes, the text tells us—and the music shows Šiškov to us, peering into their depths. Filka's distorted reaction to Akulka has, up to this point, been Šiškov's also; and her parents are no more capable of penetrating the mystery. They take her to be leading Šiškov on, and abuse her—as Šiškov has—to the same music, Example 51. Again her impenetrability forces others to a mistaken, disastrous reaction; for it is soon clear that there is no such implication. Čerevin, a versatile interlocutor whose questions (at times penetrating, at others naïve) always have the effect of drawing Šiškov out, now asks the crucial question: was she really so easy to get? The character of the music changes at once, and a real flow and clarity invade the orchestra as Šiškov, beginning the phase of the story which will prove Akulka's innocence, at last becomes the protagonist of his own drama. Šiškov is no longer so eager to repress Čerevin's desire to hear the story; he loses the detached objectivity with which he has so far told of all except his hated rival Filka; as his own role becomes central, he becomes animated and involved. And with this involvement comes a humanity which redeems even Šiškov: Janáček shows his self-disgust, shows also that his crime was inevitable.

Šiškov was seduced by Akulka's mystery. The new warmth invades the textures the moment his mother puts the idea of asking to marry her into his head, and it continues to flower in the orchestra, overriding even Filka's contempt for him. We are about to witness the first real human contact to be made in the story: between Šiškov and Akulka. And the music gathers increasing momentum as we are taken from wedding to bridal bed, illuminating the almost unutterable tenderness of the girl:

> she sat there white,
> not a drop of blood in her cheeks,
> hair like flax,
> big eyes,
> as if she were dumb,
> so strange!

and Šiškov's contempt for himself and his brutality; the heart-rending attempt to absorb the fact of Akulka's virginity, the tremulous power of her love, bestowed on her husband as Akulka's only gift to any other human; the uncomprehending outcry of remorse and rage against Filka which we hear that love provoke in him; and the delicate, impassioned, utterly sincere apology when he has calmed that impulse:

> 'Darling Akulina, dear child,
> forgive me!
> I too took you for impure.'

The delicacy which the orchestra has sustained throughout the scene is now transmuted to a gentle, throbbing ostinato. Akulka sits there, in smiles and tears; and both Janáček and Šiškov are alive to the wonder and the beauty of the fact that her first emotion is a paradoxical one. But then their ways part; for Janáček remains totally understanding, while Šiškov loses the humanity and breadth of emotion to which his closeness to Akulka raised him: he can now react only with empty rage. The parents are broken; so too, in a different sense, is Šiškov. His attempt to stand up against Filka is exposed by the music as hollow and histrionic; roughed up by Filka and his cronies, he is too weak to oppose them, or his mother. But he is a violent man, and has the need to release his violence—which he can only do by taking it out on his wife. Hideously ugly music, the brutality of the narrative, the anger of the old convict—roused to curse Šiškov, 'You bastard, dog's flesh!'—bring the section to a halt only when all the convicts for a moment resume a dramatic role, shout at Šiškov to shut up. He concludes in terms of utter self-contempt. 'I was sorry, but I still beat her! Beat her up!' But the music has illuminated the effect of his violence on Akulka. The repentance is too late. As we find out in the final stages of the narrative, she has retreated back from her physical and emotional contact with Šiškov into privacy.

A merciful calm precedes the close. Šiškov for the last time asks his interrogator not to hurry him: the story has taken time to unfold, not merely because of its complexity, but because of its measured extent, our need for clarity and Šiškov's need for calm to take reckoning of himself at each turning-point in the action. But the remainder is bound together by an ever-increasing, irresistible plunge. The initiative is now with Filka; a sparse but real energy emerges in the orchestra, reflecting the narrator's joy at his rival's departure. But the joy is delusory. The orchestral motion gradually becomes more steady and measured as Filka is heard sobering up, beginning his final, triumphal farewells. And when Akulka encounters him there is no interruption to the placid, downward flow of the sustained triads. We recognize with horror that there is nothing tentative about the meeting. It is part—the final part—of Filka's farewell. As he confesses his love and begs forgiveness, the descents merely change their note-value and turn from brashness to stability to match the completeness of his recantation.

'My heart, my darling
I have loved you three long years!
Forgive me, honourable daughter of an honourable father!
I'm a bastard, I am guilty!'
And deeply he bowed himself before her.

The tension is released, by two chords each of a breve in length (the tempo is maestoso), the first intolerable, the second a release. And we are left breathless. Filka's confession is so complete, the scene so poignant, that Akulka's reaction becomes of the first importance. She has retreated into privacy—this Example 50 tells us, returning pianissimo to express her fright and her terror. But then, urged by his sincerity—she, like us, has just heard Filka's true self for the first time—she reveals herself, also for the first and only time. As never before, Example 50 is developed: it flowers into an exquisite, dolcissimo melody as she replies:

'Forgive me too, you're a good young man,
I have no hatred for you.'

Aljeja cries out in his sleep—and it is vital that his part be sung by a female voice, or the effect is lost: the eruption of the music is that of Akulka's pain, the violence of Šiškov as he went to her and demanded to know what she said. And her purity is also truthfulness: his violence leads her to repeat her revelation, display intact her existence in all its simplicity and depth. Once again Example 50, now once more totally self-enclosed and presented in the most tenuous instrumentation:

'I am in love with him,
more than all the world
I love him!'
'Damn you!'

She has condemned herself to death. Šiškov cannot penetrate her mind, for he has destroyed all the emotion towards him which she showed on the night of the wedding. His jealousy and hatred are total. He resolves instead to destroy her body. A terrible night passes, and is succeeded by a more ghastly dawn: violence, apocalyptic separations of orchestral line, Luka's death-cry, and the literal 'leaping up' of the sun in Šiškov's narrative, bring the music near to breakdown. But as Luka dies—he will never know the fate of the girl he loved and destroyed—the orchestra gathers in increasing tension. Šiškov brings his wagon to a halt in the forest, and speaks. 'Get out, Akulka! This is your death!'

Example 45 declares itself in a form strained beyond belief; the camp and the outside world are in the process of fusion. And as the phrase devolves on to a remorselessly sustained, tremolo discord, we gaze with Akulka into the face of death as never before in opera. She peers into an abyss. For the girl and the audience, time stands still: this ghastly tremolo is a figuration for the end of life implacable beyond all imagination. It is sustained beyond the limits of tolerance, and the trombones summon Šiškov inexorably to the deed. He cuts her throat, killing to remove the unbearable enigma which has tortured his passions. And now he has his reward. With Akulka's death, we are thrust back into the house of the dead. For here too a man has died.

Notice the phrasing of the old convict's words: not a convict, but a *člověk*, a human being. And in the face of Luka as it sets into death, Šiškov recognizes Filka Morozov. The recognition brings him to hoarse, chaotic near-disbelief which involves all the convicts in incredulous outcry. The old convict barely salvages the moral 'even he was some mother's child'. Šiškov learns nothing: he curses Filka dead as he cursed him in life 'Dog's flesh! Dog's flesh!' But from his total failure to comprehend *we* are given, in this moment, an equally total illumination. The lunacies of violence have, in previous Acts, been chiefly the prerogative of the camp: the circumstances which led Luka and Skuratov there are trivial in comparison with the brutality of the opera's setting. But now we have been taken out, to our world; and the entire process has been reversed. Violence, the whole wretched tragedy of Šiškov, Filka and Akulka is the stuff of life; our own world is one of ultimate incapacity to communicate: Akulka's opaque privacy and Filka's desperate response have led her to death, and the two men in her life, directly and indirectly, to the house of the dead. In the moment of *anagnorisis*, of tragic recognition, our world floods into that of the hospital with glaring light. And even as Šiškov curses, even as the body is taken out and Šiškov expends his last energies in poisonous hatred for the corpse of the man who brought him to prison, Janáček dares to draw his moral. 'Even he was some mother's child.' Someone, once, loved even Filka.

In the recognition which makes us contemplate two parallel deaths, Janáček has vindicated his motto. And this is why the tutti outcry is not bestowed on either moment of death, but reserved for this moment. As the sounding out of Example 45 just before Akulka's murder has prefigured, the two worlds are now one. The characters of Šiškov's story are totally unjustified:

233

Akulka's silence and passivity, the catalyst of the entire sequence of events, led her to death; Filka and Šiškov cemented that tragedy by their violence of reaction. Two are dead, the third condemned to living death and trapped in futile, repetitive hatred. But even these have in them 'hearts of gold'. In the music now, Janáček's compassion oversets even Šiškov's hatred and the trumpet call in which all the fatal, tragic irony of the story has been gathered. And rightly so. Akulka and Filka have shown their moral worth in their mutual declaration; and even Šiškov is redeemed by the degree of insight and self-disgust with which he has narrated his own part in the events, shirking nothing of his own brutality.

We have confronted the most terrible events in this opera, and been made to recognize their meaning. We are ready for the light.

The interlude transports us to the open air. And the first impression of the music is that of a successful striving for space. But against the upward movement there is the evolution to a tenuous, but unmistakably march-like theme; chains clatter, and the prisoners' groans are heard behind the scene. We are being returned to sunlight—but also to the pain of the convicts' daily work. With the rise of the curtain there is a sudden, striking musical contrast. In the setting of Šiškov's monologue, Janáček's idiom reached extremes of concision and compression: here in the final scene the forms are looser, the music more expansive. The expansiveness is, in dramatic terms, that of release, the catharsis after the night of purgatory; but it is also more: the gathering of width prefigures a delusory dream of human contact. The final scene does not establish a world which could overshadow the reality of Šiškov's story; instead we are treated to an extended irony, a scene of mock union which is almost a comic parody of the confrontation of Šiškov and Filka.

With the commandant drunk, playing with his knowledge that Petrovič is to be freed, the hierarchies of reality are for a moment broken; his maudlin apology and self-abasement are set with ironic, leisurely richness. In the world of the camp which we now know to be our own, men are equal only in such moments— and the woodwind circle in mocking irony round sentiments which are impermanent, while Petrovič (quite reasonably)

234

speaks as though stunned: he can hardly believe his ears. To match this the prisoners' march music becomes relaxed, their chorus of lamentation less doleful, merely a muted reminder of reality. And the scene goes even further towards the world of dreams. The march finally unmasks itself (figure 36) as the commandant embraces Petrovič: it is a mildly altered version of that which introduced the opera as a whole; and now triplets which were in that introduction abrupt and harsh float gently in to illustrate the escape of Petrovič's actual dream, about his mother. He who has entered the house of the dead *may* leave, and if he does so it is to the same music, transmuted to ecstasy by the almost complete psychological unreality of the event. Petrovič's dream was no accident: he is free.

His chains are struck off, the music leading up to this by swift but arduous attempts to rise. The release is marked by the blacksmith: 'his chains are off', but the moment is shot through with pain: the bitterness of the ending rivals even that of *Kát'a Kabanová*. For the dream ends. Reality is pain, the pain of separation even in what we call freedom. As Petrovič is released from his chains, the cry of the prisoners becomes truly plangent for the first time in this scene; and Example 45 returns, now separating the orchestra into vast divisions of heights and depths, suffering and silence. Aljeja and Petrovič are wrenched apart by emotion; and the opera assumes its closing movement. Again the circling triplets from the introduction—but now with vigour: the dream has become, for Petrovič, reality. Kissing his chains, he hails 'new life! Glorious freedom!' and the eagle which like him was crippled in Act I now becomes free also. But what has he learnt from the experience of the camp? And is the outside world truly better than this one? The chorus hails freedom—but the music here gives the feeling of merely marking time. And the end is inevitable. The orchestra gradually gathers full force and Janáček's customary concision; Petrovič and Aljeja are literally parted; and at the guard's third cry of 'March!' the working party is forced off. Their cry is now one of real anguish; and the march is unleashed at full force as the curtain falls. The house of the dead remains, its pain undiminished by Petrovič's departure; and the 'idealistic' triplets of the dream world are crushed in the closing tutti by the lacerating power of the march and the rattle of chains. Freedom and captivity are one: the limits of mortality are defined in these pages as nowhere else, as the march seems to echo on, radiating outwards from the world of the prison into our own.

In every opera, Janáček presents men and women who are human beings like us; he does so with the deepest understanding, neither raising metaphysical doubts nor offering a pessimistic view of mankind, but snatching some consolation for mortality even from the jaws of extreme suffering. Janáček offers six operas of very different richness, united by their tragic stance, their consciousness of the inevitability of disastrous action and the place of man in his universe. Despite their completely alien style, they yet unite imaginative width with rigorous restraint in a manner which is wholly classical; intellect and emotion unite to illuminate a vast range of truth, offering to all who will listen a triumphant demonstration of the worth and dignity of individual man. Janáček confronts reality with utter objectivity, facing man increasingly at his least congenial and finding in him none the less something of a value which he can assert.

This positive assertion is not made with ease, or any lack of consciousness of the difficulty of Janáček's task. On the contrary, these works are so fraught with truth, so bereft of idealism or faith, that they raise only one final question: what is the value to us of this terrifying illumination? Why do we flinch under the burden of Janáček's exhibition of what it is to be man or woman in this tormented century?

Janáček's tragic operas heal our wounds, make sense of our existence: they have within them much of what it is to live.

Synopses

JENŮFA
(Její pastorkyňa—Her foster-daughter)

Opera in three Acts after a drama of Moravian rural life by
GABRIELA PREISSOVÁ
Play: 1890
Opera composed: ?1894–1903
First performance: Brno, 21 January 1904

CHARACTERS:
Grandmother, housekeeper in the mill *(contralto)*
Laca Klemeň ⎱ her grandsons, stepbrothers *(tenor)*
Števa Buryja ⎰ *(tenor)*
Kostelnička Buryjovka, a widow, her daughter-in-law *(soprano)*
Jenůfa, Kostelnička's foster-daughter *(soprano)*
Miller ('Old man') *(baritone)*
Mayor *(bass)*
Mayor's wife *(mezzo-soprano)*
Karolka, their daughter *(mezzo-soprano)*
Shepherdess *(mezzo-soprano)*
Barena, serving girl in the mill *(soprano)*
Jano, cowhand *(soprano)*
Aunt *(contralto)*
Recruits, musicians, servants from the mill, customers of the
   mill, village people, children

237

The first Act is set at the Buryja mill, the second and third in Kostelnička's room. Between Acts 1 and 2 there is an interval of half a year, between Acts 2 and 3 one of two months.

Act 1 *A solitary mill in the hills*
Late afternoon

Jenůfa is waiting with Grandmother Buryja and Laca for the return of Števa, by whom she is pregnant. Today Števa, the owner of the mill, has been before the recruiting board, and if he has not been conscripted, Jenůfa hopes to persuade him to marry her; if he has, the marriage will be impossible, her condition will soon become known and the shame will drive her to suicide.

Laca waits in equal anxiety: desperately in love with Jenůfa, he is jealous and embittered by her love for Števa, and by his inferior position in the household.

Though she chides Jenůfa for her restlessness and her inability to work today, Grandmother Buryja appreciates her value. And the next scene reveals this further. Jano rushes in; Jenůfa has taught him to read, and he begs for more tuition. Too preoccupied to fulfil her usual role of teacher, she gently postpones the lesson, assuring him she will teach him to write as well. Laca pays no attention to Jano's jubilation—or to Jenůfa's growing introspection.

The miller arrives, fresh from town. Laca asks him to sharpen his knife, which gives him the opportunity to tease Jenůfa with the whipstick on which he has been working, and taunt her about her love for Števa. Provoked, Jenůfa disappears into the house for a few moments; and the miller draws Laca out into admitting his love for Jenůfa and how it has affected him. But this penetrating scrutiny of his motives leads Laca to a passionate outburst —which makes the miller break his news: Števa has not been conscripted.

Jenůfa is delighted, Laca furious at the injustice. Kostelnička, passing across the stage in time to hear the news, is incredulous.

The recruits now approach, with Števa prominent among them. Mill-workers and others come out to meet them. Jenůfa forces Števa to come to her, and reproaches him for his drunkenness. For this she has to endure Števa's flaunting of his easy conquests before her; he then makes her join him in a wild dance.

Kostelnička has been watching from the doorstep since Števa arrived. She now intervenes, stops the dance and refuses to allow Jenůfa to marry Števa until he can prove his worth by staying sober for a whole year. The recruits and villagers depart.

Jenůfa, left alone with Števa, vainly tries to make him realize how desperate her position is—but perceives her failure even before his Grandmother returns to ease him off to bed.

Laca has overheard all this. He comes forward to taunt Jenůfa about how easily the boastful Števa was deflated by Kostelnička. Jenůfa provokes him, defiantly asserting that she can wear proudly even a discarded posy which one of Števa's women has given him. Laca knows that Števa sees nothing in her but her apple-blossom cheeks, and, ostensibly approaching to offer her the posy and steal a kiss, slashes her cheek with his knife when she repulses him. Agonized, Laca declares that he has loved her all his life; Barena, who has observed the final moments of the quarrel, says it was an accident. The miller is sure it was deliberate. Appalled at what he has done, Laca takes to his heels.

Act 2 *A Slovak chamber*

Jenůfa has been concealed in Kostelnička's house during her pregnancy, and has borne a baby boy, Števuška, a week before the action of this Act begins. Kostelnička's pride has been deeply hurt; she is obsessed by shame for the disgrace which has happened to the foster-daughter of whom she was so proud, and had prayed fervently that the child might not live.

She gives Jenůfa a sleeping-draught and sends her to bed; for she has sent for Števa, who now arrives. Like everyone else in the village, he believes that Jenůfa is in Vienna, but Kostelnička tells him that a son has been born to him and begs him to marry Jenůfa. He offers money to support the child provided that the identity of its father is not disclosed, but he refuses to marry Jenůfa despite Kostelnička's entreaties. He says that Jenůfa's loss of beauty and changed character have caused him to fall out of love with her, and that he has become engaged to Karolka. Jenůfa cries out in her sleep, Kostelnička goes to attend her and Števa takes the opportunity to make his escape.

Laca enters, asking after Jenůfa, whom he will always love.

239

He wants to marry her; but when Kostelnička resolves to tell him the truth that Jenůfa has borne a child of Števa's, his immediate reaction is one of horror, and Kostelnička, seeing Jenůfa's last chance of happiness vanishing, tells Laca that the child has died. She then tells him of Števa's engagement to Karolka and sends him to find out when their wedding will take place.

Left alone, she contemplates hiding the child. But she realizes this is impossible, and in agony of mind she resolves to murder it. Near to madness, she rationalizes the deed by convincing herself that the baby is too young to have sinned yet: 'God will surely take him.' Determined to save her pride and Jenůfa's honour, she carries the baby into the night and drowns it in the river.

Jenůfa awakes from her drugged sleep, finds her baby and Kostelnička gone, and assumes that Kostelnička has taken the child to the mill to show to Števa. She sings an Ave Maria for his welfare. Kostelnička returns, feverish and half-frozen, and tells Jenůfa that for two days she has lain in fever, during which time her baby died and was buried. She tells her of Števa's desertion, and urges her to turn to Laca, a man whose love she can depend on. Laca now returns; he has recovered from his shock, and asks Jenůfa to marry him. Knowing now that Laca wants her, she accepts with tender resignation. Kostelnička begins to bless the couple; but the blessing degenerates into a bitter heaping of curses on Števa, an icy blast of wind forces the window open, and Kostelnička begins to realize the full significance of her deed. The weight of guilt forces her to moral breakdown.

Act 3 *Kostelnička's room from Act 2*

This is the day of Jenůfa's wedding to Laca. Kostelnička has been very ill: she is nervous, distraught and reduced to restless inactivity. A neighbour, the shepherdess, has come to help out with the wedding preparations; the mayor and his wife arrive. While they are inspecting the trousseau, Jenůfa and Laca are left alone. Laca speaks of his remorse, his love for Jenůfa, and of his reconciliation with Števa, who is expected shortly together with his fiancée. When they arrive, Karolka makes the customary greetings to bride and groom, adding a pert comment on the simplicity of Jenůfa's wedding. She then teases Števa about their own wedding, expected to take place in two weeks' time.

Barena leads in an excited group of girls who bring flowers and sing a song for Jenůfa, after which Grandmother Buryja blesses the couple. As Kostelnička is on the point of giving them her blessing also, a commotion is heard outside the house, and Jano bursts in. He describes the discovery of a frozen baby beneath the ice.

All except Števa, Kostelnička and Grandmother Buryja rush out, and when Jenůfa cries out that she recognizes the child as hers, the crowd of villagers who have gathered accuse her of having murdered it. As their threats increase and they bear down on Jenůfa, Laca holds them back by the sheer violence of his intervention. Their hysteria is quelled.

But to save Jenůfa, Kostelnička must confess her guilt; and she explains not only her imagined motives but her real ones. Had the baby lived, two lives would have been ruined. Even so, she now recognizes the true implications of her action; and she seeks only Jenůfa's forgiveness to give her the strength to face up to the consequences of her action. After a moment of revulsion, Jenůfa, now mature, raises Kostelnička up with understanding, forgiveness and the promise of God's mercy. Kostelnička accepts her future suffering and the knowledge of salvation; she is led away by the mayor; the villagers follow.

Jenůfa and Laca are left alone, and now that all have gone, she urges him to go too. She wants him to know that she forgave him long ago for slashing her cheek; he sinned only out of love, just as she did too. He was always for her the best of men; too good now to endure the humiliation which he will have to suffer if married to her, the disgraced foster-daughter of a murderess.

When Laca declares that he would bear far more than that for her, that the world does not matter as long as they are together, she realizes for the first time that she loves and is in love with him, 'that great love, with which God is content'.

DESTINY
(Osud)

Three romantic pictures by Fedora Bartošová (story outlined by the composer; dialogue versified by Miss Bartošová)
Opera composed: 1903–7
First performances: Brno and Stuttgart, 25 and 26 October 1958
Neither can be regarded as a première, since both were productions of extensive rearrangements which violated Janáček's musical and dramatic intentions. There has yet to be a production of this opera in the form in which Janáček wrote it.

CHARACTERS:

Act 1
Lhotský, a painter (*baritone*)
Konečny, an old friend of Živný (*baritone*)
Miss Míla Valková (*soprano*)
Dr. Suda (*tenor*)
Živný, a composer (*tenor*)
Miss Stuhlá (*soprano*)
Míla's mother (*mezzo-soprano*)
Chorus: 1. teachers; 2. students and girls, with echo;
   3. spa guests

Act 2
Živný, Míla
Doubek, their son (*soprano*)
242

Jean and Nanny, their servants (*silent*)
Míla's mother, a madwoman

Act 3
Živný
Verva, a student (*baritone*)
Součková and Košinka, female students (*soprano* and *alto*)
Doubek, a student, Živný's son (*tenor*)
Hrázda, a student (*tenor*)
Chorus of students

Act 1 *A fashionable spa*

Guests promenade in the park in front of a hotel at the spa.
Students and girls stand on a bridge and call out across the valley
for an echo. All are united in their praise of the sun, which gives
them renewed life and health.

Míla enters, elegantly dressed. Lhotský presents her with a
bouquet, and they are joined by Dr. Suda, who offers her an
elegant compliment. But bitter memories dominate her thoughts,
even as she lifts her veil to take her cup of spa water. And she
suddenly sees Živný, who is standing in the distance, engaged in
conversation. Her companions—who now include Konečny—
notice her disturbance, and speak of Živný and of the opera he is
writing, the obituary of an unfortunate love. Míla begs that they
walk on, and arranges their promenade in such a way as to contrive a meeting with Živný. He finally finds this unavoidable, and
introduces himself to Lhotský and Suda—but ironically, doubt-
ing his own ability as a composer and making pointed reference
to his obsession with the griefs of love. 'Your own or someone
else's?' Míla asks. 'Perhaps you know.' Živný and Míla make
clear to the others that they want to be left alone. When they are,
she asks at once if he has come for his child. Živný has come
for the echo of the voice which has given meaning to his life, to
claim his right to her and the child.

A party of schoolmistresses begins to appear, and Živný and
Míla retreat. Miss Stuhlá ushers her colleagues indoors for a
rehearsal; her efforts are mocked by a group of male students and
girls, who are preparing for an excursion. Dr. Suda and Lhotský
reappear, in a jovial mood and accompanied by a bagpiper. They

are asked to join the excursion party—which they do. The students and girls take Suda's sunshade and make a banner with the colours of the Czech flag out of it, by tying ribbons to it. Meanwhile Lhotský and Suda assemble musicians to accompany the outing.

Indoors, Miss Stuhlá's rehearsal begins, interrupted by sarcastic comments from Lhotský and Suda, with whom she argues. Finally she and her teachers shut the window, again to laughter from the students and the girls. Míla's mother enters looking for Míla, but Lhotský brushes her off with a casual remark; she goes, but not before she has overheard a gossip inquiring where Živný is, in terms which imply that he is staying at the spa.

Dr. Suda proposes that the excursionists sing 'a little hymn to the sun', and is joined in it by Lhotský, the students and the girls as they march off. The sound of their singing and playing slowly fades into the distance.

Miss Stuhlá and the teachers emerge from the salon and pass across the stage, abusing the excursion party now that it is at a safe distance. Míla's mother again enters anxiously, looking for her daughter, and finally wanders off in the direction which the outing has taken.

It is in the heat of midday. A few guests recline in the shade; but otherwise all is still. Živný and Míla return, and an extended dialogue begins. Živný evokes at length the power and the ecstasy of their first love, and finally sings of the prejudice Míla's mother had against him as a poverty-stricken composer. Míla hails the sun, begs that its heat may consume her grief. She explains: her parents introduced her to a well-groomed, suitable prospective husband, but he had only to leave the house and she was away to meet Živný. She recalls how, conducting the première of one of his own works, Živný accepted the gift of a red rose from her with special affection; and how they were parted, when she was taken from Prague to an isolated village. And then she sings of the dreamlike, ecstatic recollections of their moments together in Prague which came to her; and finally of her travail, and the birth of their child. They resolve to leave together.

As dusk falls, the excursion begins to return. Two of its members arrange a rendezvous for the next day; Konečny passes across the stage with a young widow, reciting a love poem to her. Some of the young men comment knowingly on the obvious attraction between Živný and Míla, while one woman asks another why Míla did not come with them. Other people try to stop them interfering, but Míla has been affected; she begs Živný to leave with her. He disarms her anxiety: why should they live by the opinions of others? They declare their complete love for each other.

But Míla voices another fear; that her mother will not endure the fact of their reunion. Živný and Míla leave, resolved to elope. As they go, Dr. Suda gathers the party together for a final celebration in the hotel.

Míla's mother enters, looking for Míla. Lhotský shrugs his shoulders—he doesn't know where she is; but one of the gossips maliciously tells her that Míla has left with Živný. She reacts with horror.

All the remaining excursionists have returned to the hotel, and it is now quite dark. Electric lights come on on the promenade. A student is heard in the distance, pleading for his girl to give him a kiss, and to make a rendezvous. She refuses—but they disappear together into the darkness. Míla's mother is left alone, wandering around. She broods on her daughter's elopement with Živný, until suddenly she sees it as nothing but utter, disastrous misery.

Act 2 *Živný's study*
A winter evening, four years later

Živný is at his piano, Míla beside him. Light shines on them from a standard lamp. Doubek, who is six, plays with books and papers from a cupboard.

Živný is contemplating his score, 'the echo of our life'. There are two kinds of pages: those which express their true love—when, he asks, will they fly away in brilliance?—for the opera is still incomplete; the others imply that Míla betrayed him: Živný denounces them. Even thinking about them disquiets Míla, who regards them as a proof of her guilt.

Behind the scenes Míla's mother, now maddened, cries out: 'What are they saying?' Živný tries to ignore her, and recalls his first love letter to Míla—playing lightly on the piano as he does so. He goes on to speak of her answer, and of the inevitability of their union. He hails it as destiny. Míla, disturbed, begs him to

245

stop; but her mother echoes his cry, and his song, ironically. Živný for the first time acknowledges this 'dreadful echo'. Míla weeps: 'so many years of harmony, and still no mercy'. Živný tries to comfort her—but his feelings develop into a torrent of self-accusation for the attempt made in his first draft to slander her and portray her as a cold deceiver. Finally he sets on the score and hurls it to the ground. 'All lies, base suspicion! Only born of madness!'

When Živný began to recall their first moments together, Míla sent Doubek off to play somewhere else. He now returns, and asks her a question which penetrates her heart: do you know what love is? She gently tries to put him off—but she sees her offence as real; even her own child denies that she truly knows what love is. And now her mother enters, abusing the young couple sarcastically. She parodies Živný's song of love again, and proceeds to accuse him of seducing her daughter for her money. Míla tries to restrain her mother as she retreats, clutching her jewel-box warily; while struggling to prevent her from falling from the balcony, she herself is dragged from it by her mother.

Živný rushes out. Doubek, left alone on the stage, stares at the door as it slowly shuts. Živný returns with his wife's dead body, and lays it on the divan. Sinking to the floor beside her, he invokes the lightning which has struck, begs its thunder to descend on him also.

Act 3 *Great Hall of a Conservatoire*

The students are singing through the closing pages of Živný's opera, which is to receive its première that evening. The images of both text and music are violent; a storm illustrates the truth 'it is not wise to challenge God', and the opera ends with a tenor solo which calls for lightning to come in all its searing, destructive glory.

'Strange ending,' Verva comments, and the students, aware that a storm is gathering around them too, relieve their feelings with a grotesque dance, which Součková accompanies on the organ. Verva begs them to stop, and tells them about Živný's opera. He has private information about it from Živný himself; there is no real ending: 'that is in the hand of God and remains there.' Verva begins to explain Živný's opera. It is autobiographical—Lenský, the composer who is its hero, is Živný himself.

Součková interrupts. The girls are determined to go and ask Živný in person to explain the mysteries of his opera. But before that—and with Doubek, now a student, present—Verva plays over to them a scene which we recognize at once as that between Míla and Doubek from Act 2 of Janáček's opera.

The reaction to this fragment of Živný's opera is mixed. The girls find it merely clever—but the male students are more deeply involved. At this moment Živný himself enters, aged and looking pale. They ask him to talk about his opera, and Lenský the composer. Živný consents willingly. 'I knew him very well.'

Lenský, he begins, was inspired. But his compositions were melancholy at first. Suddenly something joyful flared up in him for the first time—and it was said that he had fallen in love.

As the stage darkens with the gathering storm, Živný continues. He speaks of the joy and grief with which 'Lenský's opera' was filled in such terms that Verva and Součková are in no doubt that he is speaking of his own life. And now Živný, in mounting excitement, tells of Lenský's tragedy and of his defiance; the pain of separation from Míla led him to pour out work of such cruelty and bitterness that it would ruin her life.

They met and were reunited. But 'How could they realize, that their melodies of love would so soon grow pale in the lightning of death?' Živný closes his monologue in the pain of overwhelming recollection, bringing his story to the point where his opera broke off—Lenský's search for truth in 'the music of God', confronting the fury of storms and the glory of lightning. And stage events now merge with the narrative of recall: he is given a glowing, complete vision of Míla's sorrowful, angelic face in all her beauty. But thunder and lightning strike the hall, extinguishing the lights. Doubek cries out; Živný lies stunned; and the students huddle by the organ. Verva sends Součková for a doctor; but Živný revives, and his final vision is calm. He hears Míla weeping—a sound beyond the apprehension of the others; and Verva whispers quietly to the other students, 'Perhaps this is music from the last Act?' But Živný, overhearing, reacts violently: 'From the last Act? That is in the hands of God and remains there!'

The vision has gone. Živný leaves the hall, with difficulty, supported by his son.

KÁT'A KABANOVÁ

Opera in three Acts
after A. N. OSTROVSKY'S
The Storm in the translation by
V. ČERVINKA
Play written: 1859
Opera composed : 1920–1
First performance: Brno, 23 October 1921

CHARACTERS:
Savël Prokofjevič Dikoj, a merchant (*bass*)
Boris Grigorjevič, his nephew (*tenor*)
Marfa Ignatěvna Kabanova (Kabanicha), a rich merchant's
   widow (*alto*)
Tichon Ivanyč Kabanov, her son (*tenor*)
Katěrina (Kát'a), his wife (*soprano*)
Váňa Kudrjáš, teacher, chemist and mechanic (*tenor*)
Varvara, a ward in the Kabanov household (*mezzo-soprano*)
Kuligin, a companion of Kudrjáš (*baritone*)
Gláša and Fekluša, servants (*mezzo-soprano*)
Passer-by, woman from the crowd (*alto*), inhabitants of the
   town of both sexes.

The drama takes place in the town of Kalinov on the shore of
the Volga in the 1860s. Two weeks elapse between the second
and the third Acts.

Act 1 Scene i *A park on the banks of the Volga. On the left, the Kabanov house*

A sunny Sunday afternoon; the family are away in church. Váňa Kudrjáš is sitting on a bench, contemplating the river and praising its beauty. The matter-of-fact servant Gláša, who has come out of the house, scoffs at his reflections, but both swiftly take refuge, Váňa in the park and Gláša in the house, as Dikoj approaches, bullying Boris. Boris, he complains, is a layabout and always follows him around—not surprisingly, since both have reasons for visiting this particular house. Dikoj goes to the door; Gláša tells him with malicious pleasure that Kabanicha is still at church. He spits on the ground and leaves. Boris is now joined by Váňa, who asks him why he chooses to live with Dikoj and be bullied by him. Boris explains: he and his sister will not inherit their grandfather's wealth unless they obey their uncle. Only the need to dissuade Dikoj from forcing his sister to live in Kalinov as well keeps Boris there.

The return of the other servant-girl, Fekluša, warns that the family are returning from church. Boris confesses his love for Kát'a to Váňa. They take refuge behind the house and watch the approach of Kát'a, Varvara, Kabanicha and Tichon. When they arrive he laughs bitterly and runs off.

Kabanicha is ordering Tichon to depart immediately for the market at Kazan, and takes the opportunity which his reluctance offers to lecture him on putting his wife above his mother. When Kát'a intervenes on Tichon's behalf she is roughly rebuffed, but with a gentle 'words like these were best unspoken', she goes into the house. Tichon wants the best of both worlds: 'I love you both'—but his mother replies that if he treats Kát'a softly, sooner or later she will take a lover. When Kabanicha goes, Tichon tries to confide in Varvara, but she retorts: he goes on at Kát'a just like his mother. Tichon leaves in silence, her taunt of 'drunkard' ringing in his ears. Varvara goes into the house.

Act 1 Scene ii *A room in the Kabanov household*

Varvara and Kát'a are sewing, as the sun streams through the window. Kát'a tells of her happy childhood, and then slowly describes the visions she used to see in church, of angels singing,

249

then of vast cathedrals in the heavens and of herself soaring through a space filled with invisible choirs. But suddenly she sees a terrible sin tempting her; faintly she describes her desires, and her nightly dreams. Varvara tries to prompt her to tell more, but Kát'a reacts hysterically, and throws her arms round Tichon's neck as he enters dressed for his journey. Varvara rushes from the room. Kát'a tries desperately to persuade him to stay, or to take her with him. When she sees that both are impossible she tries to swear an oath to him that she will never speak to or think of any other man. He refuses to accept it, and raises her from her knees as Kabanicha comes in. She makes Tichon tell his wife how to conduct herself in his absence. All the instructions which Tichon would not give for his wife's peace of mind he now gives at his mother's dictation. Kát'a breaks down and Kabanicha leaves them alone, returning after a few moments with Varvara and Gláša for the formal leave-taking. Tichon kneels to his mother, then kisses her. At her command he goes to his wife, but Kát'a suddenly embraces him passionately. Tichon tears himself from her and goes off rapidly.

Act 2 Scene i *A comfortable workroom*

Kabanicha, Kát'a and Varvara are busy with needlework. Kabanicha reproaches Kát'a with failing to make the conventional show of weeping at her husband's departure, and then leaves the room. Varvara has obtained the key to the gate by the summer-house, which Kabanicha had hidden. She leaves it to Kát'a, who slowly turns it over and meditates on the inescapable shame it offers. Eventually she resolves to see Boris whatever may happen, and leaves the house.

Kabanicha, who has been heard talking outside, enters with a lamp followed by Dikoj, who is drunk. He makes coarse and ludicrous advances to her, which she repels.

Act 2 Scene ii *A hollow thick with shrubs, below the walls of the Kabanov garden*

It is almost entirely dark. Váňa appears with a guitar, and sings a song while waiting for Varvara. But Boris is the next to arrive: Váňa tries hopelessly to dissuade him. Varvara arrives singing;

she tells Boris to wait while she and Váňa go down by the river. Kát'a appears, at first silent and with her eyes fixed on the ground. In a long and ever more animated dialogue she acknowledges that she has, by secretly leaving the house, committed herself irrevocably. She embraces Boris passionately.

Varvara returns with Váňa, and tells them to go off together. She chats with Váňa about the arrangements she has made for their meeting to be safer, while the voices of Boris and Kát'a are heard from the distance, pledging eternal love. The nightwatchman passes, and Varvara warns Váňa that it is time to go. Calling the other couple back, they slowly make their way up the path to the gate, singing alternate verses of a love song. But as Varvara reaches the top, Boris and Kát'a enter below, and she suddenly calls out, taunting them. Kát'a walks slowly up the path, alone.

Act 3 Scene i *In the foreground, an old ruined house. Grass and shrubs here and there. In the background the river bank and a view of the Volga*

Heavy rain is falling. Kuligin and Váňa Kudrjáš rush to take shelter in the old house, followed by a number of townspeople. They talk about the murals around them, which depict the punishment of sinners in hell. Dikoj brushes his way angrily through the crowd, and gets into an argument with Váňa, who wants lightning conductors installed in the town. Dikoj rebukes him, declaring forcibly that storms are God's punishment for wrongdoing. Váňa makes a sophisticated retort, and walks casually away, to Dikoj's greater annoyance. The rain eases and all leave; for a moment the stage is empty and the orchestra silent.

Varvara enters quickly, looking all round her. Boris and Váňa appear and she beckons Boris to her. Tichon, she whispers, has returned and Kát'a is wandering around wildly like a demented being; Kabanicha is watching her every move. At this moment the renewed and steadily growing storm drives Kát'a herself in. Boris hides at the back. As the crowd comment on the scene Váňa tries to reassure Kát'a; but she has caught sight of Boris, and his presence makes her increasingly strained. They are suddenly joined by Tichon, Kabanicha and Dikoj, who points

251

accusingly at Kát'a. As they comment on her, a flash of lightning illuminates the paintings, and Kát'a sinks to her knees and confesses. Tichon tries to take her in his arms; Kabanicha and Dikoj demand the name of her lover. Varvara tries to protect Kát'a, but she shouts Boris's name over the full fury of the storm. Suddenly she tears herself from Tichon and rushes out. The crowd scatters in panic.

Act 3 Scene ii *The Volga; a deserted spot on its banks*

It is now quite dark, in the deep calm that follows the storm. Small search parties are out looking for Kát'a, and one consisting of Tichon and Gláša passes across the stage. They are heard calling in the distance as Varvara enters with Váňa. Kabanicha, besides giving her opinion that adulteresses should be buried alive, has tried to lock Varvara up at home. She decides to go away to Moscow with Váňa. As they disappear into the night Kát'a appears. She sings a long and dreamlike monologue, interrupted briefly by the appearance of Kuligin, singing. He glances curiously at her as he goes out. Distant wordless singing is heard, like a sigh of the river, as she voices her fear of the growing darkness. A drunkard passes silently across the stage. Kát'a now wishes only for death. Suddenly she runs to the river bank and calls in an ecstatic vision for Boris. He hears her, rushes in and they embrace. Dikoj has ordered him to leave the town at once and for ever. As Kát'a, her reason almost going, tries to give him her last farewell, the voices of the Volga return to call insistently for his departure. As Boris goes, the voices summon Kát'a softly, for the last time. She approaches the river and throws herself into it.

Her fall is observed, and all the searchers are drawn to the spot. Dikoj goes down into the water. Kabanicha tries to restrain Tichon, but he accuses her: 'You, you alone have killed her.' Dikoj lays the body of Kát'a on the ground and goes away in agitation. Tichon falls on the corpse, calling out Kát'a's name. The crowd stare in horror; but Kabanicha has the last word.

ADVENTURES OF THE VIXEN BYSTROUŠKA
(Příhody lišky Bystroušky)

Opera in three Acts after RUDOLF TĚSNOHLÍDEK's *The Vixen Bystrouška.*
Story written: 1920
Opera composed: 1921–4
First performance: Brno, 6 November 1924

CHARACTERS:
The forester *(bass)*
His wife *(alto)*
The schoolmaster *(tenor)*
The parson *(bass)*
Harašta, in business as a poultry vendor *(bass)*
Pásek, an innkeeper *(tenor, from chorus)*
Bystrouška *(soprano)*
Mrs. Pásková, the innkeeper's wife *(soprano, from chorus)*
The fox *(soprano)*
Little Bystrouška *(child soprano)*
Frantík, Pepík, two boys *(sopranos from chorus)*
Lapák, a dog *(mezzo-soprano)*
The cock *(soprano)*
Chocholka, a hen *(soprano)*
A cricket, a grasshopper and a little frog *(child sopranos)*
Flies, blue dragon-fly, squirrel, forest insects *(ballet)*
The woodpecker *(alto)*
The mosquito *(tenor)*

The badger (*tenor*)
The owl (*soprano*)
The jay (*soprano*)

Act 1 Scene i *How they caught the vixen Bystrouška*

A ravine in the forest, on a hot, sultry summer afternoon. The badger, smoking a pipe, pokes his head out of his den; flies and a blue dragon-fly dance around him. As the forester approaches, all these creatures disappear. Hot and inebriated, he takes a nap, his trusty gun by his side. A cricket and a grasshopper enter, and entertain themselves with music and a dance. Soon a mosquito joins them, attracted by the forester's red nose. Its alcohol-tainted blood induces him to perform a slightly tipsy dance, and a little frog tries to catch him—only to realize that little Bystrouška has run on to the stage. She stops dead on seeing a frog for the first time. When she calls to her mother, asking what the frog is and whether it is edible, the little frog leaps in terror right up on to the forester's nose. The forester awakes with a start, sees little Bystrouška, and jubilantly picks her up to take her home as a pet for his children.

After he has gone, the dragon-fly returns, and, unable to find Bystrouška, sadly folds her wings.

Act 1 Scene ii *Bystrouška in the yard of the forester's home; Bystrouška in politics; Bystrouška escapes*

The forester is at home on an autumn afternoon. His wife, re-proaching Bystrouška for the fleas she has brought in, none the less gives her milk.

Lapák and Bystrouška are left alone; the dog consoles her, disclosing that his lot is just as bad as hers, especially during the mating months, when he—knowing nothing about love—can only dedicate himself to art. But the melancholy songs which he sings nightly are not appreciated: he is beaten instead.

Bystrouška, too, is inexperienced in love. But she has learnt quite a few things from the scandalous behaviour of the forest birds, and she tells Lapák about them. All her talk of love makes Lapák amorous, but Bystrouška immediately puts him in his place.

254

Pepík and Frantík come home and tease Bystrouška. Frantík tickles her snout with a stick, and is bitten by the proud, independent animal—who tries to escape during the ensuing turmoil. But she is caught and tied up.

Night passes; and as if in a dream, we see Bystrouška appear in the form of a maiden, while she weeps in her sleep. At dawn she resumes the form of a vixen.

In the morning, the cock arrogantly reproaches Bystrouška: her trouble is caused by being unproductive—she does not lay eggs. The stupid hens smugly support his argument. Bystrouška is provoked: she makes an impassioned speech, apparently inciting them to rebel and create a new order free of exploitation by the cock and by mankind. But their apathy disappoints her; declaring that she would rather bury herself alive than endure the sight of their backwardness, she goes to the rubbish heap and pretends to do just that. Chocholka urges the cock to go and see if Bystrouška has suffocated; she seizes and kills him, and then slaughters as many hens as she can reach. Then, defying the forester who tries to beat her, she bites through her confining rope and successfully escapes.

Act 2 Scene i *Bystrouška expropriates*

Bystrouška has returned to her forest, and resumes her life efficiently. She acquires a home by ridiculing the badger and inciting the forest insects to rail against him until, in a huff of ruffled dignity, he leaves his den in the ravine and she immediately takes possession of it.

Act 2 Scene ii

The 'gentlemen's parlour' at Pásek's inn is patronized by the parson, the schoolmaster and the forester. They are playing cards, the schoolmaster with singular inattention. The forester is sure this is because he is in love, and teases him remorselessly. When the schoolmaster retaliates by turning the conversation to the vixen who outwitted the forester, the forester retorts angrily.

The preoccupations of parson and schoolmaster are disturbed; the schoolmaster leaves angrily, and the parson is summoned against his will to see some new tenants. Left alone, the forester launches into an extended praise of alcohol. But he bursts out angrily again when Pásek reminds him about the vixen.

Act 2 Scene iii *Bystrouška's flirtations*

The schoolmaster makes his way home through the forest, swaying under the effects of drink and musing at length on what has just happened at the inn and on Terynka, with whom he has long been blindly and romantically in love. In his state of euphoria he takes Bystrouška, whose eyes are glowing in the darkness behind a patch of sunflowers, for Terynka, and goes to embrace her. She runs out as he falls headlong over the fence into the sunflowers. Bystrouška hides behind a bush.

Now the parson appears; he remembers how he was falsely accused, when he was a young student of theology, of making a girl who had attracted him pregnant. As he concludes his reflections, the forester approaches. He catches sight of Bystrouška and takes a couple of wild shots at her. The schoolmaster and the parson leap up, and run for their lives in opposite directions.

Act 2 Scene iv *Bystrouška is won and falls in love*

On a warm moonlit night Bystrouška is resting near her house when a fox called Zlatohřbítek ('Goldenstripe') approaches. She is immediately attracted to him—as he to her. His manner is dutifully formal as he pays his addresses to her and offers to escort her, provided her mother does not object. But she tells him that she has long since been independent. His joy becomes amazement when she tells of her clever victory over the forester, and his admiration increases when he learns that she is a house owner and non-smoker. He rushes off to gather a feast of rabbits for her, and after they have eaten it together he delicately raises the subject of love. When she confesses that she returns his love, they disappear together into her den. The owl and the jay gossip maliciously; the sun rises, and the couple return. Bystrouška whispers tearfully into her lover's ear, and he replies with a sigh that they had better go to the parson at once. The woodpecker acts in this capacity: dispensing with banns, he marries them at once and the entire forest unites in the most joyful of wedding festivities.

256

Act 3 Scene i *Bystrouška outwits Harašta from Líšen. How the vixen Bystrouška died*

On an autumn day, Harašta is walking through the edge of the forest; he comes across a dead hare and is just about to appropriate it when he sees the forester, whom he tries to convince of his honesty. He is going to marry Terynka—a prospect which he views with mixed feelings. And he claims that he resisted a temptation to take the dead hare without any prompting.

The forester, left alone, discovers fox prints by the hare; he deliberately leaves it untouched, and sets a trap. As soon as he is gone, Zlatohřbítek and Bystrouška appear with their cubs and immediately sense that something is wrong. The cubs scamper around, undeceived by the trap, and a tender love scene between the two mature foxes follows. Bystrouška insists on remaining by the path, even when she sees Harašta on his return journey with a basket of chickens for his bride. She pretends to be lame so that he will think her an easy prey. Her ruse succeeds, Harašta is tripped up, and the entire fox family seize the contents of his basket. Humiliated and desolate at the thought of his failure in Terynka's eyes, he shoots to kill, and Bystrouška dies.

Act 3 Scene ii

Pásek's inn is unnaturally quiet. The forester tells the schoolmaster that he found Bystrouška's den empty, but hopes to give his wife a new muff. Mrs. Pásková overhears and tells them that Terynka is wearing a new muff today, as her wedding gift from Harašta. The schoolmaster is broken-hearted at the news. The forester tries to console him by asking him what on earth he could do with a woman like that. Both men are getting old; he himself feels the need to return home through the forest, much earlier than usual.

Act 3 Scene iii *The little vixen 'as like her mother as egg to egg'*

The forester climbs slowly through the ravine, now at peace with the forest. He remembers his youth, and all the passionate life of the early days of his marriage—an experience which he and his wife shared with the forest. Sitting down to rest, he sees a vision of the forest's renewal in summer as the wood-nymphs return to their homes; and he falls asleep.

In his dream, the insects and animals of 1.i reappear; all except Bystrouška. But then a new little vixen runs up to the forester, the image of her mother. He reaches out for her, but catches instead, to his shock, a little frog. He isn't the same frog either: it was his grandfather whom the forester encountered in Act 1. Recognizing nature's eternal pattern of renewal, the forester lets his gun fall to the ground.

MAKROPULOS

(Věc Makropulos—The Makropulos thing)

Opera after the comedy of the same title by KAREL ČAPEK
Play written: 1921–2
Opera composed: 1923–5
First performance: Brno, 18 December 1927

CHARACTERS:
Emilia Marty *(dramatic soprano)*
Albert Gregor *(tenor)*
Vítek, a solicitor's clerk *(tenor)*
Kristina (Krista), his daughter *(mezzo-soprano)*
Jaroslav Prus *(baritone)*
Janek, his son *(tenor)*
Dr. Kolenatý, a solicitor *(bass-baritone)*
A stage-mechanic *(bass)*
A cleaning woman *(alto)*
Hauk-Šendorf *(operetta tenor)*
A chambermaid *(alto)*
Male-voice chorus

Act 1 *The clerk's room at Dr. Kolenatý's office*

Vítek is filing away the last documents in the case of Gregor
versus Prus. He muses on the mortality of things and is led to an
impassioned outburst (borrowed from Danton) against the behaviour of aristocrats. Albert Gregor interrupts him: he is one
of the present litigants in the case, impatient to know if a decision

259

has been reached. Kolenatý has been in court all morning; Vítek telephones, only to find that he has already left. Vítek's regrets for the imminent demise of a hundred-year-old lawsuit drive Gregor to distraction. At this point Krista arrives. She is a young opera singer, full of admiration for the performance of the great and beautiful opera singer Emilia Marty. Gregor asks Marty's age, but Krista says that nobody knows it. Krista chatters on, but suddenly Kolenatý arrives, ushering in Marty herself. Vítek leaves on tiptoe, followed by his daughter. Marty reveals that her business is connected with the Gregor case, and when Kolenatý introduces Gregor, she condescendingly allows him to stay while the lawyer tells her about it. He does so: the Prus estates belonged around 1820 to Baron Josef Ferdinand ('Pepi') Prus, who died 'childless and intestate' in 1827. There were three contestants for the inheritance: his cousins Emerich Prus and Baron Szepházy, and Ferdinand Karel Gregor, whose claim rested on a visit paid by Baron Prus to the Director of the Academy where Ferdinand was a student, during which he stated that he was putting the estate in trust for him; also on the fact that Ferdinand Gregor received the revenues of the estate and the title 'owner and proprietor'. Emerich Prus counter-claimed that there was no valid will to this effect, and that Baron Prus had while dying made a verbal arrangement in favour of some other person, one 'Herr Mach Gregor'—in Czech, Řehoř Mach.

Marty has several times interrupted the narrative in impatient, involved disagreement; now she declares passionately that Pepi must have meant Ferdi Gregor. Kolenatý points out that no individual called 'Řehoř Mach' could be discovered. Marty explains: Ferdi was Pepi's son by an opera singer called Elian Macgregor. Gregor is excited; Kolenatý sceptical. He concludes his narrative: the case has continued for generations, assisted by the Doctor Kolenatýs, and thanks to this one the present Gregor is about to lose the case, that very day. 'What do you need to win the case?' 'A written will.' Marty now tells them where to find one: in Prus's old house there is a filing cabinet, and in it under the year 1816—when Pepi got to know Elian—there are her letters, an old document and Prus's will, signed and sealed. Kolenatý is incredulous, Gregor believes her; he threatens to sack his lawyer if Kolenatý refuses to go and see if the will is there. Under pressure, Kolenatý consents, furious.

Left alone with Marty, Gregor speaks of the wonderful faith which she and her beauty have inspired in him; of his desperation, and his mad quest for the Prus millions. He asks her how she knows about the will and the documents, but she rebuffs him coldly. Only when he asks about Elian Macgregor and her love for Pepi does she speak with any warmth—but even then she remains withdrawn. Her manner goads Gregor to make advances to her, with mounting urgency; she begs him to leave her alone. He has already offered her money, and been contemptuously rejected. Now he declares himself ready to do anything for her; she demands that he give her the Greek document which is among Pepi's papers. When he pleads that he knows nothing of it she orders him to find out where it is and bring it to her— 'That was why I came'; and begins to leave. Her departure is interrupted: Kolenatý returns, followed by Baron Jaroslav Prus, present occupant of old Pepi's house and Gregor's opponent in the lawsuit. The will has been found, the letters, and something else as well. But Emilia learns from Prus that Gregor cannot yet give her the letters or the Greek document. There is no written proof that this son Ferdinand was actually Ferdinand Gregor. Marty promises to meet the objection: she will send the necessary paper to Kolenatý. 'Really? Do you carry these things around with you?' 'Would that surprise you? Why?' Kolenatý, defeated, begs Gregor to get himself another lawyer.

Act 2 *The stage of a large theatre, empty, in some disorder from the previous night's performance*

A cleaning woman and a stage-mechanic discuss Marty's success and her endless succession of admirers. These appear to include Jaroslav Prus, since he enters and asks after her. Learning that she will soon pass that way he retires into the wings. The two workers leave the stage, and are succeeded by Krista and Janek. Janek is in love with Krista and tries to steal kisses from her, but Krista is preoccupied with her future as a singer, and disturbed by the fact that she always finds herself thinking about Janek instead. She wonders if Marty is in love with anyone; as Janek steals another kiss, Prus interrupts. Marty appears at once; tired, strained, fending off admirers in the wings. Prus introduces his son; Janek is so dazzled that he can say nothing but 'yes' to all her questions. When she has humiliated him, Vítek and Gregor arrive. Gregor has put a present for her in his bouquet, but she rejects it contemptuously. Vítek's innocent attempt to pay her a compliment by comparing her to Strada elicits a diatribe against all the great sopranos of the past hundred years, and Marty then proceeds to humiliate Krista as well by asking if she has made love to Janek yet.

Hauk comes in and falls to his knees before her, weeping. He is a senile diplomat who tells her that she reminds him of a gipsy girl he used to know in Spain fifty years ago. Marty raises him to his feet, calls him by his Christian name, and speaks passionately to him in Spanish, finally asking him to leave. He does so, his strength revived by the re-creation of his dream.

Vítek asks Marty to sign a photograph of herself for his daughter; Marty is at first reluctant, but confers the favour out of affection for Krista. She then tells them all to go, except Prus, with whom she needs to speak. He tells her that he has looked through the filing cabinet; there is an old sealed document there. He calls Elian Macgregor a prostitute; Marty reacts with violence, which is only gradually calmed. He has read the letters; they contain sexual references which show that the most depraved roué would be hard put to rival Elian's experience. Prus abruptly changes the subject: what was Elian's real name? The letters are just signed E.M. But he has looked up the parish register: Ferdinand's mother was really called Elina Makropulos. Marty is furious at the revelation. Prus will keep the estate—and the sealed document—until some Mr. Makropulos comes forward to claim it. Despite Prus's irony she is confident that one will; but asks what his price is for the document. He merely bows and leaves.

Gregor returns, now madly in love. But she repels him, out of increasing tiredness and cold. He tries to put into words the perverse feelings she arouses in him, at once attracting and repelling; but she uses his love to insist that he retrieve the paper she has sent to Kolenatý: 'We must have one in the name Makropulos.' 'And will you love me?' 'Never, do you understand, never.' He is first furious, then desolate. She falls asleep, and he leaves, half-enraged, half-tender towards her.

Janek appears, infatuated with Marty; she rouses herself to seduce him into stealing the document from his father's house.

By desperate pleading she wins his consent, but Prus now emerges from the wings and dismisses his son contemptuously. Prus and Marty confront each other. He admits that he was waiting for her. 'Then give me the document.' He undertakes to bring it to her—that night.

Act 3 *A hotel room*

Prus and Marty dress after their night together. Prus is completely disillusioned: she has cheated him, it was like embracing a corpse. She simply demands the document and opens it to ensure that it is what she has sought. Prus feels abject self-contempt.

They are interrupted by the chambermaid: she says that a servant is at the door asking for a Mr. Prus; after a moment's hesitation, Prus goes out to see him. Marty gets the girl to do her hair and orders breakfast; but the chambermaid is so distracted by the manservant's pitiful condition that she can hardly do the job properly. When Prus comes back and dismisses the maid, the reason becomes obvious. Janek has killed himself and made clear in his suicide note that he died for Marty. 'Father, be happy, but I. . . .' Marty's cynicism provokes Prus almost to physical violence against her, but they are again interrupted—by Hauk. Prus stalks from the room. Hauk has come to take Emilia back to Spain, and stolen his wife's jewels to pay for the journey. Marty agrees to leave with him, but the chambermaid now ushers in Gregor, Kolenatý, Vítek, Krista, Prus—and a doctor, who takes Hauk back into custody.

Kolenatý has compared the handwriting on the paper Marty has sent him with that on Vítek's photograph, and accuses her of forgery. Marty swears that the paper was written by Elian Macgregor but refuses to say when. She tries to fight her way out, pulling a revolver from a drawer; but Gregor seizes it from her. She goes into the bedroom, saying she must dress and have breakfast. While she is out, Gregor, Vítek and Kolenatý search her luggage; they find a variety of documents in various names all bearing the initials E.M. When Kolenatý orders Vítek to bring her back, she is dressed, but also drinking freely from a bottle of whisky. She gradually confesses, at first hysterically but with ever-increasing calm. She is Elina Makropulos; she is 337 years old. Her father was the court physician to the Emperor Rudolf the second. She was Pepi's mistress and Ferdi's mother; she is a distant ancestor of Albert Gregor. Ferdi was called Ferdi Gregor, but she had to give his real name in the parish register: Ferdinand Makropulos. She has changed her own name many times—how else could one live for three hundred years? She once gave the document, for which she has come back, to Pepi—who kept it, hoping that she would. And at last she has come; it contains *věc Makropulos*, the thing that gives three hundred years of life. Her father invented the formula for the Emperor, who made him try it out on his daughter. She lay ill for a few days—but then recovered. Rudolf had her father arrested as a fraud; she escaped over the border to Hungary, taking the paper with her. Pepi was the only man to whom she ever showed it; and now she has come back to recover it and renew her span of life, which is running out.

Increasing weariness overtakes her as she tells the last part of the story, and under this strain and Kolenatý's relentless questions she collapses. At last they believe her. They carry her into the bedroom and send for a doctor. But there is nothing he can do; he returns, supporting her. She looks like an apparition, a mere shadow of herself. They apologize for their maltreatment of her; and in an extended monologue she renounces the *věc*. Her long life has given her nothing but complete emptiness, the death of the soul. Holding up the formula which grants eternal life, she begs for someone to take it, finally forcing Krista to accept it. She takes the document—and burns it. As the paper is completely burnt up, Elina Makropulos dies.

FROM THE HOUSE OF THE DEAD
(*Z mrtvého domu*)

Opera in three Acts after F. M. DOSTOEVSKY's *Diary from the House of the Dead*
Op. posth.
Book written: 1860
Opera composed: 1927–8
First performance: Brno, 12 April 1930

CHARACTERS:
Alexandr Petrovič Gorjančikov (*baritone*)
Aljeja, a young Tartar (*soprano*)
Filka Morozov, in prison under the name of Luka Kuzmič
   (*tenor*)
A large convict (*tenor*)
A small convict (*baritone*)
The commandant (*bass*)
A very old convict (*tenor*)
Skuratov (*tenor*)
Čekunov (*baritone*)
A drunken convict (*tenor*)
A cook (*baritone*)
A blacksmith (*baritone*)
A priest (*baritone*)
A young convict (*tenor*)
A prostitute (*soprano*)
A prisoner (in the roles of Don Juan and the Brahmin) (*bass*)

SYNOPSES

Kedril (*tenor*)
Šapkin (*tenor*)
Šiškov (*bass*)
Čerevin (*tenor*)
Two guards (*tenor, baritone*)
Voice behind the scene (*tenor*)
The knight, Elvira, the cobbler's wife, the priest's wife, the miller, the miller's wife, the clerk, devils (silent roles in the play and pantomime performed by the prisoners)
Chorus of prisoners

Act I *The yard of a Siberian prison camp on the bank of the river Irtyš*

It is early morning; the sun rises. The prisoners leave their barracks to wash. In a corner of the yard several prisoners torment a lame eagle, while others go into the kitchen. Soon Aljeja appears. Most of the prisoners are silent and frowning; many cross themselves. They wash themselves with water from buckets. Two groups of convicts mention with laconic excitement that a new prisoner, one of the aristocracy, is to arrive this day. Luka, who is withdrawn and comments only occasionally, remarks sardonically on the half-serious quarrel between the large and the small convict, which holds our attention until the entry of the new prisoner, Petrovič.

The commandant enters, and rapidly lays down what is to be done with him: a haircut, chains and the sale of his fine clothes. He proceeds to torture Petrovič, who tells him he is a political prisoner; enraged, the commandant orders him to be flogged.

While Petrovič is taken away the prisoners turn to the lame eagle. The large convict urges it to surrender; the small convict says it will never do so. The others agree, and hail the eagle as 'Tsar of the forests', urging it on to freedom. But the eagle cannot yet fly again.

They are interrupted: the guard pushes them off to work. As some prisoners leave to work outside the camp, they sing of home and of the torture they endure, all in vain. Those left begin to sew mailbags.

Skuratov sings snatches of popular songs and recalls events from his life before imprisonment. He has been driven mad by his consciousness of loss, and Luka is terse with him to maintain his own sanity. Skuratov dances until he collapses, and then lies immobile; Luka concentrates intensely on his task and on the quality of the thread he is using.

Gradually he begins to recall the events which brought him to prison. He remembers that there were twelve others on trial with him; one was an old man who kept pleading for his freedom for the sake of his children.

It was Luka's misfortune to be serving in the army under a major who made life intolerable for everyone. Luka alone, however, stood up against him and told him that he was neither Tsar nor God, as he liked to claim. Luka had a knife concealed; each provoked the other; Luka stabbed the major to death.

While telling his tale, Luka has still been concentrating on his task. He calls at this point for thread and scissors, and then tells of the flogging he received after murdering the major. He thought he was dying.

Petrovič is brought back, crippled after receiving his hundred lashes. All the prisoners stop working and watch the gates close after him.

Act 2 *On the banks of the river Irtyš. It is possible to see far into the Kirgiz steppe*

A year has passed. The Western sun shines in a sky of greyish-blue. In the steppe, a hut is visible, its chimney smoking; distant singing is heard, but soon overlaid by the sound of the convicts at work. Some prisoners are repairing a boat; others lay bricks. Aljeja, Skuratov and Petrovič are among those passing bricks.

The dialogue between Petrovič and Aljeja reveals their close relationship, and Petrovič agrees to teach Aljeja to read and write. The cook, passing across the stage, announces a holiday and a theatre. A priest enters, accompanied by the commandant, to bless the convicts, and they set to their Easter holiday feast with enthusiasm. Skuratov says he has been imprisoned in Siberia just because he fell in love. The convicts are interested, and want to hear his story; as it unfolds, it is occasionally interrupted by the drunken convict, who says it is all lies.

Skuratov was a young soldier who fell in love with a German

girl called Luise, who returned his affection but insisted he should marry her before she gave up her innocence. But before Skuratov could do this, Luise's aunt persuaded the girl to consent to be married to a rich relation. Skuratov got her to come and tell him this; finding that the relative was old, ugly, fat and arrogant, he took a pistol and shot him on the wedding day. He was flogged and sent to prison. And Luise? No one knows what happened to her. The convicts, moved by his story, break out into wild snatches of song to relieve their feelings.

The entertainments now follow: the parts are played by chained convicts, on a stage built from parts of a boat and in crudely improvised costumes. First comes the play, *Kedril and Don Juan*. Kedril is the Don's manservant; he reaps the profits of his master's adventures, always keeping to one side and escaping the damnation which overtakes Juan at the end of the play. The convicts laugh and applaud, and the actor who has played Kedril announces the pantomime, *The Miller's Lovely Wife*.

She receives a variety of lovers in her husband's absence. They include Don Juan, disguised as a Brahmin. When the miller returns, they are all routed out from their various hiding-places; but Juan fights the miller off and dances with his wife until they collapse, sparks flying from him.

After the entertainment, dusk falls. A young convict talks to an ugly prostitute, whom he obviously knows. They disappear together into the darkness; today even convicts have money. Elsewhere, Antonič and Šapkin exchange greetings; we hear Luka singing offstage; and then the small convict approaches Petrovič and Aljeja truculently, trying to make them befriend him. They are drinking tea. Luka approaches them also: 'Oh, the gentlemen are drinking!' The small convict insists that there are no gentlemen here: all are equal. This cry is taken up by other prisoners; Petrovič calms them by offering tea to them all. But in the barracks, Čekunov continues Luka's sad song; and the small convict, unable to contain his resentment any longer, hurls a bucket at Aljeja, who falls, seriously injured. Petrovič cries out; the prisoners think Aljeja has been killed; but when they lift him up, he is alive. 'God has saved him.' The guards force them all back into the barracks.

Act 3 Scene i *The prison hospital; camp beds in a row*

The very old convict is sitting on a large Eastern European stove; Petrovič is sitting beside Aljeja, who is lying in fever. Luka is dying; he taunts Čekunov as if he were the serf of Aljeja and Petrovič, to whom he has brought tea. Čekunov defends himself; but Luka is overcome by a fit of coughing, and the old convict invokes the Lord's mercy on him. Šapkin tries to take the minds of the others off Luka's suffering by telling the story of his own. He and his friends were tramps, who were caught trying to rob the house of a rich merchant. The chief of police rapidly sent the others off to jail, but kept Šapkin behind and forced him to write, while tugging at his ear till it almost came off—all because Šapkin reminded him of a large-eared clerk who had run off with some money.

Skuratov is now quite mad; he cries out again and again for Luise. The others silence him, and have to force him down on to a bed. The lights are put down for the night.

And now Šiškov begins to tell his tale to Čerevin, asking him to be patient, saying that he will tell all. He first evokes the picture of a rich man before whom all bowed, a landowner and cattle dealer with many serfs, so wealthy that his every word was worth a rouble to the poor. He had two sons and a daughter named Akulina. 'That was your wife?' Again Šiškov counsels patience; it will take time for this story to unfold. One Filka Morozov was after her. At this point Luka, dying, cries out twice in agony.

Morozov went to the old man and demanded that they split up their partnership. And he boasted that he wouldn't marry Akulka; he had slept with her for a year and didn't want her any more. He would tell everyone that she'd lost her honour; no other man would marry her.

Again, the dying Luka cries out twice. The old landowner, Šiškov continues, sobbed till the ground shook; Filka drank and had women day and night. Fascinated, Čerevin asks if Filka still kept on with Akulka.

Once more, he is asked to have patience—for Šiškov must now recall how Filka tarred Akulka's door and her parents beat her so that neighbours heard her crying all day. Šiškov himself joined Filka in shouting insults and treating Akulka like a common whore—but she met his taunts with wide-eyed silence, which her mother took to be leading Šiškov on. 'Was she really so easy to get?' Čerevin asks. Šiškov explains. His mother told him to marry Akulka; he ignored Filka's threats—though he drank from the day Filka heard of it until the wedding, and took a whip to the bridal chamber because of what he had been told. It was not needed; Akulka was honest—as well as tender and loving. Why did Filka tell such lies about her?

Šiškov was filled with the desire to kill Filka. He sought him out—but Filka's cronies held him while Filka told him he was too drunk on his wedding night to know if Akulka had been a virgin. Šiškov took the humiliation out on Akulka, whom he thrashed until she could hardly stand. He now abuses himself so much for this that all the prisoners shout at him to shut up.

In the ensuing calm Čerevin asks if he became friends with Filka after that. But Šiškov still cannot be rushed. He continues: Filka took the place of Ivanov's son as a soldier, and demanded his right in return to the highest degree of hospitality before he left. He slept with the daughter, forced the women to bathe him in wine, made them tear down the fence to make an entrance for him. Finally, on the day on which he had to go, he sobered up— and while making his farewells encountered Akulka. He told her he had loved her for three years, and begged her forgiveness. She readily granted it; Šiškov, overhearing, forced her to explain. 'I am in love with him. More than all the world, I love him.' Šiškov resolved to kill her. After a sleepless night, he took her out into the forest and cut her throat.

But in the hospital Luka has died, just before the end of the story. As the convicts crowd round the corpse, Šiškov recognizes in the dead man's features as they set into death the man who was Filka Morozov. All are astounded; the old convict murmurs that even Filka had a mother. As the guards take the body out, Šiškov curses it again and again. Petrovič is summoned out of the hospital.

Act 3 Scene ii *The prison yard as in Act 1. The sun is shining; convicts stand prepared to go off for work*

The commandant is drunk; he humbles himself before Petrovič, and finally tells him that an order for his release has come through. Petrovič's chains are struck off. But his joy is mingled with the pain of parting from Aljeja, who comes to him from the doorway of the hospital. The convicts release the eagle; its wound now healed, it leaves the prison like Petrovič.

The convicts have a moment to rejoice in the bird's freedom; then they are marched off to return to work.

Some Further Reading

The only good biography is that by Jaroslav Vogel, *Leoš Janáček, His Life and Work*, published by Artia, Prague. The English translation appeared in 1962 under the imprint of Paul Hamlyn. Milena Černohorská's essay *Leoš Janáček* (Editio Supraphon, Prague, 1966), and Bohumír Štědroň's collection of documents, *Leoš Janáček in Letters and Reminiscences* (Topičova Edice, Prague, 1946) are valuable complements to Vogel's book. Both have been published in English-language editions.

I know only three works of interpretation which express deep understanding of Janáček's music. All are brief, but cogent and well-written: unfortunately, none has been translated into English. *Leoš Janáček* by Max Brod (in German; Universal Edition, Vienna, no. 8169); *Janáček*, by Daniel Muller (in French; Editions Rieder, Paris, 1934); and 'Umělecký profil Leoše Janáčka' (Artistic profile of Leoš Janáček) by Jan Kunc, in *Odkaz Leoše Janáčka České Opere*, by Leoš Firkušný (Brno, 1939).

Karl H. Wörner's 'Katjas Tod', contributed to the published proceedings of the 1958 Janáček Congress in Brno (pp. 392–8), is the only adequate treatment as music-drama of any scene in a Janáček opera.

A large amount of scholarship has been devoted to Janáček and his work, principally in Czech and German. I have found this literature of little value for the interpretation of Janáček's operas.

The Scores

The most glaring deficiency of Janáček scholarship is the continuing lack, nearly fifty years after the composer's death, of adequate editions of the majority of the six operas discussed here. The chief reason for this is the feeling of some early conductors that Janáček's instrumentation was too sparse and rough in comparison with that of standard repertory composers; they indulged in extensive reorchestration. Recent conductors (especially Rafael Kubelik and Charles Mackerras) have felt that this alteration of Janáček's intentions was misguided and that his original orchestration is perfectly practicable, and have given performances of the late operas in which they have reverted when and where possible to Janáček's original version. I agree with their views, and have taken pains in this book to discuss only Janáček's own final version of the musical text of each opera, where that can be established. Unfortunately, the editions in print frequently reflect earlier attitudes; notes are therefore needed on the accuracy of the current published versions of each opera.

Jenůfa
Full score: UE 13980 (hire only)
Study score: UE 13600
Vocal score: UE 5821

Janáček revised this opera himself between the Brno première and the Prague performances; most of this work was done before 1908. These revisions consisted chiefly of cuts, to tighten up the dramatic argument of some over-repetitive passages, and rewriting of vocal lines to increase the independence of and the dialogue between voice and orchestra. But the chief conductor at the Prague National Theatre, Karel Kovařovic, made extensive reorchestrations and a number of cuts and adjustments to the vocal line, as a condition of accepting the opera for production there in 1916.

All these alterations are of very great interest. But they are entirely ignored by the editor of the published full and study scores, J. M. Dürr. He prints a post-Kovařovic musical text, and concerns himself minutely with the suggested emendations of conductors since Kovařovic. He also includes a 75-bar section, Kostelnička's narrative in Act 1, which Janáček himself cut before the 1908 edition of the vocal score; but no indication is given of what Janáček wrote and what he did not. And there is even an absurd redistribution of vocal parts (one of Kostelnička's cries at the end of Act 2 is given to Jenůfa!), for which there is no authority whatsoever.

I have discussed the opera as Janáček wrote it, in the post-1908 version; my source is a conducting score from the National Theatre, now in the Janáček Archive in Brno, in which Kovařovic's alterations are clearly marked off from Janáček's original work, in red ink.

The Universal Edition vocal score follows Kovařovic's version. (Incidentally, since this and all the other Universal Edition vocal scores are published with Czech and German words only, readers who have German but no Czech should be warned that the translations by Max Brod are considerably free—and in particular that his arrangement of *Adventures of the Vixen Bystrouška* bears almost no resemblance to the original libretto. Tolerably accurate English translations accompany the Supraphon recordings.)

A new edition of the full score which makes plain what Janáček wrote is clearly needed; in the meantime, readers are urged to try and obtain the Czech-language vocal score (*Její pastorkyňa*, edited by Vladimír Helfert for Hudební matice umělecké besedy, Prague, 1934, no. 89). Helfert prints Janáček's original vocal parts, and distinguishes Janáček's orchestration from Kovařovic's as far as is possible in the instrumental indications of a piano reduction.

The opera has been twice recorded by Supraphon, once under

Vogel and once under Gregor; the second recording was a co-production with EMI. Both recordings use the Kovařovic version; Gregor balks at two of the most outrageous emendations—but outweighs this gesture towards authenticity by using gratuitous extra percussion elsewhere, at the suggestion of other conductors.

Destiny (published as *Osud*)
Full score: Dilia 1178 (hire only)
Vocal score: Dilia—(hire only)

The full score is passable. It has been cut about (literally) in order to reflect the flashback arrangement of the Acts made for the 1958 productions, and contains a large number of obvious musical errors, but is otherwise accurate. The vocal score is an impossible collage of alterations by arrangers, inaccurate beyond hope of rescue.

I have worked from the 1905 MS. version in the Janáček Archive, which contains the modifications made by Janáček in 1906 and 1907.

The opera has been recorded by Supraphon, under František Jílek. Janaček's original order is followed, and the musical text is essentially accurate.

Kát'a Kabanová
Full score: UE 7070 (hire only)
Vocal score: UE 7103

The full score is an edition by Mackerras which restores the composer's intentions (the opera had been extensively re-orchestrated by Talich). Mackerras includes as optional alternatives extended versions of the orchestral postludes to 1.i and 2.i; Janáček wrote these after the completion of the opera at the request of a producer.

Despite his return to Janáček's orchestration, Mackerras believes that the close of 2.ii (from after figure 20) is impracticable in Janáček's orchestration, and has offered a rearrangement, printing Janáček's original as an appendix. My discussion and Example 22 follow Janáček's own orchestration.

The vocal score is accurate but for some minor misprints and omissions. It prints only Janáček's original, shorter interludes after 1.i and 2.i.

The only recording (Supraphon, under Krombholč) uses the Talich version.

Adventures of the Vixen Bystrouška published (as *Das Schlaue Füchslein*)
Full score: UE 7560 (hire only)
Vocal score: UE 7564

The full score is of a substantially augmented orchestration made by Talich in 1937, and the instrumental indications of the vocal score reflect this rather than Janáček's original. In preparing the music examples for this book I have consulted Janáček's manuscript; but it has not always been possible for me to discover Janáček's original intentions, as substantial sections of this MS. are lacking.

Readers who have German but no Czech should be warned that Max Brod's *Bearbeitung*, printed in both scores, is a travesty of the original libretto in letter and spirit. In pursuit of his reinterpretation of the opera Brod even persuaded Janáček to add to the score the choral intervention in 3.ii (5 and 6 bars after figure 20), which is rightly omitted from the gramophone versions. A relatively accurate English translation of the original libretto comes with both recordings.

The opera has twice been recorded by Supraphon, under Neumann and Gregor. Both use the Talich reorchestration, except that at one or two points Gregor reverts to the original. But the Neumann interpretation is superior on all musical and dramatic grounds.

Makropulos (published as *Die Sache Makropulos*)
Full score: UE 14851 (hire only)
Vocal score: UE 8656

Conductors have not tampered seriously with Janáček's most daunting opera. The full score was carefully corrected by Universal Edition in 1970, and indicates Janáček's original orchestration clearly at the few points where it is still considered technically impracticable. My examples follow Janáček's wishes at these points: Gregor's recording for Supraphon, the only one yet made, does not. The vocal score is reliable.

From the House of the Dead (published as *Aus Einem Totenhaus*)
Full score (edited by Kubelik): UE 8235 (hire only)
Vocal score: UE 8221

Janáček died while in the process of revising his copyist's MS. of this score, and there is a genuine difficulty in deciding how much more he would have added had he lived to complete it. What is not in doubt is that the first editors, Janáček's pupils Bakala and Chlubna, grossly overdid the task of completing the orchestration, at points even reversing Janáček's visible intentions; and for the examples in this book I have used Rafael Kubelik's edition of the full score, which attempts to add as little as possible to what can certainly be established as Janáček's original intentions. But even this edition is not now felt to return sufficiently far—a version was performed in Brno in 1974 in which virtually nothing was added to the MS. orchestration; and a new critical edition is needed which will make clear what Janáček actually wrote, distinguishing it from such additions as the editor feels to be necessary for performance.

Bakala and Chlubna also composed an optimistic ending at the request of the first producer: in it several parts of 3.ii are altered, and the closing march is replaced by a stirring chorus in praise of freedom with an exultant tutti close in B major. This astonishing travesty of the composer's style and intentions is still printed as the end of the opera in the vocal score, though Janáček's original has been added as an appendix to recent reprintings. The orchestral indications throughout the vocal score reflect the Bakala and Chlubna instrumentation.

The opera has been recorded twice: from the Holland festival of 1954, under Alexander Krannhals, in German and in the Bakala/Chlubna edition, for Philips; and by Supraphon, under Gregor. The Supraphon recording uses Janáček's original ending, but does not go as far towards removing the Bakala and Chlubna 'touching-up' of the score as the Kubelik edition. Gregor also makes an unauthentic repeat during the interlude in Act 3; this presumably reflects a need for extra time for changing scenery in the Prague production on which the recording is based.

277

Index